A MICROCOMPUTER
FINITE ELEM

G A Mohr
BE MEngSc PhD

H R Milner
BE MEngSc DIC PhD FIEAust MIIE

Heinemann : London

Dedication
To Courtney Balthazar Oppenheim
Mohr 1906–1986
A brilliant, modest and honest
academic.

William Heinemann Ltd
10 Upper Grosvenor Street, London W1X 9PA

LONDON   MELBOURNE   JOHANNESBURG   AUCKLAND

First published by Pitman Publishing Pty Ltd 1986
First published in Great Britain by William Heinemann Ltd 1987

British Library Cataloguing in Publication Data
Mohr, G. A.
    A microcomputer introduction to the
    finite element method.
    1. Finite element method – Data processing
    2. Engineering mathematics – Data processing
    3. Basic (Computer program language)
    I. Title   II. Milner, H. R.
    620'.001'515353   TA346.F5

ISBN 0 434 91262 X

Printed in Great Britain by
Thetford Press Limited, Thetford, Norfolk

Contents

Preface

This introductory text provides newcomers to the finite element method with a simple, but practical introduction to the subject. It outlines the underlying theory of finite elements and provides programs (for low cost personal computers) which enable the student to gain confidence through solving practical problems.

The programs listed in the text were developed over a period of several years on various microcomputers, and drawn together and supplemented for a short course at Auckland University in 1984. For this course a computer with only 29K bytes of free RAM was used in order to demonstrate that even the smallest machines can be used for finite element analysis. Since that time, the programs have been modified to run on an IBM compatible machine and further programs have been added.

The authors are grateful to the many students who have used and acted as critics of the programs. The dc network and truss programs, for example, were used by all second year engineering students at Auckland in 1983 and 1984, in a very successful educational experiment.

We also wish to express our gratitude to the mentors and professional colleagues who have guided and assisted us over the years.

HRM, GAM
December 1985

Introduction

The first paper describing the finite element method (FEM) for the analysis of continua was presented by Turner, Clough, Martin and Topp at a conference in Pittsburgh, Pennsylvania, in 1954[1] although the name was coined some time later. This paper, in common with many other early papers, was concerned with plane stress and strain problems, typically, where a slice of dam was analysed. Concurrently, there were parallel developments in the analysis of skeletal frame problems and this symbiotic relationship spurred a rapid development of the FEM.

In the 1960s attention shifted towards the technically more difficult finite element stress analysis problems of plates in bending and shell structures. There was also a broadening of the scope of the method to include simple field problems such as those of heat flow and seepage of fluids through porous media. The second half of this decade saw the first three major conferences on the subject (1965, 1968 and 1970) held at Wright–Patterson Air Force Base in Ohio. The structural origins of the method were apparent in the conference title, Matrix Methods in Structural Mechanics, although papers on nonstructural applications were included.

While Turner, Clough, Martin and Topp co-authored the first paper on continuum finite elements[1] — a collaboration between Berkeley Civil Engineers and the Boeing Corporation — they were not the only workers active at this time. Argyris, working in Stuttgart, was the other prime mover and he published extensively in the journal *Aircraft Engineering* in 1954–55; his papers were reprinted as a text in 1960[2]. He also opened the first Wright–Patterson Air Force Base conference with his landmark paper of some two hundred pages.[3] The first text on the subject was written for students in 1968 by Przemieniecki[4], convenor of the first conference on the method. This was followed shortly afterwards with a text by Zienkiewicz and Cheung.[5] These texts brought the method to the attention of a large number of academics who progressively introduced the teaching of finite element analysis into their postgraduate and, subsequently, their undergraduate programmes. Other texts have followed and today the method is widely taught.

As the preceding paragraph suggests, the method was initiated by aeronautical and civil engineers as a means of analysing stresses in aircraft structures and buildings. The stiffened shell structures which aeronautical engineers sought to analyse led to the FEM becoming among the more demanding tasks presented to digital computers in any field of application. The data card decks used for the analysis of a Boeing 707 aircraft were reported to require a large trolley for their conveyance and, undoubtedly, the computer program did also. The large package programs subsequently developed for FEM analysis can only be run conveniently on the largest of digital computers. PAFEC, for example, one of the largest of such programs, comprises a total of 250 000 lines of code which has absorbed 250 man years of development work. Presently some 20 people are employed full time in its continuing development and maintenance. It requires large machines to run efficiently, although there are versions available in Australia which run, with some inconvenience, on PRIME 750 computers.

There are many even larger programs (as well as more compact programs) used in teaching, the best known being E L Wilson's SAP programs written at Berkeley in the 1960s. These smaller programs have also been used extensively in practical engineering analysis of framed structures, plates and simple shells.

Such smaller programs are easily run on the modern 'minicomputer' having a high speed memory of around 10 Mb. With further improvement in processing power and the lower costs of computers even personal computers (PCs) now offer the engineer the opportunity to carry out finite element analysis for a wide variety of situations. This book shows how many finite element programs, useful as analysis tools and for teaching, can be run on PCs.

The machine used to develop many of the programs given in the present book (an SV-328) has a monochrome monitor, simple cassette unit and a modest sized CPU (30 Kb ROM, 80 Kb RAM with 30 Kb user free RAM).

Modern PCs are a little faster, have enhanced graphics facilities and much more RAM, commonly in the region of 350 Kb. They are usually fitted with floppy and, occasionally, hard disks for mass storage of data and programs. However, the largest program given herein requires only around 16 Kb (the amount likely to be available to most engineering students using privately owned PCs). Compilers, as distinct from interpreters, are available for PCs for most computer languages including BASIC, FORTRAN, PASCAL and C and these speed execution considerably. Having access to such equipment seems incredible to the authors given that the cost of machines, such as the Sinclair, is comparable, in today's terms, to the cost of a slide rule when they were students in the 1960s. For students who purchase such machines the range of analytical tools available to them is, by comparison, extended enormously. One of our objectives is to show how much one can achieve in analysing FEM problems with minimal 16 Kb machines, anticipating the day when all students have such equipment. However, because of the widespread availablity of the IBM PC and compatibles, all programs listed in this book are written for these machines in BASICA. Users of other machines may need to key in the programs.

References

1 M J Turner, R W Clough, H C Martin and L J Topp, 'Stiffness and deflection analysis of complex structures', *Journal of Aeronautical Science*, vol 23, 1956, p 805. (Originally presented at a conference in Pittsburgh, Pennsylvania in 1954.)

2 J H Argyris, *Energy Theorems and Structural Analysis*. Butterworth, London, 1960. (Reprinted from *Aircraft Engineering*, 1954–55.)

3 J H Argyris, 'Continua and Discontinua', Paper delivered to conference 'Matrix Methods in Structural Mechanics', Wright–Patterson Air Force Base, Ohio, 1965.

4 J S Przemieniecki, *Theory of Matrix Structural Analysis*, McGraw–Hill, New York, 1968.

5 O C Zienkiewicz and Y K Cheung, *The Finite Element Method in Continuum Mechanics*. McGraw–Hill, London, 1968. (Now expanded and appearing as O C Zienkiewicz and R L Taylor, *The Finite Element Method*, 4th edn, McGraw–Hill, London, 1984.)

CHAPTER 1

Applications of the Finite Element Method

To begin we introduce some applications of the finite element method to illustrate its scope and power. Further examples, along with simple programs, follow.

1.1 Structural modelling

The appeal and utility of the finite element method of structural analysis is attributable to its ability to model* structures of complex geometry as an assemblage of simple elements (or modules). The main requirement is to have, for a range of elements of varying shapes, exact or approximate solutions of the governing differential equations for arbitrary boundary conditions. For example, the flat plate in Fig 1.1a can be regarded as an assemblage of the simple triangular or quadrilateral elements shown or as a combination of the two. If the plate is, in turn, supported on columns then this 'modelling' can be extended to include the columns shown in Fig 1.1b, represented as line elements. Solutions of the plate and beam equations within the elements provide all the information necessary to compute the behaviour of the whole structure. Computer programs which contain a library of such elements, with coded solutions of the governing differential equations, can be used to develop and analyse models of the most complex of geometric shapes.

Although the models drawn in Fig 1.1 appear simple to devise the simplicity is often illusive. Engineering students will be familiar with analysing frame structures using line (or beam) elements and it may not have occurred to them that such structures can also be analysed as an assembly of two dimensional (plane stress) or three dimensional elements in which the subdivision can be as coarse or as fine as desired. The use of a line element model is appropriate if we require only bending moments and shears

---

* An assemblage of elements such as shown in Fig 1.1 is described as a mathematical model because it is a representation of the real object. The model can be used to predict the real object's behaviour.

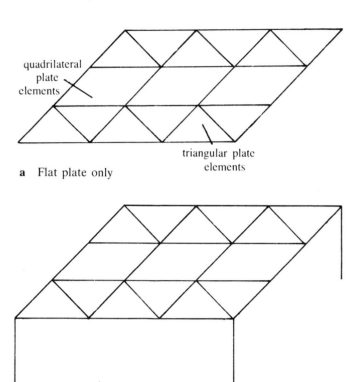

a Flat plate only

b Flat plate supported on columns

Figure 1.1 Finite element models of plates showing mixtures of element types

but modelling with two or three dimensional elements may be appropriate in regions where information is sought concerning local stress concentrations. It follows, therefore, that finite element modelling involves more skill than merely subdividing a structure according to a prescribed set of rules which cover all possible situations; there is art or judgement involved in selecting the appropriate elements and in deciding on the level of refinement.

The extension of the finite element beyond the domain of stress analysis (a generic term which applies equally to computing bending moments in skeletal frames) to heat and fluid flow and other applications was, historically, a later development. Such applications recognise finite element analysis as a technique for solving differential equations in general rather than those associated only with stress analysis. Some examples which illustrate the point are given later.

1.2 Skeletal elements

One of the simplest stress analysis problems which can be solved by the finite element method is the computation of nodal displacements and member axial loads of two dimensional pinjointed trusses. Fig 1.2 shows such a structure modelled using elements with four displacement freedoms. Typically element end nodes, such as 7 and 10 of element (7–10), are each assumed to have two associated displacement components u and v. Commonly, displacements are computed first and element axial loads are obtained directly from these displacements.

While the particular structure shown in Fig 1.2 is statically determinate and can be readily analysed by hand methods using the principles of statics, the finite element method provides an alternative and universally applicable approach more suited to automatic computation. In order to carry out such an analysis it is necessary only to define the geometry, member properties and loads. The geometry is defined simply and naturally by specifying the co-ordinates of the nodes, shown numbered, within a global co-ordinate system. Elements are described by specifying the nodes which they connect and this information, along with member property (Youngs modulus and cross-sectional area) load and the boundary condition data, is used to solve the problem. Even with the more advanced two and three dimensional elements described below, the same basic information of nodal coordinates, connectivity information, element properties, loads and boundary conditions is all that is necessary.

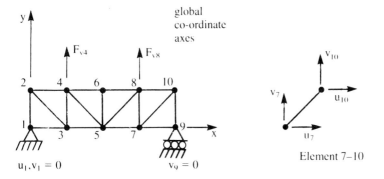

Figure 1.2 Pinjoined truss showing typical element

A problem which has similarities to the one described above is illustrated in Fig 1.3. It involves a continuous beam on rigid supports modelled with elements each having two extensional degrees of freedom. The element cannot be used to model frame structures in which sidesway occurs.

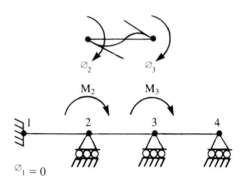

Figure 1.3   Continuous beam showing typical element

In Fig 1.4 a rigid jointed frame is shown. It has been modelled using beam elements which each have six freedoms. This element combines extensional (u) and flexural (v and ø) freedoms enabling plane frames undergoing sidesway to be analysed. While there is a natural division of the structure, additional arbitrary nodes and elements can be included (as created by node 5).

This beam element can also be used to model (in an approximate way) curved arches as a series of straight segments.[1] However, where there is very high curvature, conventional beam theory is inaccurate and special curved beam theories should be employed. Furthermore, it is a relatively simple matter to develop programs which analyse approximately the amplification of deflections which arise due to axial load, ie take into account the so-called P–δ effect. The frame is first analysed using its original nodal co-ordinates and these are progressively updated by adding the deflections to them until the deflections stabilise (if the structure is stable) or increase indefinitely (if the structure is unstable). However, in order to make an accurate analysis of this type, an element with a modified element stiffness matrix should be used.

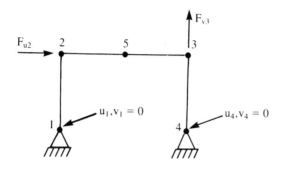

Figure 1.4   Rigid frame showing typical element

1.3   Two dimensional plane stress and plate bending elements

In Fig 1.5 we come across the first continuum problem in which the fineness of the element mesh and node locations are almost completely arbitrary. The problem involves analysing a cross-sectional slice of an earth dam using triangular plane stress elements having six freedoms, viz two in-plane displacements, u and v, at each node. The mesh shown in the example is relatively coarse and, in practice, a considerably larger number of elements should be used[2].

This element differs from the elements of Section 1.2 in that it involves phenomena in a two dimensional domain; displacements u and v are each functions of co-ordinates x and y. Because the governing partial differential equations have no known analytical solution for arbitrary boundary conditions, the element stiffness matrix must be determined from approximate solutions of the governing differential equations. Much of this book is devoted to showing how such solutions are derived.

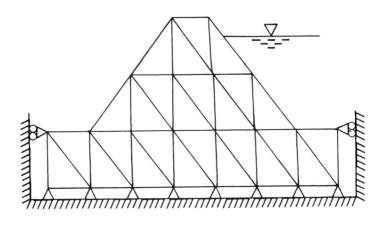

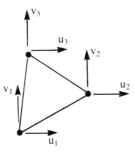

Figure 1.5 Earth dam with coarse grid of triangular membrane elements with six freedoms

The modelling of flat plates by the finite element method is geometrically similar to plane stress modelling. However, an additional and unexpected, mathematical difficulty arises in selecting admissible plate deflection functions for the solution of the governing differential equations. These problems are discussed in detail in Chapter 9.

Fig 1.6 shows a typical plate problem involving a perforated slab modelled using nine-freedom thin plate bending elements. Once again, a larger number of elements than indicated is generally required, particularly when we require accurate stress results near the corner of the hole. Where relatively thick slabs are being analysed, ie where the ratio of span to thickness is less than ten, thick plate elements should be used[2] which take the effect of shear deformations into account. The same comment applies to the analysis of thick shells.

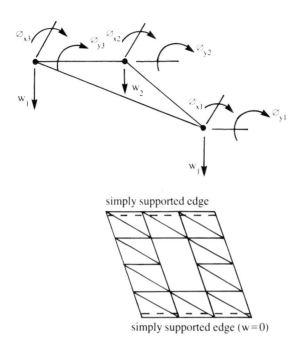

simply supported edge (w = 0)

Figure 1.6 Perforated slab and typical element

1.4 Three dimensional elements

Three dimensional analysis involves a simple extension of two dimensional analysis. The addition of the third dimension generally leads to more data preparation, computation and cost. Fig 1.7 illustrates a typical problem in which wedge shaped elements, with 18 freedoms, have been used to analyse the behaviour of a small column pad footing as well as foundation material below. The boundary conditions require careful consideration in this case. Special techniques are required to deal with the infinite subgrade using the few elements shown in Fig 1.7[3].

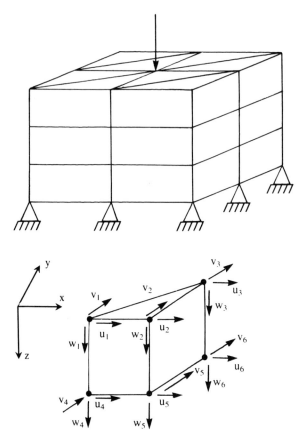

Figure 1.7 Foundation represented using wedge elements

1.5 Axisymmetric elements

Axisymmetric problems constitute a very important sub-class of three dimensional problem which can be reduced to a two dimensional problem and analysed with considerable economy. These analyses may be derivatives of the three dimensional solid or shell type.

Fig 1.8 shows axisymmetric thin shell elements, with six freedoms, used to represent a perforated thin spherical shell. Such elements have limited application compared to doubly curved shell elements but are very economical when they can be used.[5]

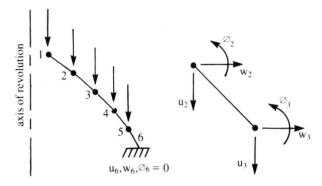

Figure 1.8 Perforated spherical shell

In Fig 1.9 axisymmetric solid elements with twelve freedoms are used to represent a thick cylindrical caisson. The midside nodes shown allow the development of elements having curved sides, referred to as isoparametric elements, capable of accurate modelling of the curved shapes which occur at the base of the caisson. Thin and thick shell elements can also be used for such problems. Thin shell elements do not give especially accurate results as thin shell theory ignores shear deformations and is unable to adequately describe the high shear that must be transferred at the rim of the base.[4] Thick shell elements provide much more accurate results in this case.

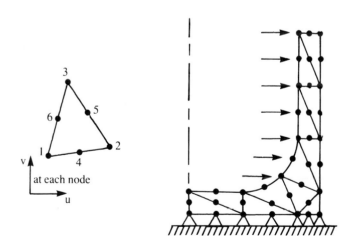

Figure 1.9 Cylindrical caisson with radial loading

1.6 Flat shell elements

In Fig 1.10 we see a combined plane stress and thin plate bending element having five degrees of freedom at each node used to model a stiffened steel plate. In this type of problem it is also necessary to include a sixth 'drilling freedom' ϕ_z at each node. The element can also be used to analyse cylindrical shells corresponding to modelling arches or cylinders with straight beam elements. As it suffers the same advantages and disadvantages, it is not an accurate approach for deeply curved shells.

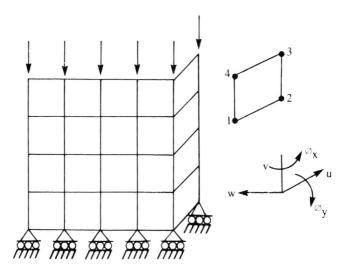

Figure 1.10 Folded plate elements used to represent a stiffened steel plate

Fig 1.11 shows a flat facet element of triangular shape and having six degrees of freedom per node.[3] Again, the element is a combination of a thin plate bending and plane stress elements. A difficulty in using it is the large number of elements required to represent the often complex geometry. Where curvature is high and geometry complex it is usually best to model using the elements described in Section 1.7.

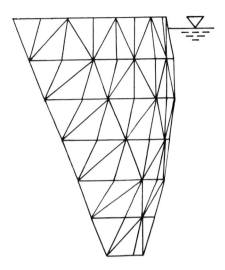

Figure 1.11 Arch dam modelled with triangular facet elements

1.7 Curved shell elements

Curved rectangular cylindrical shell elements are shown in Fig 1.12 in the analysis of an octant of a pipe subjected to pinching loads, ie loads applied across a diameter. Such elements, like axisymmetric elements, have limited application but do allow analysis in cases where the structure is axisymmetric but the loads are not. It is the doubly curved shell elements illustrated in Fig 1.13 which can be used more generally.

Unfortunately, the properties of doubly curved shell elements are difficult to derive, largely because the derivation of the accurate triangular plate bending element needed as their basis is, in itself, a formidable problem.[2] If only the simplest bending and plane stress elements are used as the basis for doubly curved shell elements there is little improvement in the accuracy compared to that obtained when using flat shell elements. However, some accurate doubly curved shell element formulations are now available in commercial finite element computer programs.

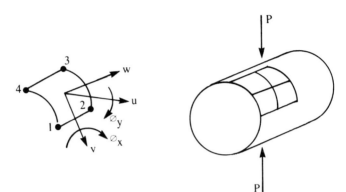

Figure 1.12   Cylindrical shell elements

A further difficulty with doubly curved shell elements occurs when dealing with general shell shapes. In special cases, such as in cylindrical and spherical shell analyses, surface co-ordinates are easily specified but, for shells with variable curvatures, the differential geometry of curved surfaces must be used to calculate curvatures and arc lengths.[6]

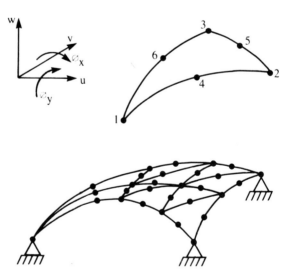

Figure 1.13   Doubly curved triangular shell elements

1.8 Potential flow elements

Fig 1.14 shows a gravity dam resting on an isotropic foundation the seepage under which is described by Poisson's equation $\partial^2\phi/\partial x^2 + \partial^2\phi/\partial y^2 = C$; $C = 0$ in this case. The problem can be solved, approximately, using the small number of rectangular potential flow elements shown. The left and right hand boundaries and the rock under the soil stratum are assumed to be impervious and the other boundary conditions are the pressure heads, ie the water depths, at the nodes in contact with the water to the left and right of the dam.[7] The fact that finite element analysis can be used to solve this problem should be no surprise to stress analysts if for no other reason than the fact that the torsion of prismatic line elements is also governed by Poisson's equation. The extension from torsion to seepage analysis involves no more than a noting of the appropriate analogies.

Further extensions to an even wider range of problems are not

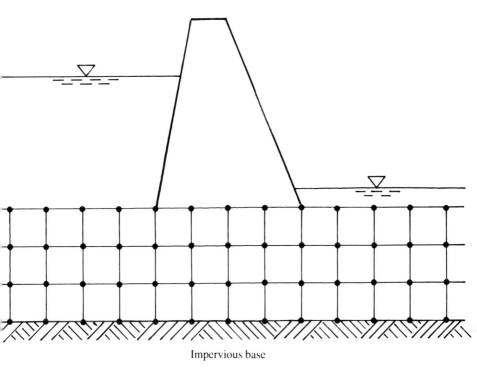

Impervious base

Figure 1.14 Mesh of potential flow finite elements used to determine water pressure under a dam

restricted, fortunately, by reliance on analogies between the particular problem and some stress analysis problem. It is actually possible, in principle, to apply finite element analysis to the solution of any problem in mathematical physics. However, we restrict ourselves to only a few non-structural applications.

1.9 Structural design with finite elements

Perhaps the most interesting application of finite elements is in the design of structural shapes where the designer seeks to achieve more economical structural forms. Structural design is undertaken by repetitive application of elastic analysis and, in general, element sizing computations until all design criteria are satisfied and a mathematically defined optimal condition is reached. Fig 1.15 shows the development of an optimally shaped arch which has been analysed iteratively using flat shell elements.[3] In the iterative process the optimality criteria eliminate inefficient bending effects as far as possible and minimise the integral of the membrane stresses over the surface.

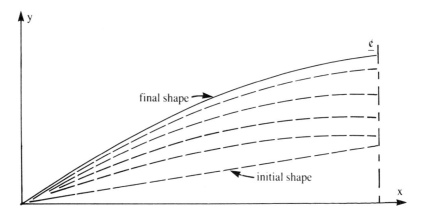

Figure 1.15 Iterative development of optimal arch shape

As a further example Fig 1.16 details the finite element mesh used to obtain the pseudo optimum shape of the arch dam shown in Fig 1.11.[3] Initially the abutments were regarded as fixed and the dam wall thickness uniform. The shape was adjusted to optimise a ratio of actual stresses to fully stressed design stresses.

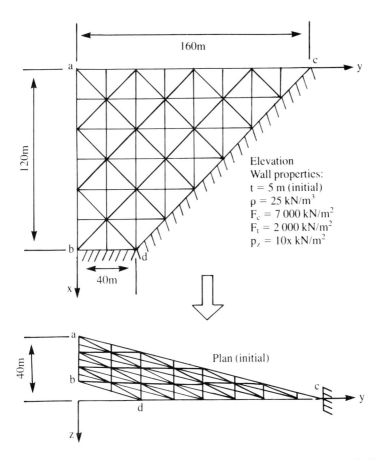

Figure 1.16 Ilerative design of an arch dam using flat triangular shell elements

After eight iterations, the shape of the crown cantilever profile obtained was Shape I of Fig 1.17. Further improvement in the design was obtained by rotating the abutments about the base in small steps. Design Shape II in Fig 1.17 was chosen when the optimality measures were at a minimum. The final step in the procedure was to iteratively adjust the thickness of individual elements until a fully stressed design was obtained.

The development of optimisation techniques is an active area of research.[9] Such applications are the most rewarding and challenging areas of finite element development.

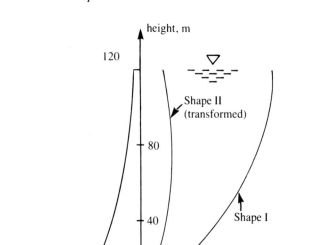

Figure 1.17 Optimum shape and thickness for the crown cantilever of the arch dam of Fig 1.11

1.10 Concluding remarks

In this introductory text, space does not permit discussion of the more advanced problems illustrated in the present chapter. Simple programs dealing with the problems discussed in Sections 1.1, 1.2 and 1.7 are given in Chapters 4,5,7,8 and 9. Chapters 3 and 6 describe simple network and vibration problems respectively and Chapter 10 indicates the many additional problems which can be solved by the finite element method.

References

1 G A Mohr and R Garner, 'Reduced integration and penalty factors in an arch element', *International Journal of Structures*, vol 3(1), 1983, p 9.

2 O C Zienkiewcz and R L Taylor, *The finite element method*, 4th edn, McGraw-Hill, London, 1984.

3 G A Mohr, 'Analysis and design of plate and shell structures using finite elements', PhD thesis, University of Cambridge, 1976.

4 G A Mohr, 'Application of penalty factors to a curved quadratic shell element', *Computers and Structures*, vol 14, 1981, p 15.

5 N C Knowles, A Razzaque and J B Spooner, 'Experience of finite element analysis of shell structures', in D G Ashwell and R H Gallagher, *Finite elements for thin shells and curved members*, Wiley, London, 1976.

6 G A Mohr and N B Paterson, 'A natural numerical differential geometry scheme for a doubly curved shell element', *Computers and Structures*, vol 10, 1984, p 443.

7 J J Connor and C A Brebbia, *Finite element techniques for fluid flow*, Butterworth, London, 1976.

8 K F Reinschmitt, C A Cornell and J F Brotchie, 'Iterative design and structural optimisation', *Journal of the Structural Division ASCE*, vol 92, 1966, p 281.

9 G Sander, and F Fleury, 'A mixed method of structural optimisation', *International Journal for Numerical Methods in Engineering*, vol 13, 1978, p 385.

CHAPTER 2

Some Basic Finite Element Concepts

In this chapter we introduce some basic finite element concepts. Initially, we discuss the subdivision of a domain into a mesh of finite elements. The choice of mesh must account for the low order polynomials used, within elements, to represent the problem variables such as displacements. If the polynomial is only linear then it cannot represent a quadratic or higher order variation with complete accuracy. The accuracy of the analysis will depend largely on how many elements are chosen, how accurately these elements can represent the variables within the element and the specific nature of the problem ie whether or not it involves singularities which cause the stresses to vary asymptotically with respect to distance.

Next, we discuss methods of solving the differential equations within elements and finally methods of using these solutions to obtain a set of simultaneous algebraic equations for the complete structure. The use of the element solutions, once they have been derived in algebraic form, is a routine computer task; their derivation involves the greatest conceptual difficulty.

2.1 Discretising the domain and forming the element equations

We introduce the notion of mesh choice and the solution of differential equations within elements by reference to a heat flow problem.

Differential equations of heat flow

Heat flow in a two dimensional domain is governed by two laws. First, according to Fourier's law of heat conduction, the rate of heat flow q_x in the x direction, is given by

$$q_x = -k_x \partial T / \partial x \qquad 2.1$$

where k_x is the coefficient of thermal conductivity. A similar expression applies for the y direction

$$q_y = -k_y \partial T/\partial y \qquad\qquad \textbf{2.2}$$

Heat flow behaviour is also governed by a continuity condition. If we examine an infinitesimal element dxdy of the domain it is easy to show that, for conservation of heat,

$$\partial q_x/\partial x + \partial q_y/\partial y = 0 \qquad\qquad \textbf{2.3}$$

Substituting equations 2.1 and 2.2 into equation 2.3 we obtain, if $k_x = k_y$,

$$\partial^2 T/\partial x^2 + \partial^2 T/\partial y^2 = 0 \quad \text{or} \quad \nabla^2 T = 0 \qquad \textbf{2.4a}$$

where $\nabla^2(\ ) = \partial^2(\ )/\partial x^2 + \partial^2(\ )/\partial y^2$ is the Laplacian operator. The governing differential equation 2.4a, is called Laplace's equation which, taken in conjunction with the boundary conditions, enables the temperature to be determined within the domain.

In the one dimensional case equation 2.4a reduces to

$$k_x d^2 T/dx^2 = 0 \quad \text{or} \quad d^2 T/dx^2 = 0 \qquad\qquad \textbf{2.4b}$$

Equation 2.4b is mathematically analogous to the governing differential equation for a prismatic truss element, viz $EAd^2u/dx^2 = 0$ or $d^2u/dx^2 = 0$, where $u = u(x)$ is the displacement in the x direction along the element. We emphasise this analogy to underline the generality of finite element analysis.

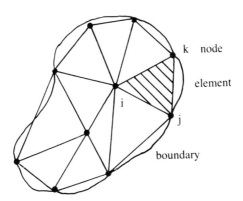

Figure 2.1 Domain discretised into triangular finite elements

Differential equation solutions within elements

Solving a differential equation, such as equation 2.4a, by the finite element method involves a two stage process. First we solve it algebraically but approximately within a general class of elements for arbitrary boundary conditions. Taking care to ensure continuity of the variables at the inner boundaries and to satisfy external boundary conditions, we then link these element solutions to obtain a solution for the complete domain. Approximate solutions within elements are necessary because partial differential equations cannot be solved exactly for arbitrary boundary conditions.

To obtain these approximate solutions we use expressions, called interpolation functions, to represent the variables within an element. In heat flow, for example, these functions allow the variation of temperature within the element to be expressed in terms of temperature values at the corner point nodes of the triangular elements of Fig 2.1. Through this procedure the problem is finally reduced to solving for the nodal temperatures from which the temperature anywhere within the element can be found.

Element interpolations

In general we write element interpolations in the form

$$T = \Sigma f_i T_i = \{f\}^t \{T\} \qquad 2.5$$

where T_i are the temperatures at the element's nodes and f_i are the interpolation functions corresponding to each of the nodal values. $\{T\}$ and $\{f\}$ are respectively the vectors of nodal temperatures and interpolation functions for the element. Each interpolation function, f_i, expresses the variation of temperature within the element due to a unit change in temperature at node i while all other nodal temperatures are held to zero.

As an example of such an interpolation consider the one dimensional line element shown in Fig 2.2a representing a metal bar. If a linear interpolation is used this has the form

$$T = (1 - x/L)T_1 + (x/L)T_2 = f_1 T_1 + f_2 T_2 \qquad 2.6$$

where $\{f\} = \{1 - x/L, x/L\}$ and T_1 and T_2 are the temperatures at nodes 1 and 2.

If an additional node exists at the centre, as shown in Fig 2.2b, we can use a quadratic, ie a second order polynomial, interpola-

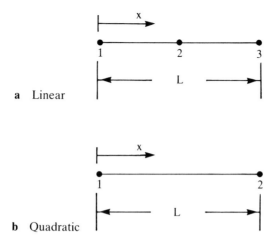

a Linear

b Quadratic

Figure 2.2 Two and three freedom dimensional elements

tion involving the three nodal temperatures T_1, T_2, T_3 now available. To obtain the interpolation we write initially $T = a + bx + cx^2$ and eliminate a, b and c by substituting $T_1 = T_{x=0}$, $T_2 = T_{x=L/2}$ and $T_3 = T_{x=L}$. This leads to

$$T = (1 - 3x/L + 2x^2/L^2)T_1 + (4x/L - 4x^2/L^2)T_2$$
$$+ (-x/L + 2x^2/L^2)T_3 \qquad 2.7$$

We can now differentiate the interpolation function twice and substitute it into equation 2.4b to obtain

$$d^2T/dx^2 = (4/L^2)T_1 + (-8/L^2)T_2 + (4/L^2)T_3 = 0 \qquad 2.8$$

relating the nodal temperatures within the element. This approach already provides a useful method of obtaining element equations in which we could also employ higher order polynomials in the hope of obtaining a better approximation. Such an approach is an example of the point collocation method in which the differential equation is satisfied exactly at chosen points. Point collocation is classified as a method of weighted residuals (MWR).

General approaches to solving differential equations within elements

Quite generally, in the finite element method, the approaches used to fit the interpolation function to the problem variables belong in one of the categories:

1 method of weighted residuals,
2 energy or variational methods

There are many variants of these general methods. The most widely used energy method is based upon the principle of minimum potential energy. The most widely employed weighted residual method, used in association with the finite element method, is the Galerkin method.

Generally weighted residual methods are used in fluid mechanics and like applications and energy methods are used in solid mechanics applications, as in the present text.

Heat flow element by the Galerkin method

Consider an example of one dimensional heat flow, governed by the differential equation $d^2T/dx^2 = 0$, for which we derive the finite element relationships by the Galerkin method. We designate the approximate interpolation function for T by T_a ($= \Sigma f_i T_i$), to distinguish it from the exact distribution T, and substitute into the differential equation. Because T_a does not satisfy the differential equation exactly, we obtain a small residual error, ie $d^2T_a/dx^2 = R$. In the Galerkin method we multiply this error, in turn, by each of the interpolating functions, f_i, integrate over the length and equate the result, on each occasion, to zero, ie we write,

$$\int_0^L f_i(R)dx = \int_0^L f_i(d^2T_a/dx^2)dx = 0 \qquad \textbf{2.9}$$

Rewriting equation 2.9 in matrix notation leads to

$$\int_0^L (\{f\}d^2(\{f\}^t)/dx^2\{T\})dx = \{0\} \qquad \textbf{2.10}$$

where $\{0\}$ is a null vector.

Because the nodal temperatures $\{T\}$ are constants these are moved outside the integral so we can write

$$\int_0^L (\{f\}\{f_{xx}\}^t dx) \ \{T\} = \{0\} \qquad \textbf{2.11}$$

where we have denoted $d^2\{f\}/dx^2$ as $\{f_{xx}\}$.

This expression may be used to form the element expressions although, because $\{f\}$ and $\{f_{xx}\}^t$ are not derivatives of the same order, the resulting element equations will be unsymmetric, ie the coefficient matrix formed from $\{f\}\{f_{xx}\}^t$, in parentheses, will be unsymmetric. Furthermore, if our interpolation is only linear, f_{xx} vanishes.

We overcome this lack of symmetry and, in the process, reduce the order of interpolation required by applying integration by parts to the interpolation product in equation 2.10 giving

$$\int_0^L (\{f\}\{f_{xx}\}^t\{T\})dx$$

$$= \{f\}\{f_x\}^t\{T\}\bigg|_0^L - \int_0^L (\{f_x\}\{f_x\}^t dx)\{T\} = \{0\} \qquad \textbf{2.12}$$

The first term on the RHS involves only element boundary terms so that the final element equations may be written as

$$\{q\} - k\{T\} = \{0\} \qquad \textbf{2.13a}$$

where
$$k = \int_0^L \{f_x\}\{f_x\}^t dx$$

$$\{q\} = \{dT/dx\} \qquad \textbf{2.13b}$$

are respectively the element coefficient matrix and the vector of temperature gradients at the ends of the element.

As k now involves first derivatives only we can use the simple linear element of Fig 2.2a. Note that at $x = 0$ we have $f_1 = 1$ and $f_2 = 0$ and at $x = L$ we have $f_1 = 0$ and $f_2 = 1$. Differentiating the interpolation functions of equation 2.6 we obtain

$$\{f_x\} = d\{(1 - x/L), (x/L)\}/dx = \{-1/L, 1/L\} \qquad \textbf{2.14}$$

Substituting this result into the first of equations 2.13b we obtain

$$k = \int_0^L \begin{bmatrix} -1/L \\ 1/L \end{bmatrix} [-1/L \quad 1/L] dx = (1/L) \begin{bmatrix} 1 & -1 \\ -1 & 1 \end{bmatrix} \qquad \textbf{2.15}$$

The equations for the element of Fig 2.2 are therefore

$$(1/L)\begin{bmatrix} 1 & -1 \\ -1 & 1 \end{bmatrix}\begin{bmatrix} T_1 \\ T_2 \end{bmatrix} = \begin{bmatrix} -(dT/dx)_1 \\ +(dT/dx)_2 \end{bmatrix}$$ **2.16**

Although we considered the example $d^2T/dx^2 = 0$ for the purpose of demonstration, the same exercise can be repeated, in principle, for any ordinary $\pounds(x) = 0$ or partial $\pounds(x,y) = 0$ differential equation in which $\pounds$ represents a differential operator.

One dimensional truss element by the energy method

To demonstrate the method of minimum total potential energy we consider the problem of the two freedom truss element shown in Fig 2.3 which is, as we have already pointed out, mathematically analogous to the heat flow problem.

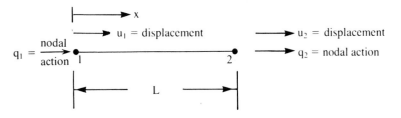

Figure 2.3   Two freedom one dimensional truss element

This element has two displacement freedoms u_1 and u_2, one at each node. The displacement at any point within the element is again given, as in the temperature problem, by the linear interpolation

$$u = (1 - x/L)u_1 + (x/L)u_2 = f_1u_1 + f_2u_2$$ **2.17**

The strain at any point now follows as

$$\varepsilon = du/dx = d(\{f\}^t\{u\})/dx = [-1/L \quad 1/L]\{u\}$$ **2.18**

or $$\varepsilon = B\{u\}$$ **2.19**

where $B = [-1/L \quad 1/L]$ is called the strain interpolation matrix. The stress at any point is given by Hooke's law as

$$\sigma = E\varepsilon$$ **2.20**

where E is Young's modulus.

Corresponding to the nodal freedoms u_1 and u_2 we define interelement reactions q_1 and q_2 which are analogous to the flux terms of equation 2.16. These are the forces exerted by the other elements of the truss on this particular element to hold it in equilibrium.

We evaluate the element total potential energy Π_e as the sum of the strain energy in the element and the work done by the interelement reactions as

$$\Pi_e = \tfrac{1}{2}\int \varepsilon_x \sigma_x dV - \{u\}^t\{q\} \qquad 2.21$$

Substituting equations 2.19 and 2.20 into equation 2.21 leads to

$$\Pi_e = \tfrac{1}{2}\{u\}^t\left(E \int B^t B dV\right)\{u\} - \{u\}^t\{q\}$$

$$= \tfrac{1}{2}[u_1 \quad u_2]\, k \begin{bmatrix} u_1 \\ u_2 \end{bmatrix} - [u_1 \quad u_2]\begin{bmatrix} q_1 \\ q_2 \end{bmatrix}$$

$$= \tfrac{1}{2}(k_{11}u_1^2 + k_{12}u_1u_2 + k_{21}u_2u_1 + k_{22}u_2^2) - (u_1 q_1 + u_2 q_2)$$
$$2.22$$

where k is the stiffness matrix given by equation 2.24.

Using the principle of minimum total potential energy to minimise Π_e we obtain

$$\partial\Pi_e/\partial\{u\} = \left(E \int B^t B dV\right)\{u\} - \{q\} = \{0\}$$

$$= k\{u\} - \{q\} \qquad 2.23a$$

The expression $\partial\Pi_e/\partial\{u\}$ is taken to mean that the scalar Π_e is differentiated, in turn, with respect to each term of the displacement vector $\{u\}$, ie we perform

$$\partial\Pi_e/\partial u_1 = k_{11}u_1 + k_{12}u_2 - q_1 = 0$$
$$\partial\Pi_e/\partial u_2 = k_{21}u_1 + k_{22}u_2 - q_2 = 0 \qquad 2.23b$$

The detailed steps involved in computing the matrix k of equation 2.23a are as follows

$$k = E \int B^t B dV = EA \int B^t B dx$$

$$= (EA)\int_0^L \begin{bmatrix} -1/L \\ 1/L \end{bmatrix}[-1/L \quad 1/L]dx$$

$$= (EA/L)\begin{bmatrix} 1 & -1 \\ -1 & 1 \end{bmatrix}$$

$$= \begin{bmatrix} k_{11} & k_{12} \\ k_{21} & k_{22} \end{bmatrix} \qquad \textbf{2.24}$$

in which k is known as the element stiffness matrix (ESM).

2.2 Assembling and solving the system equations

To obtain solutions to finite element problems, element expressions, such as equations 2.16 and 2.23b, must be combined to obtain the equations for the complete domain. The system of equations obtained is then solved to complete the problem.

In the case of the energy method the objective of the assembly process is to obtain the structure total potential energy by summing the element total potential energies, ie to carry out the summation $\Pi = \Sigma\Pi_e$. Because minimising Π_e at the element level leads to a relationship linking between the element end actions, the element stiffness matrix and displacements it follows, by analogy, that minimising at the structure level will lead to a relationship between the applied nodal loads, nodal displacements and the structure stiffness matrix, ie

$$\Pi = \Sigma\Pi_e = \Sigma(\text{Element strain energy})$$

$$+ \Sigma(\text{PE of element end actions})$$

$$= \Sigma(\text{Element strain energy}) + (\text{PE of nodal loads})$$

In this expression we have used the relationship, PE of nodal loads = Σ(PE of element end actions), in view of the joints being in equilibrium. We illustrate the application of this principle in the summation process described below.

An analogous principle applies when the Galerkin method is used as in the heat flow example. The Galerkin error products for the individual elements are simply summed to obtain that of the entire domain, ie summing element Galerkin error products is the same process as adding element total potential energies. This universal summation process for the element equations is demonstrated below for the three element steady state heat flow problem shown in Fig 2.4.

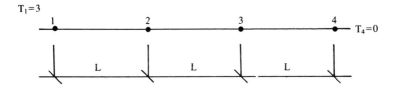

Figure 2.4 Three element heat flow problem using linear elements 1–2, 2–3, 3–4

Example of assembly and solution procedures

The element equations for the heat flow example are given by equation 2.16 and, after assembly, appear as follows

$$(1/L)\begin{bmatrix} 1 & -1 & 0 & 0 \\ -1 & 2 & -1 & 0 \\ 0 & -1 & 2 & -1 \\ 0 & 0 & -1 & 1 \end{bmatrix}\begin{bmatrix} T_1 \\ T_2 \\ T_3 \\ T_4 \end{bmatrix} = \begin{bmatrix} 0 \\ 0 \\ 0 \\ 0 \end{bmatrix} \qquad 2.25$$

In this example it is relatively easy to see what has happened. The element matrices have the overlapping pattern indicated as a result of some nodes being shared by elements. As there are no specified nodal heat fluxes at the nodes the interelement fluxes on the right side of equation 2.16 cancel because of their alternating signs. Where external heat fluxes occur at the nodes these will appear on the right hand side of equation 2.25.

To solve equations 2.25 we note that T_1 ($= 3$) and T_4 ($= 0$) are specified boundary conditions. We move these known variables to the right hand side by multiplying the corresponding columns by their values and placing them in the right hand side vector. We then omit the first and fourth equations so that we are left with

$$(1/L)\begin{bmatrix} 2 & -1 \\ -1 & 2 \end{bmatrix}\begin{bmatrix} T_2 \\ T_3 \end{bmatrix} = \begin{bmatrix} 3/L \\ 0 \end{bmatrix} \qquad 2.26$$

Solving equation 2.26 we obtain $T_2 = 2$ and $T_3 = 1$ as expected.

2.3   Convergence of finite element solutions

Extrapolation techniques

In skeletal problems, such as the analysis of trusses and frames, there is a natural discretisation of the problem in which the nodes can be chosen to coincide with the member intersections without loss of solution accuracy. In general, however, the domain is a continuum and the accuracy of any finite element analysis depends on the number of nodes and elements chosen and the order of the polynomial approximating functions within each element.

Suppose we use elements of length 'h' (in one dimension this is clear and in two dimensions it is the average length of the element sides) and these involve an interpolation of order p, ie a polynomial of the form $u = c_1 + c_2x + c_3x^2 + \cdots + c_{p+1}x^p$. To form the element matrices we differentiate this polynomial m times, eg in the temperature problem $m = 1$, which means the largest term missing from the element stiffness matrix computation is $(\text{const.})h^{p-m+1}$.

The missing term is referred to as the truncation error, said to be of order h^{p-m+1} and is denoted by $O(h^{p-m+1})$. It can be shown that symmetric element matrices k of the type used above involve an error in the energy product of $O(h^{2p-2m+2})$.[1,2] This result is surprising in some respects because errors in the load terms do not appear and integration over the length h of the element does not affect the result. It is easy to show this is correct,[3] however, and that we can extrapolate finite element solutions from two coarse meshes to obtain better solutions rather than use a single very fine mesh.[1]

To obtain the required extrapolation formula, we write the solutions for a nodal variable u obtained with two meshes, with element sizes h_i and h_j ($h_i > h_j$), as

$$u_i = u^* - (\text{const.})h_i^N \qquad \qquad 2.27$$

$$u_j = u^* - (\text{const.})h_j^N \qquad \qquad 2.28$$

where u^* is the extrapolated solution. Eliminating the constant from equations 2.27 and 2.28 and solving for u^* we obtain the extrapolation formula[1]

$$u^* = u_j + (u_j - u_i)/[(h_i/h_j)^N - 1] \qquad \qquad 2.29$$

where $N = 2(p - m + 1)$ is the order of the element truncation error.

Extrapolation of secondary quantities such as stresses or fluxes, which are calculated from the nodal variables, is more complex. Space does not permit detailed examination of this point but it can be shown that, in stress analysis problems solved using the displacement method described in Chapters 8 and 9, the stress truncation error is of the order $O(h^2)$.[1]

Admissibility criteria

The discussion above refers to conditions under which the interpolations comply with certain admissibility criteria. Considerable attention has been directed to the question of whether, as the element size decreases, the solution accuracy improves. For this to happen it is necessary that:

1 all rigid body modes be represented,
2 all constant strain modes be represented.

If we consider the truss element of Section 2.1, it is usual to use the interpolation $u = c_1 + c_2x$. However, if, instead, we use $u = c_1x + cx^2$ then automatically we have $u = 0$ at $x = 0$. Clearly, as the element size decreases, the elements become subject to more constraint and overall the solution tends to $u = 0$ throughout irrespective of the load. The use of $u = c_1 + c_2x^2$ or $\varepsilon = 2c_2x$ ultimately implies that $\varepsilon = 0$ throughout with element refinement and causes a similar difficulty. The same arguments also apply for two and three dimensional elements.

Interelement continuity

It is not actually necessary for element interpolations to imply that strains and displacements along element boundaries match exactly, in order to achieve acceptable solutions to finite element problems. For line elements such matching automatically occurs but, in two and three dimensional problems, this may not happen, eg along the sides of triangular elements between the nodes. This issue is addressed in Chapter 9 in connection with plate bending analysis where it presents a serious problem.

References

1 G A Mohr and I C Medland, 'On convergence of displacement finite elements, with an application to singularity problems', *Engineering Fracture Mechanics*, vol 17, 1983, p 481.

2 O C Zienkiewicz, *The Finite Element Method*, 3rd edn, McGraw–Hill, New York, 1977.

3 O C Zienkiewicz and K Morgan, *Finite Elements and Approximation*, Wiley, New York, 1983.

CHAPTER **3**

Steady State Network Problems

In this chapter we further develop the type of analysis introduced in Chapter 2 and show how simple one dimensional finite elements, with only two freedoms, can be used to analyse a wide variety of important engineering problems. These include electrical current flow in dc and ac networks and the flow of fluids in hydraulic networks. Problems of this nature are among the most practically important in engineering.

3.1 dc networks

Element expressions Fig 3.1 shows a typical resistance element of a dc network in which the nodal variables are the electrical potential values V_i and V_j measured in volts. We obtain the element equations directly from Ohm's law which we take in the form

$$V_i - V_j = I_{ij}R \qquad 3.1$$

where R is the resistance in ohms and I_{ij} is the current, in amperes, flowing from node i to j. It is taken as positive if $V_i > V_j$ which is equivalent to assuming that current flows from points of high voltage to points of low voltage.

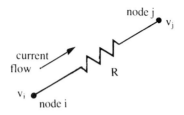

Figure 3.1 Two freedom resistance element of a dc network

At nodes, a flow in to or out of that node from an element is designated by $(I_i)_n$, where n is the element number and i the node number. If the flow is coming from an external current source, ie one which supplies a fixed current irrespective of the nodal voltage, we designate it $(I_i)_e$. At nodes, $(I_i)_n$ and $(I_i)_e$ are taken as positive if the flow is into the node.

In the case of flows from elements, we have, for end i, that $(I_i)_n = I_{ij}$ and, for end j, $(I_j)_n = -I_{ij}$. Substituting these expressions into equation 3.1 leads to

$$V_i - V_j = (I_i)_n R \qquad \textbf{3.2a}$$

$$-V_i + V_j = (I_j)_n R \qquad \textbf{3.2b}$$

Writing equations 3.2 in matrix form, we obtain the expressions for element n as

$$\begin{bmatrix} G & -G \\ -G & G \end{bmatrix} \begin{bmatrix} V_i \\ V_j \end{bmatrix} = \begin{bmatrix} (I_i)_n \\ (I_j)_n \end{bmatrix} \qquad \textbf{3.3}$$

where $G = 1/R$ is the conductance.

Note also, that this result can be derived by the use of interpolation functions and the application of the weighted residual or variational methods introduced in Chapter 2. Using such approaches, we commence with the governing differential equation $dV/dx = -I_{ij}r$, where x is the length along the conductor and r is the resistance per unit length. Next we choose, say, a linear interpolation function for the potential V and, by forming a weighted residual expression, derive equation 3.3. The direct procedure was used above because it is more straightforward.

Network expression Equation 3.3 can be used as a standard expression for each resistive element of the complete circuit. In forming the system equations we also need to use Kirchoff's current law which states that the sum of the currents flowing into and out of a node from all sources (elements and external sources) is zero, ie

$$\Sigma(I_i)_n + (I_i)_e = 0 \qquad \textbf{3.4}$$

To illustrate the use of equations 3.3 and 3.4 consider the circuit of Fig 3.2. Using the assembly procedure of Section 2.2 and the element conductance matrices of equation 3.3 we obtain, after noting equation 3.4, the system equation

$$C\{V\} = \begin{bmatrix} G_1+G_2 & -G_1 & -G_2 & 0 \\ -G_1 & G_1+G_3 & 0 & -G_3 \\ -G_2 & 0 & G_2+G_4 & -G_4 \\ 0 & -G_3 & -G_4 & G_3+G_4 \end{bmatrix} \begin{bmatrix} V_1 \\ V_2 \\ V_3 \\ V_4 \end{bmatrix} = \begin{bmatrix} 0 \\ 0 \\ 0 \\ 0 \end{bmatrix} \quad 3.5$$

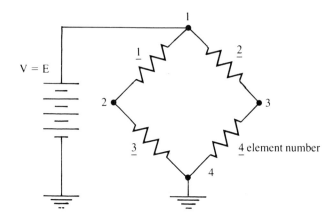

Figure 3.2   Simple dc network

Element 1, with its conductance G_1, has its conductance matrix added as a 2 × 2 block to the top left corner of the system matrix because its node numbers are consecutive. Element 2, on the other hand, connects nodes 1 and 3 so that the entries in its conductance matrix are placed at locations (1,1), (1,3), (3,1), (3,3) in the system matrix. If its conductance, G, and node numbers I and J have just been read as data the computer code to carry out the assembly would read as

$$C(I,I) = C(I,I) + G$$
$$C(I,J) = C(I,J) - G$$
$$C(J,I) = C(J,I) - G$$
$$C(J,J) = C(J,J) + G$$

where C(,) is the circuit conductance matrix. For resistor (1–3), I = 1 and J = 3.

Readers should work through this assembly exercise and, when doing so, may find it helpful to write the voltages which apply to each column at the top of the initially empty system matrix. Furthermore, during this assembly process, because there are no current inputs from external sources in this problem, the application of equation 3.4 leads to the RHS vector being null.

Boundary conditions and equation solution If we now attempted to solve equation 3.5 as it stands, we would find the matrix C is singular. It is necessary to specify the potential of at least two nodes in the network. In specifying a voltage we are implying the node is physically connected to a voltage source which provides a constant voltage irrespective of the magnitude of the current drawn from it. In this case the value of V_1 is taken equal to E and V_4 is taken equal to zero.

The introduction of the zero voltage condition is quite straightforward. The $V_4=0$ condition is introduced by placing 1 in position $C(4,4)$ and 0 in all other $C(4,J)$ and $C(I,4)$ positions, ie zeroing column 4 and row 4 except for the term on the leading diagonal. If other zero voltages exist then an identical procedure is followed for the corresponding rows and columns. If a set of non-zero voltage conditions is to be introduced then we first carry out a shift of origin procedure by subtracting the specified voltages from $\{V\}$ to produce a set of virtual voltages. Let the specified voltages be $\{E\}$ and the virtual voltages be $\{v\}$, then

$$\{v\} = \{V\} - \{E\}$$

and $\qquad \{I\} = \{0\} = C\{V\} = C\{v\} + C\{E\} \qquad$ **3.6a**

or $\qquad\qquad C\{v\} = -C\{E\} \qquad\qquad$ **3.6b**

In vector $\{E\}$ zeros are introduced at nodes where the voltages are zero or unspecified; elsewhere the non-zero values are introduced. The RHS is formed from the matrix product $C\{E\}$ and, since wherever V is specified as non-zero v will be zero, then zero virtual voltages can be treated as described above for treating the $V_4 = 0$ condition. After solution for $\{v\}$, actual voltages are recovered using

$$\{V\} = \{v\} + \{E\} \qquad \textbf{3.6c}$$

Applying this to the present problem leads to

$$\begin{bmatrix} 1 & 0 & 0 & 0 \\ 0 & G_1+G_3 & 0 & 0 \\ 0 & 0 & G_2+G_4 & 0 \\ 0 & 0 & 0 & 1 \end{bmatrix} \begin{bmatrix} v_1 \\ v_2 \\ v_3 \\ v_4 \end{bmatrix} = \begin{bmatrix} 0 \\ G_1E \\ G_2E \\ 0 \end{bmatrix} \qquad \textbf{3.6d}$$

The solution of the equations for the virtual voltages in this case is extremely simple although, in general, a computer routine, such as Gauss or Gauss–Jordan reduction, has to be used. Equation 3.6d leads to

$$V_1 = v_1 + E = 0 + E = E$$
$$V_2 = v_2 + 0 = G_1E/(G_1 + G_3)$$
$$V_3 = v_3 + 0 = G_2E/(G_2 + G_4)$$
$$V_4 = v_4 + 0 = 0 \qquad\qquad 3.7$$

In the description above it may wondered why we have presented the equation solution process as involving four simultaneous equations, when it is possible to delete rows and columns 1 and 4, and solve the reduced system

$$\begin{bmatrix} G_1+G_3 & 0 \\ 0 & G_2+G_4 \end{bmatrix} \begin{bmatrix} v_2 \\ v_3 \end{bmatrix} = \begin{bmatrix} G_1E \\ G_2E \end{bmatrix} \qquad 3.8$$

In general, the rearrangement of the equations in this form is difficult to code into computer programmes and, in most problems of any significant size, there are comparatively few boundary conditions in relation to the number of unknown nodal variables. Therefore, solving the equations with a few additional trivial equations is not especially inefficient.

BASIC program for dc networks   The BASIC program below can be used to solve any dc network problem. It uses the dimensioned arrays

C(20,20)   the system conductance matrix

V(20)   initially the right hand side matrix which, after the application of Gauss–Jordan reduction (see Section A.11), contains the solutions for the nodal voltages.

The data is read using INPUT statements and is required in the order:

1   # nodes, # elements, # specified voltages(NP,NE,NS)
  (# = number of)
2   node numbers for each element and its resistance(I,J,R). There will be NE such lines.
3   node number and any specified voltages — NS such lines.

For the problem of Fig 3.2 above, with E = 1 and R = 1 for all resistors, the data required would be

Problem paramaters
        4,4,2   (NP,NE,NS)

Element detail

Node i,	Node j,	Resistance	
1,	2,	1	
1,	3,	1	
2,	4,	1	NE lines
3,	4,	1	

Nodal voltages

Node	Voltage	
1,	1	
4,	0	NS lines

and the program will return the solutions

$V_1 = 1$, $V_2 = 0.5$, $V_3 = 0.5$, $V_4 = 0$.

Listing of program *DCNET*

```
10 DIM C(20,20),V(20):A$=" ##        ##.####":B$=" ##"
20 FOR I=1 TO 20
30 V(I)=0
40 FOR J=1 TO 20
50 C(I,J)=0:NEXT J:NEXT I
60 PRINT "Input"
70 PRINT "(No .of nodes)  (No. of resistors)   ";
80 PRINT "(No. of specified voltages)"
90 INPUT NP,NE,NS
100 FOR K=1 TO NE
110 PRINT "Input (NodeI),(NodeJ),(Resistance) for Elem
ent";
120 PRINT USING B$;K:INPUT I,J,R
130 C(I,I)=C(I,I)+1/R
140 C(I,J)=C(I,J)-1/R
150 C(J,I)=C(J,I)-1/R
160 C(J,J)=C(J,J)+1/R
170 NEXT K
180 FOR K=1 TO NS
190 PRINT "Input specified voltages (node),(voltage)":
INPUT N,S
200 FOR I=1 TO NP
210 C(N,I)=0:V(I)=V(I)-S*C(I,N)
220 C(I,N)=0:NEXT I
230 V(N)=S:C(N,N)=1:NEXT K
240 FOR I=1 TO NP
250 X=C(I,I):V(I)=V(I)/X
260 FOR J=I+1 TO NP
270 C(I,J)=C(I,J)/X:NEXT J
280 FOR K=1 TO NP
290 IF K=I GOTO 330
300 X=C(K,I):V(K)=V(K)-X*V(I)
310 FOR J=I+1 TO NP
```

```
320 C(K,J)=C(K,J)-X*C(I,J):NEXT J
330 NEXT K
340 NEXT I
350 PRINT:PRINT "Node        Voltage"
360 FOR I=1 TO NP
370 PRINT USING A$;I,V(I):NEXT I
380 END
```

Note Further code can be added to calculate the current flow in each element and any other quantity of interest such as the power dissipation. To extract this information, the node numbers of each resistor are stored in an array NO(20,2) and the following code added

```
11  DIM NO(20,2),R(20)
95  PRINT USING B$;:INPUT NO(K,1),NO(K,2),R(K)
344 PRINT "Element      Current"
345 FOR N=1 TO NE
346 I=NO(N,1):J=NO(N,2)
347 CN=(V(I)-V(J))/R(N):PRINT USING A$;N,CN:NEXT N
```

3.2   Loop current formulation of dc network problems

An alternative approach to dc network problems is through the use of loop currents. As an example, consider the circuit shown in Fig 3.3.

We assume loop currents a,b,c flow in each closed loop of the circuit shown and use Ohm's law, equation 3.1, to determine the voltage drops in each element. Noting that, by Kirchoff's voltage law, their sum around each closed loop must be zero, we obtain the three equations (taking $R = 1$ and $E = 1$)

$$a + 5(a - c) + 4(a - b) = 0 \qquad \textbf{3.9}$$

$$b + 4(b - a) - 2 = 0 \qquad \textbf{3.10}$$

$$5(c - a) + c + 1 = 0 \qquad \textbf{3.11}$$

Rearranging these we obtain

$$10a - 4b - 5c = 0 \qquad \textbf{3.12}$$

$$-4a + 5b + 0c = 2 \qquad \textbf{3.13}$$

$$-5c + 0b + 6c = -1 \qquad \textbf{3.14}$$

Using Gauss elimination to solve the equations leads to the results a = 0.29114, b = 0.63291, c = 0.07595

and the voltages at nodes 2 and 4 are calculated as

$$V_2 = 2 - 0.63291 = 1.36709$$
$$V_4 = 1 + 0.07595 = 1.07595$$

As we compute currents in this problem, rather than voltages, it is termed the dual of the one solved in Section 3.1. For hand solution the dual problem is sometimes simpler in that it often involves fewer unknowns. The formulation in terms of voltages is, however, easier to program.

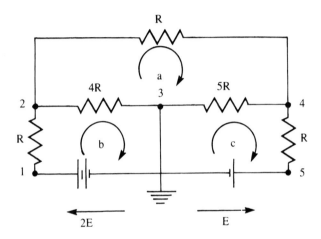

Figure 3.3   dc circuit with loop currents

3.3   ac networks

In steady state ac circuits the voltage and current vary with time but the pattern of variation is cyclic, ie the same pattern, usually sinusoidal, repeats indefinitely.

Basic sources of impedance to ac flow

The magnitude and phase of the time varying current in an ac network are determined by the three basic circuit elements whose instantaneous values of voltage, v, and current, i, are related by the equations:

a pure resistor

$$v = iR \qquad 3.15$$

where R is the resistance,

a pure capacitor

$$i = C(dv/dt) \qquad 3.16$$

where C is the capacitance and t is time,

a pure self-inductor

$$v = L(di/dt) \qquad 3.17$$

where L is the self inductance.

Expressions for basic circuit components   Let us suppose an element is carrying an alternating current. Assume the driving voltage v, applied across the element, is given by

$$v = V_m \sin \omega t \qquad 3.18$$

$$= \sqrt{2}V \sin \omega t \qquad 3.19$$

where V_m is the peak voltage and V the root mean square (rms) voltage. We now determine expressions for the flow of current through these basic elements.

For a purely resistive element we have, from equations 3.15 and 3.19, that

$$i = \sqrt{2}V \sin \omega t \qquad 3.20$$

The impedance, Z_R, is defined as the ratio, (voltage function/current function) and is given by

$$Z_R = v/i = \sqrt{2}V \sin \omega t / (\sqrt{2}V \sin \omega t / R) = R \qquad 3.21$$

Following the same procedure for a purely capacitive element leads to

$$Z_C = v/i = (1/\omega C) \sin \omega t / \sin (\omega t + \pi/2) \qquad 3.22$$

which shows that the current through a capacitor leads the voltage by $\pi/2$.

Finally, for an inductive element,

$$Z_L = v/i = (\omega L)\sin\omega t/\sin(\omega t - \pi/2) \qquad \textbf{3.23}$$

and the current lags the voltage by $\pi/2$.

Phasor notation   The above expressions are very clumsy and no circuit analysis could conveniently proceed using them. More convenient expressions are obtained by introducing complex variable notation and transforming the problem to the frequency domain. In the frequency domain, we write relationships between the rms voltages and currents in which the complex operator, j, indicates the phase relationships. Introducing such notation, equations 3.21–3.23 take the form

$$Z_R = V/I = R$$
$$Z_C = V/I = -j/\omega C$$
$$Z_L = V/I = j\omega L$$

For a resistor, if we choose the input voltage to have the form $v = \sin\omega t$, ie zero phase angle, then the current is also real. For capacitors and inductors, the choice of voltage for the time reference leads to the current being purely imaginary, ie $\pm\pi/2$ out of phase with the voltage. More generally, however, we could regard both the voltage and current as being complex. In fact, this becomes necessary in a circuit having many nodes and elements because the voltage at a particular node or the current in a particular element may have any phase relationship to the reference input voltage.

Expressions for subassemblies   While it is possible to regard ac networks as composed of an assemblage of the above elements it is preferable, for computational purposes, to use larger building blocks and to treat the more basic circuit elements as special cases. Consider first a resistor, capacitor and inductor in series for which it can be shown that

$$V_1 + jV_2 = (I_1 + jI_2)[R + j(\omega L - 1/\omega C)]$$
$$= (I_1 + jI_2)[R + jX] \qquad \textbf{3.24}$$

where $X = \omega L - 1/\omega C$ and the subscripts 1 and 2 on the voltages and currents indicate the real and imaginary parts.

For a parallel circuit with the same basic elements we obtain, by similar procedures,

$$V_1 + jV_2 = (I_1 + jI_2)[1/R + j(\omega C - 1/\omega L)]^{-1} \qquad \textbf{3.25a}$$

$$= (I_1 + jI_2)[G + jB]^{-1} \qquad \textbf{3.25b}$$

where $G = 1/R$ and $B = \omega C - 1/\omega L$.

We can also develop further expressions for subassemblies having, say, a resistor and inductor in series and a capacitor in parallel and other combinations. However, whatever combinations we use these can always have their voltage–current relationship written in the general form

$$V_1 + jV_2 = (Z_1 + jZ_2)(I_1 + jI_2) \qquad \textbf{3.26}$$

where Z_1 and Z_2 are the real and imaginary components of impedance. We can also form the inverse of equation 3.26, viz

$$I_1 + jI_2 = (Y_1 + jY_2)(V_1 + jV_2) \qquad \textbf{3.27}$$

where Y_1 and Y_2 are the complex components of the admittances and are related to the impedances by

$$Y_1 = Z_1/(Z_1^2 + Z_2^2) \qquad \textbf{3.28}$$

$$Y_2 = -Z_2/(Z_1^2 + Z_2^2) \qquad \textbf{3.29}$$

Networks by the nodal voltage method   The nodal method for ac networks is a generalisation of the same procedure given in Section 3.1 for dc networks. To form the element matrix equation we consider a typical element having nodes designated by the numbers 1 and 2 and complex admittance $Y_1 + jY_2$. We assume the complex potentials at nodes 1 and 2 are, respectively, $V_{11} + jV_{12}$ and $V_{21} + jV_{22}$* and that the current is $I_1 + jI_2$. Assuming that current flowing out of a node is positive we can write the relationship between nodal potentials and currents as

$$\begin{bmatrix} (I_1 + jI_2)_n \\ -(I_1 + jI_2)_n \end{bmatrix} = (Y_1 + jY_2)\begin{bmatrix} 1 & -1 \\ -1 & 1 \end{bmatrix}\begin{bmatrix} V_{11} + jV_{12} \\ V_{21} + jV_{22} \end{bmatrix} \qquad \textbf{3.27}$$

where $(I_1 + jI_2)_n$ and $-(I_1 + jI_2)_n$ are respectively the currents flowing out of nodes 1 and 2 into element n; see Section 3.1.

Next we assemble the system equations and use Kirchoff's law which, as before, requires that the sum of currents flowing out of a node be equal to the nett input from external sources. This leads to the expression

$$[Y_1 + jY_2]\{V_1 + jV_2\} = -\{I_1 + jI_2\} \qquad \textbf{3.28}$$

---

* The potential differences used in equations 3.24–3.27 are related to the node potentials by $V_1 = V_{11} - V_{21}$ and $V_2 = V_{12} - V_{22}$.

where $\{V_1 + jV_2\}$ and $\{I_1 + jI_2\}$ are the vectors of nodal voltages and current input from external sources respectively for the entire network.

To solve such equations we separate real and imaginary parts which leads to

$$(Y_1V_1 - Y_2V_2) = I_1$$
$$(Y_2V_1 + Y_1V_2) = I_2 \qquad \qquad 3.29$$

Equation 3.29 can be written as

$$\begin{bmatrix} Y_1 & -Y_2 \\ Y_2 & Y_1 \end{bmatrix} \begin{bmatrix} V_1 \\ V_2 \end{bmatrix} = \begin{bmatrix} I_1 \\ I_2 \end{bmatrix} \qquad \qquad 3.30$$

showing that, when solving ac networks, the dimensions of the coefficient matrix double and the system is unsymmetric. In other respects the solution procedures are similar to those for dc networks.

3.4   Pipe networks

Steady state pipe network problems must, like all equilibrium problems, satisfy conservation, continuity and constitutive relationships. In linear skeletal frames these are respectively dealt with by ensuring conservation of energy, equilibrium and the use of Hooke's law. In pipe networks the analogous requirements are met in the same way as they are in electrical networks by using

$\Sigma q = 0$ at junctions (conservation),
$\Sigma p = 0$ around closed loops (continuity),
$p = Rq^2$ in each branch (constitutive).

Again, the first two are, once again, Kirchoff's laws and the third is Darcy's law (analogous to Ohm's law) which is nonlinear. Usually the exponent is slightly less than two but here we take two for the sake of convenience.

This problem possesses dual forms. One approach is to use nodal pressures as variables[1] and to solve the problem along similar lines to that outlined in Section 3.1 for dc networks. The alternative is to use loop flows[2] as variables; see Fig 3.4.

It is assumed that the branch flows comprise a loop, L_i, and base flow, B_{ij}. The base flows are chosen to satisfy the demands D_j by some systematic approach such as by setting

$$B_{ij} = D_j \qquad \qquad 3.31$$

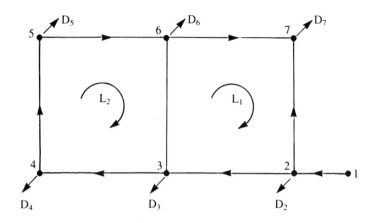

Figure 3.4 Pipe network showing loop flows

As each branch is introduced into the problem, equation 3.31 is employed provided D_j has not been satisfied by an earlier base flow. This process satisfies the conservation requirement stated above. The loop flows are now introduced to provide head balance and satisfy the continuity requirement. It follows that the total flow Q_{ij} is given by

$$Q_{ij} = B_{ij} + \sum_{ij} L \qquad \qquad 3.32$$

and that there will no head loss around a loop provided

$$\sum_1 R_{ij} Q_{ij}^2 = 0 = \sum_1 R_{ij} \left(B_{ij} + \sum_{ij} L \right)^2 \qquad \qquad 3.33$$

$\sum_1$ signifies summation over all branches in a loop and $\sum_{ij}$ signifies summation over branch ij. An equation of the type 3.33 can be written for each loop.

As the problem is nonlinear, an iterative solution technique must be used. If we assume the 'unproductive' loop currents are small then the problem can be linearised by neglecting the squares of the loop flows. Equation 3.33 simplifies to

$$\sum_1 R_{ij} B_{ij}^2 + \sum_1 R_{ij} \left(2B_{ij} \left(\sum_{ij} L \right) \right) = 0 \qquad \qquad 3.34$$

where, because the B_{ij} terms are known the problem is linear.

If it is considered necessary to take account of the nonlinear effects the loop flows can be estimated using equation 3.34 and a better estimate formed from

$$\sum_1 R_{ij}\left(2B_{ij}\left(\sum_{ij}L\right)\right) = -\sum_1 R_{ij}B_{ij}^2 - \sum_1 R_{ij}\left(\sum_{ij}L^2\right) \quad 3.35$$

This loop flow technique is used in some commercially available computer programs. It resembles the flexibility method of structural analysis used for truss and frame structures where statically determinate forces are first eliminated and the problem solved for a set of unknown redundant forces. In the pipe flow case the loop flows are designated as redundants whereas, in structural problems, the selection of the redundant forces requires considerable additional programming.[3]

3.5 Exercises

1 Using the nodal potential method of Section 3.1 verify that the solutions to the problem of Fig 3.2 are $V_2 = 0.5$, $V_3 = 0.5$ if $E = 1$ and $R = 1$.

2 Rework the exercise of (1) using the loop flow method of Section 3.2 (Hint: Use two loop flows).

3 Check through the working of the loop flow problem of Fig 3.3 carefully to ensure that you understand this technique. Also solve this problem using the nodal potential method of Section 3.1. Check that you obtain the same solution as obtained in Section 3.2.

4 Type the program given in Section 3.1 into your microcomputer.

5 Run the problem of Fig 3.2 to check that your program works.

6 Run the problem of Fig 3.3 as an exercise in applying your program. Check the answers against those given in Section 3.2. (Assume $E = 1$ and $R = 1$.)

References

1 S H Crandall, *Engineering Analysis*, McGraw-Hill, New York, 1956.

2 W O Skeat (ed), *Manual of British Water Engineering Practice*, 4th edn, Heffer and Sons, Cambridge, 1969.

3 J S Przemieniecki, *Theory of Matrix Structural Analysis*, McGraw-Hill, New York, 1968.

CHAPTER 4

Analysis of Truss Structures

In this chapter we describe finite element analysis of truss structures, ie structures involving elements linked together by pinned joints which are assumed to transmit only axial forces to the elements. For most truss structures, provided the truss members are sufficiently slender, and their bending stiffness is negligible compared to their extensional stiffness, this is also reasonable for trusses with welded joints. At the end of the chapter we have included a short program which determines the nodal displacements in truss structures and calculates the axial load in each member. Such programs are now very widely used in engineering practice.

4.1 Element stiffness matrices for truss elements (direct approach)

We have already determined the element stiffness matrix for a one dimensional truss (or spar) element in Chapter 2 (see equation 2.24) using an energy approach and one dimensional linear interpolation. We now undertake the closely related exercise of obtaining the element stiffness matrix for a two dimensional truss element but, by way of demonstration, we use the direct processes employed in the dc network problem of the previous chapter.

Truss geometry We observe in Fig 4.1 a two dimensional truss the nodes of which are numbered. Its shape is described by two sets of data. First, we specify the nodal co-ordinates with respect to a set of global (x,y) axes. Second, we indicate the existence of an element by stating its terminal node numbers, ie a particular element will link node i to node j.

Local element stiffness matrix In general, truss elements are inclined at varying angles to the global x axis and it is therefore necessary to assign two degrees of freedom to each node; one for the horizontal movement u_i and one for the vertical movement v_i. The element stiffness matrices are evaluated, initially, with reference to a set of local axes (x^*,y^*) in which the x^* axis is parallel to the element axis. Subsequently, a co-ordinate transformation process is carried out to determine the element stiffness matrices with reference to the global axes.

Fig 4.1 shows a four freedom truss element at an angle α to the global x axis, along with its nodal displacements and corresponding end actions. We assume that the element is in tension and draw inwardly directed internal forces P at each end, as shown. (If the member is actually in compression this will be revealed by analysis and will result in the element force being a negative quantity.)

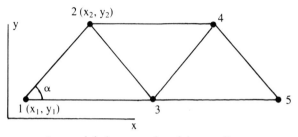

a   truss, global axes and nodal co-ordinates
b   element global displacements and end actions

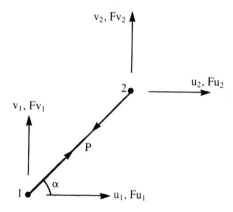

Figure 4.1   Four freedom truss elements

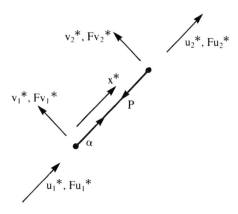

c   element local displacements and end actions

Figure 4.1   *Continued*

The load–displacement relationship for the element is given by

$$du^*/dx^* = P/EA \qquad \textbf{4.1}$$

where, in general, $P = P(x^*)$ is a function of position x^* along the element. In truss problems, since there are usually no forces distributed along the element, P is constant and we have, as the equation of equilibrium,

$$dP/dx^* = 0 \qquad \textbf{4.2}$$

On substitution into equation 4.1 and rearrangement the result is the governing differential equation for a prismatic member

$$EAd^2u^*/dx^{*2} = 0 \qquad \textbf{4.3}$$

This governing differential equation can be solved analytically leading to

$$EAdu^*/dx^* = c_1 \qquad \textbf{4.4a}$$

$$EAu^* = c_1 + c_2x^* \qquad \textbf{4.4b}$$

in which c_1 and c_2 are constants of integration.
   Substituting the boundary conditions at $x^* = 0$ and $x^* = L$ leads to

$$EAu_1^* = c_1 \qquad\qquad \textbf{4.5a}$$

$$EAu_2^* = c_1 + c_2L \qquad\qquad \textbf{4.5b}$$

giving finally

$$u^* = u_1^*(1 - x^*/L) + u_2^*x^*/L \qquad\qquad \textbf{4.6}$$

Furthermore we have, from equations 4.1 and 4.6,

$$F_{u1}^* = -EA(du^*/dx^*)_1 = -P$$
$$= -c_2 = EA(u_1^* - u_2^*)/L \qquad\qquad \textbf{4.7a}$$

and

$$F_{u2}^* = EA(du^*/dx^*)_2 = P$$
$$= c_2 = EA(-u_1^* + u_2^*)/L \qquad\qquad \textbf{4.7b}$$

Also F_{v1}^*, $F_{v2}^* = 0$.

In matrix form these can be written as

$$
\begin{bmatrix} F_{u1}^* \\ F_{v1}^* \\ F_{u2}^* \\ F_{v2}^* \end{bmatrix}
=
\begin{bmatrix} -P \\ 0 \\ P \\ 0 \end{bmatrix}
= \frac{EA}{L}
\begin{bmatrix} 1 & 0 & -1 & 0 \\ 0 & 0 & 0 & 0 \\ -1 & 0 & 1 & 0 \\ 0 & 0 & 0 & 0 \end{bmatrix}
\begin{bmatrix} u_1^* \\ v_1^* \\ u_2^* \\ v_2^* \end{bmatrix}
$$

or
$$\{q^*\} = k^*\{d^*\} \qquad\qquad \textbf{4.8}$$

where k^* is the local element stiffness matrix.

Co-ordinate transformation To obtain the global element stiffness matrix k we relate the local displacements, u^* and v^*, and end actions, F_u^* and F_v^*, to the global displacements, u and v, and end actions, F_u and F_v, respectively; see Fig 4.2. For displacements

$$u^* = u\cos\alpha + v\sin\alpha, \quad v^* = -u\sin\alpha + v\cos\alpha \qquad \textbf{4.9a}$$

which, at the nodes, becomes

$$u_1^* = u_1c + v_1s, \qquad u_2^* = u_2c + v_2s$$
$$v_1^* = -u_1s + v_1c, \qquad v_2^* = -u_2s + v_2c \qquad \textbf{4.9b}$$

In matrix notation equation 4.9b can be expressed as

$$\begin{bmatrix} u_1{}^* \\ v_1{}^* \\ u_2{}^* \\ v_2{}^* \end{bmatrix} = \begin{bmatrix} c & s & 0 & 0 \\ -s & c & 0 & 0 \\ 0 & 0 & c & s \\ 0 & 0 & -s & c \end{bmatrix} \begin{bmatrix} u_1 \\ v_1 \\ u_2 \\ v_2 \end{bmatrix}$$

or $\{d^*\} = T\{d\}$ **4.10**

In equations 4.9b and 4.10 we have used the abbreviated notation $c = \cos\alpha$ and $s = \sin\alpha$. These terms can be evaluated directly from the nodal co-ordinates using

$$c = (x_2 - x_1)/L, \; s = (y_2 - y_1)/L \qquad \textbf{4.11}$$

where

$$L = \sqrt{[(x_2 - x_1)^2 + (y_2 - y_1)^2]} \qquad \textbf{4.12}$$

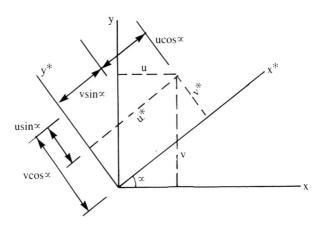

Figure 4.2   Co-ordinate transformation for displacements

In a similar fashion, the local forces $F_{u1}{}^*$, $F_{v1}{}^*$, $F_{u2}{}^*$, $F_{v2}{}^*$ at each end of the member can be related to the global forces F_{u1}, F_{v1}, F_{u2}, F_{v2} by

$$\{q^*\} = \begin{bmatrix} F_{u1}{}^* \\ F_{v1}{}^* \\ F_{u2}{}^* \\ F_{v2}{}^* \end{bmatrix} = T\{q\}$$

4.13

Equation 4.13 can be used to obtain the inverse transformation

$$\{q\} = T^{-1}\{q^*\} = T^t\{q^*\} \qquad 4.14$$

where $T^{-1} = T^t$ as matrix T is orthogonal. We obtain the final result by introducing equations 4.8 and 4.10 leading to

$$\{q\} = T^t k^*\{d^*\} = T^t k^* T\{d\}$$
$$= k\{d\} \qquad 4.15$$

where k is the transformed element stiffness matrix given by

$$k = (EA/L) \begin{bmatrix} c^2 & cs & -c^2 & -cs \\ cs & s^2 & -cs & -s^2 \\ -c^2 & -cs & c^2 & cs \\ -cs & -s^2 & cs & s^2 \end{bmatrix} \qquad 4.16$$

We emphasise that the element stiffness matrix relates the nodal displacements to the corresponding forces at the ends of elements in the form

$$\{F_{u1}, F_{v1}, F_{u2}, F_{v2}\} = k\{u_1, v_1, u_2, v_2\}$$

or
$$\{q\} = k\{d\} \qquad 4.17$$

where $\{F_{u1}, F_{v1}, F_{u2}, F_{v2}\}$ and $\{u_1, v_1, u_2, v_2\}$ are to be interpreted as vectors even though they are written row-wise for convenience.

It is not possible to write the inverse relationship of equation 4.17 because rigid body movements of any magnitude can be added to the nodal displacements without affecting the forces. This manifests itself by the matrix k being singular.

4.2 Energy formulation of the truss element stiffness matrix

It is also instructive to develop the stiffness matrix for the 4 freedom truss element using the energy approach introduced in Chapter 2. This is more general than the direct approach which can be used only with line elements.

To apply the energy method we recall equation 2.17 which, for the present problem, gives the internal local displacement, u^*, in terms of the local nodal displacements u_1^*, v_1^*, u_2^*, v_2^*, viz

$$u^* = (1 - x^*/L)u_1^* + (x^*/L)u_2^* \qquad 4.18$$

A similar expression can be written for v^* in terms of v_1^* and v_2^* but this is not required because v^* displacements do not contribute to potential energy. The strain is given by

$$\varepsilon = (-1/L)u_1^* + (1/L)u_2^*$$
$$= [-1/L, 0, 1/l, 0]\{u_1^* \ v_1^* \ u_2^* \ v_2^*\}$$
$$= B\{d^*\} = \smile T\{d\} \qquad \textbf{4.19}$$

The total potential energy of the element is given by

$$\Pi_e = \tfrac{1}{2}\int \sigma^t \varepsilon dV - \{d\}^t\{q\} \qquad \textbf{4.20}$$

where $\{q\}$ = a vector of forces acting at the ends of the element. Substituting $\varepsilon = B\{d^*\} = BT\{d\}$ and $\sigma = E\varepsilon = EBT\{d\}$ we obtain

$$\Pi_e = \tfrac{1}{2}\int \{d\}^t T^t B^t (E) BT\{d\}dV - \{d\}^t\{q\} \qquad \textbf{4.21a}$$

$$= \tfrac{1}{2}\int \{d\}^t T^t (EA) BT\{d\}dx - \{d\}^t\{q\} \qquad \textbf{4.21b}$$

in view of $dV = Adx$. The total potential energy can also be written in terms of the global stiffness matrix, nodal displacements and nodal forces in the form

$$\Pi_e = \tfrac{1}{2}\{d\}^t k\{d\} - \{d\}^t\{q\} \qquad \textbf{4.22}$$

which enables us to identify the element stiffness matrix as

$$k = T^t \int [B^t (EA) Bdx]T = T^t k^* T \qquad \textbf{4.23}$$

Substituting for B from equation 4.19 and noting that B and T are constant the reader can verify, by formally evaluating the matrix products in equation 4.23, that this gives the same stiffness matrix as obtained by the direct approach in Section 4.1.

4.3   Solution of a simple truss problem

We now outline the solution process for truss problems by the finite element method and illustrate it by way of a simple example. The basic steps are summarised below for convenience:

Step 1 Read nodal co-ordinate, element connectivity and member property data for the complete structure and use equation 4.16 to compute the element stiffness matrices.

Step 2 Using the element assembly process described in Section 2.2, establish the structure stiffness matrix, K, of equation 4.24

$$\{Q\} = K\{D\} \qquad\qquad \textbf{4.24}$$

Step 3 Read in load and boundary condition data and incorporate this in equation 4.24 as discussed in Section 2.2 and restated below.

Step 4 Solve equation 4.24 for $\{D\}$ and print out the truss deflections.

Step 5 Extract the nodal displacements for each element in turn and compute the element axial loads using equation 4.17b.

Example

As an aid to understanding the overall process we describe it in detail for the simple truss of Fig 4.3.

Step 1

Using the nodal co-ordinates we obtain the direction cosines as follows

$$c = 0, \qquad s = -1 \qquad \text{for member 1}$$
$$c = -1/\sqrt{2}, \quad s = -1/\sqrt{2} \quad \text{for member 2}$$

Applying equation 4.16 to each element with these direction cosines introduced we obtain the element stiffness matrices as

$$k_1 = \frac{\sqrt{2}EA}{4L}\begin{bmatrix} 0 & 0 & 0 & 0 \\ 0 & 2\sqrt{2} & 0 & -2\sqrt{2} \\ 0 & 0 & 0 & 0 \\ 0 & -2\sqrt{2} & 0 & 2\sqrt{2} \end{bmatrix} \quad k_2 = \frac{\sqrt{2}EA}{4L}\begin{bmatrix} 1 & 1 & -1 & -1 \\ 1 & 1 & -1 & -1 \\ -1 & -1 & 1 & 1 \\ -1 & -1 & 1 & 1 \end{bmatrix}$$

$$\textbf{4.25}$$

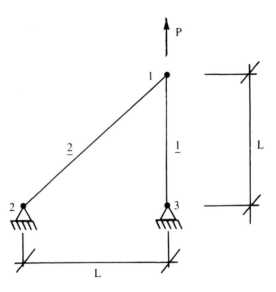

Figure 4.3   Two element truss

Step 2

Assembling these element stiffness matrices k_1 enters as a 4×4 block into the structure matrix but k_2 enters as four 2×2 blocks because its node numbers are not consecutive. The final structure stiffness matrix is

$$K = \frac{\sqrt{2}EA}{4L} \begin{bmatrix} 1 & 1 & 0 & 0 & -1 & -1 \\ 1 & 2\sqrt{2}+1 & 0 & -2\sqrt{2} & -1 & -1 \\ 0 & 0 & 0 & 0 & 0 & 0 \\ 0 & -2\sqrt{2} & 0 & 2\sqrt{2} & 0 & 0 \\ -1 & -1 & 0 & 0 & 1 & 1 \\ -1 & -1 & 0 & 0 & 1 & 1 \end{bmatrix} \qquad 4.26$$

Step 3

The load vector for the structure is

$$\{Q\} = \{0,\ P,\ 0,\ 0,\ 0,\ 0\} \qquad 4.27$$

which implies that there is only one vertically upward load at node 1.

The assembled equations for the structure are given by substituting equations 4.26 and 4.27 into equation 4.24. Before solving the system equations we introduce the boundary conditions

$u_2, v_2, u_3, v_3 = 0$. In the computer program given in Section 4.4 this is undertaken, as discussed in Section 2.2, by placing one on the diagonal and zeros in the remainder of the corresponding rows and columns. If we are solving the problem by hand, as an exercise, we simply delete those rows and columns and the reduced equations for the system become

$$\frac{\sqrt{2}EA}{4L}\begin{bmatrix} 1 & 1 \\ 1 & 2\sqrt{2}+1 \end{bmatrix}\begin{bmatrix} u_1 \\ v_1 \end{bmatrix} = \begin{bmatrix} 0 \\ P \end{bmatrix} \qquad \textbf{4.28}$$

Step 4

Equations 4.28 are solved for u_1 and v_1 leading to
$u_1 = -PL/EA \quad v_1 = PL/EA$

Step 5

Substituting these values along with the known boundary conditions into equation 4.15 using the element stiffness matrices given in equation 4.24 we obtain the axial load in each element. The reader can verify that the correct results are obtained, ie that the axial force is P in the vertical member and zero in the inclined member.

The study of such small examples aids understanding of the finite element solution of a problem and provides a good introduction to the computer program given in the following section.

4.4 BASIC program for truss analysis

The following program for truss analysis is based upon the procedure outlined in Section 4.3. Summation of the element matrices to form the structure stiffness matrix (SSM) involves a slight extension of the summation routine used in the dc network program of Chapter 3 but otherwise the procedure is the same.

Data input requirements are

Lines	Data
1	# nodes(NP), # elements(NE), # freedoms suppressed(NB), # loaded nodes(NL)
2	E, A (assumed the same for all elements)
NP lines	x co-ord(CO(I,1)), y co-ord(CO(I,2)) in order
NE lines	1st node number(NO(I,1)), 2nd node number(NO(I,2)) in order
NL lines	node number(N), x load(Q(2*N − 1)), y load(Q(2*N))
NB lines	node number(N), freedom suppressed(NF); NF = 1 for u = 0, NF = 2 for v = 0

The restriction that E and A are the same for all elements can be removed quite simply by the use of property sets. It is left as an exercise for the reader to add this feature to the present program.

The data input for the truss structure of Fig 4.4 is

6,9,3,1	Values of NP,NE,NB,NL
100,0.1	Values of E,A
0,0	Node 1 x co-ord, y co-ord
0,3	2 x co-ord, y co-ord
4,0	3 x co-ord, y co-ord
4,3	4 x co-ord, y co-ord
8,0	5 x co-ord, y co-ord
8,3	6 x co-ord, y co-ord
1,2	Element 1 Node i, Node j
1,3	2 Node i, Node j
2,3	3 Node i, Node j
2,4	4 Node i, Node j
3,4	5 Node i, Node j
3,5	6 Node i, Node j

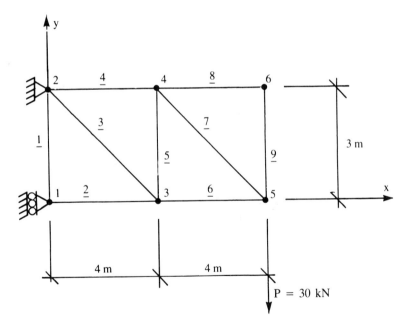

Figure 4.4   Truss (nodal d.f. u, v), E = 100, A = 0.1

4,5	7 Node i, Node j
4,6	8 Node i, Node j
5,6	9 Node i, Node j
5,0,−30	Node 5, Fx,Fy
1,1	Node 1, suppress x displacement
2,1	Node 2, suppress x displacement
2,2	Node 2, suppress y displacement

Listing of program *TRUSS*

```
10 DIM CO(10,2),NO(10,2),ES(4,4)
20 DIM S(20,20),Q(20)
30 PRINT "Input"
40 PRINT "(No. of nodes),(No. of elements)";
50 PRINT "(No. of boundary conditions),(No. of loaded
nodes)"
60 INPUT NP,NE,NB,NL
70 PRINT "Input (E),(A)":INPUT E,A
80 NN=2*NP
90 FOR I=1 TO NN
100 Q(I)=0
110 FOR J=1 TO NN
120 S(I,J)=0:NEXT J:NEXT I
130 FOR I=1 TO NP
140 PRINT "Input nodal coordinates ":PRINT"(x coord),(
y coord)"
150 INPUT CO(I,1),CO(I,2):NEXT I
160 FOR I=1 TO NE
170 PRINT "Input element end nodes":PRINT"(ni),(nj)"
180 INPUT NO(I,1),NO(I,2):NEXT I
190 FOR N=1 TO NE
200 NI=NO(N,1):NJ=NO(N,2)
210 DX=CO(NJ,1)-CO(NI,1)
220 DY=CO(NJ,2)-CO(NI,2)
230 EL=SQR(DX*DX+DY*DY)
240 CA=DX/EL:SA=DY/EL:F=E*A/EL
250 ES(1,1)=F*CA*CA:ES(1,2)=F*SA*CA
260 ES(2,1)=F*SA*CA:ES(2,2)=F*SA*SA
270 FOR I=1 TO 2
280 FOR J=1 TO 2
290 ES(I,J+2)=-ES(I,J):ES(I+2,J)=-ES(I,J):ES(I+2,J+2)=
ES(I,J)
300 NEXT J:NEXT I
310 FOR I=1 TO 2
320 FOR J=1 TO 2
330 FOR IL=1 TO 2
340 IE=2*(I-1)+IL:NR=2*NO(N,I)-2+IL
350 FOR JL=1 TO 2
360 JE=2*(J-1)+JL:NC=2*NO(N,J)-2+JL
370 S(NR,NC)=S(NR,NC)+ES(IE,JE)
380 NEXT JL:NEXT IL:NEXT J:NEXT I
390 NEXT N
```

```
400 FOR I=1 TO NL
410 PRINT"Input (node),(x load),(y load)"
420 INPUT N,Q(2*N-1),Q(2*N):NEXT I
430 FOR I=1 TO NB
440 PRINT "Input (node),(number) -   1 if u=0   2 if v
=0"
450 INPUT N,NF
460 NF=2*N-2+NF
470 FOR J=1 TO NN
480 S(NF,J)=0:S(J,NF)=0:NEXT J
490 S(NF,NF)=1:Q(NF)=0
500 NEXT I
510 FOR I=1 TO NN
520 X=S(I,I):Q(I)=Q(I)/X
530 FOR J=I+1 TO NN
540 S(I,J)=S(I,J)/X:NEXT J
550 FOR K=1 TO NN
560 IF K=I GOTO 610
570 X=S(K,I):Q(K)=Q(K)-X*Q(I)
580 FOR J=1 TO NN
590 S(K,J)=S(K,J)-X*S(I,J)
600 NEXT J
610 NEXT K
620 NEXT I
630 PRINT "NODAL DISPLACEMENTS"
640 PRINT"Node     u              v"
650 A$=  " ##    ####.###      ####.###"
660 FOR I=1 TO NP
670 PRINT USING A$;I,Q(2*I-1),Q(2*I)
680 NEXT I
690 PRINT" "
700 PRINT"ELEMENT TENSIONS"
710 PRINT"Element       Load"
720 B$=" ##       #####.##"
730 FOR N=1 TO NE
740 NI=NO(N,1):NJ=NO(N,2)
750 DX=CO(NJ,1)-CO(NI,1)
760 DY=CO(NJ,2)-CO(NI,2)
770 EL=SQR(DX*DX+DY*DY)
780 CA=DX/EL:SA=DY/EL:F=E*A/EL
790 U2=CA*Q(2*NJ-1)+SA*Q(2*NJ)
800 U1=CA*Q(2*NI-1)+SA*Q(2*NI)
810 T=F*(U2-U1)
820 PRINT USING B$;N,T
830 NEXT N
840 END
```

Notes

1 The Gauss–Jordan reduction segment (510–620) is the same as used in the dc network program. Detailed comments concerning this routine are given in Section A.11.

2 Most trusses are symmetrical about midspan under some loading conditions but, if taking advantage of this, care must be taken with boundary conditions. This requires u = 0 to be enforced at the

midspan nodes but u,v = 0 at the rigid supports and v = 0 at the roller supports.

3 Lines 430–500 deal only with displacements set to zero. Non-zero specified displacements can be dealt with in the manner used in the dc network program of Chapter 3. An alternative approach, which is easier to insert into more complex solution routines, is to add a large number β (a penalty factor) to the diagonal and β times the specified displacement to the RHS vector.

4 The program output will consist of the nodal displacements u,v followed by the member axial loads. The reader should have little difficulty obtaining analytical solutions using the method of joints and virtual work to provide comparisons.[1]

4.5 Exercises

1 Work through the truss problem of Fig 4.3 to ensure that you understand the process of element matrix calculation and assembly.

2 Type in the program of Section 4.4 and test it on the problem of Fig 4.3 using L = 1, E = 1, A = 1. Note that in metric units E and A are often input in exponential form.

3 Using *TRUSS* analyse the structures shown in Figs 4.5a and 4.5b. Assume E = A = 1.

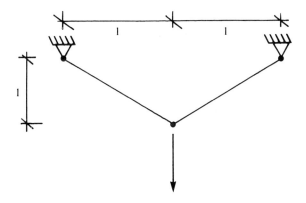

(Ans: P = 0.7071 in both
members.

Figure 4.5a

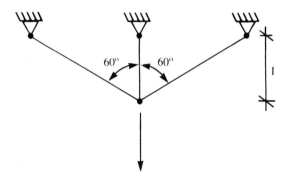

(Ans: P = 0.8 in vertical
= 0.2 in inclined
members.)

Figure 4.5b

4 Using *TRUSS* analyse the truss shown in Fig 4.6
  a analysing the whole truss,
  b analysing half the truss with u = 0 at midspan.

Compare the results.

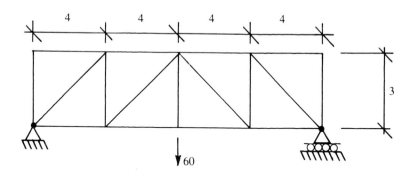

(Ans: The forces are of magnitude 0, 30, 40, and 50)

Figure 4.6

Reference

1 C H Norris, J H Wilbur and S Utku, *Elementary Structural Analysis*,
3rd edn, Prentice–Hall, Englewood Cliffs, NJ, 1975.

CHAPTER 5

Analysis of Rigid Jointed Frames

In this chapter we develop a six freedom element for the analysis of rigid jointed frames by considering, separately, the effects of axial load and bending moment. Initially the matrices are derived in terms of local co-ordinates. For bending effects nodal freedoms $v_1^*, \theta_1^*, v_2^*, \theta_2^*$ are employed and these permit the use of a cubic interpolation to derive a 4×4 stiffness matrix. The local freedoms u_1^* and u_2^* and the stiffness matrix derived for the truss element in Chapter 3 are, again, used for axial load deformations. The complete stiffness matrix for the rigid frame member, in terms of local co-ordinates, is obtained simply by combining these two stiffness matrices. Finally the combined matrix is then transformed to a global stiffness matrix to permit the analysis of general rigid jointed frames.

5.1 Direct formulation of the beam stiffness matrix

Rigid frames are modelled as an assemblage of beam elements which carry bending moments, shears and axial loads. We obtain the element properties first by direct solution of the differential equations and, subsequently, by the energy method, in Section 5.2.

Governing differential equations for bending   The behaviour of a beam in bending is governed by two relationships.

First, it must satisfy the moment–curvature relationship

$$d^2v^*/dx^2 = M_b^*/EI \qquad\qquad \textbf{5.1a}$$

in which M_b is the bending couple, taken as positive if it causes positive curvature d^2v^*/dx^2, and EI is the flexural rigidity. For convenience, we assume the x axis coincides with the member axis but the * notation is retained elsewhere for local co-ordinate quantities. Second, its behaviour must satisfy an equilibrium equation of the form

$$p^*(x) = d^2M_b^*/dx^2 \qquad\qquad \textbf{5.1b}$$

where $p^*(x)$ = load per unit length.

Equation 5.1b implies that the beam also satisfies the conditions $p^* = dV^*/dx$ and $V^* = dM_b^*/dx$ in which p is positive, if upwards, and V^* is a shear force, positive, if upward, on the right hand face of an infinitesimal element, dx. At the ends of the beam the following relationships also apply

left end   right end

$$F_{v1}^* = V_1^* = (EId^3v^*/dx^3)_1 \qquad F_{v2}^* = -V_2^* = -(EId^3v^*/dx^3)_2$$

$$M_1^* = -M_{b1}^* = -(EId^2v^*/dx^2)_1 \quad M_2^* = M_{b2}^* = (EId^2v^*/dx^2)_2$$

5.1c

The governing differential equation satisfying both the moment–curvature and equilibrium relationships is obtained by combining equations 5.1a and 5.1b leading to

$$EId^4v^*/dx^4 = p^*(x) \qquad \textbf{5.2}$$

This equation, together with boundary conditions chosen as one from each of the pairs (F_{v1}^*, v_1^*), (M_1^*, θ_1^*), (F_{v2}^*, v_2^*), (M_2^*, θ_2^*) must be satisfied to obtain a complete solution. Alternatively, a complete solution may be obtained by satisfying equations 5.1a and 5.1b simultaneously, along with the boundary conditions. We will use equation 5.2 as our starting point[1].

Solution of the governing differential equation Consider the beam element shown in Fig 5.1 in which p^* is uniform. Integrating equation 5.2 leads to

$$EId^3v^*/dx^3 = px + c_1 \qquad \textbf{5.3}$$

$$EId^2v^*/dx^2 = p^*x^2/2 + c_1x + c_2 \qquad \textbf{5.4}$$

$$EIdv^*/dx = p^*x^3/6 + c_1x^2/2 + c_2x + c_3 \qquad \textbf{5.5}$$

$$EIv^* = p^*x^4/24 + c_1x^3/6 + c_2x^2/2 + c_3x + c_4 \qquad \textbf{5.6}$$

Substituting the boundary values v_1^*, θ_1^* at $x = 0$ and v_2^*, θ_2^* at $x = L$ gives

$$EI\theta_2^* = p^*L^3/6 + c_1L/2 + c_2L + EI\theta_1^* \qquad \textbf{5.7}$$

$$EIv_2^* = p^*L^4/24 + c_1L^3/6 + c_2L^2/2 + EIL\theta_1^* + EIv_2^* \quad \textbf{5.8}$$

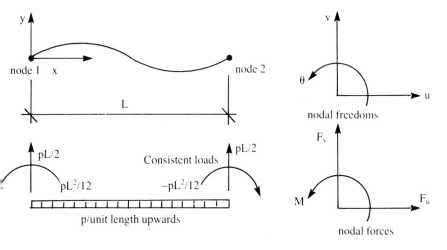

Figure 5.1 Beam element basis for deriving frame element stiffness matrix noting that $\theta^* = dv^*/dx$.

Solving, we find that c_1 and c_2 can be expressed in terms of the end moments and shears given in equation 5.1c, ie

$$F_{v1}{}^* = (EId^3v^*/dx^3)_1 = c_1$$
$$= 6EI(\theta_1{}^* + \theta_2{}^*)/L^2 + 12EI(v_1{}^* - v_2{}^*)/L^3 - p^*L/2 \quad \textbf{5.9}$$

$$M_1{}^* = -(EId^2v^*/dx^2)_1 = -c_2$$
$$= EI(4\theta_1{}^* + 2\theta_2{}^*)/L + 6EI(v_1{}^* - v_2{}^*)/L^2 - p^*L^2/12 \quad \textbf{5.10}$$

Using equations 5.3 and 5.4 with $x = L$ we obtain for the second node

$$F_{v2}{}^* = -(EId^3v^*/dx^3)_2 = -p^*L - F_{v1}{}^*$$
$$= -6EI(\theta_1{}^* + \theta_2{}^*)/L^2 + 12EI(v_2{}^* - v_1{}^*)/L^2 - p^*L/2 \quad \textbf{5.11}$$

$$M_2{}^* = (EId^2v^*/dx^2)_2 = p^*L^2/2 + c_1L + c_2$$
$$= EI(2\theta_1{}^* + 4\theta_2{}^*)/L + 6EI(v_1{}^* \quad v_2{}^*)/L^2 + p^*L^2/12 \quad \textbf{5.12}$$

Equations 5.9–5.12 are the slope deflection equations. The

terms $\pm p^*L/2$ and $\pm p^*L^2/12$ are equal to the fixed-end element reactions for uniformly distributed loading. From equations 5.9–5.12 we obtain the matrix relationship

$$\begin{bmatrix} F_{v1}{}^* + p^*L/2 \\ M_1{}^* + p^*L^2/12 \\ F_{v2}{}^* + p^*L/2 \\ M_2{}^* - p^*L^2/12 \end{bmatrix} = \frac{EI}{L^3} \begin{bmatrix} 12 & 6L & -12 & 6L \\ 6L & 4L^2 & -6L & 2L^2 \\ -12 & -6L & 12 & -6L \\ 6L & 2L^2 & -6L & 4L^2 \end{bmatrix} \begin{bmatrix} v_1{}^* \\ \theta_1{}^* \\ v_2{}^* \\ \theta_2{}^* \end{bmatrix} \quad \textbf{5.13}$$

To include axial deformations in the analysis we now introduce the truss stiffness expressions

$$P^* = \sigma_x A = EA\varepsilon_x = EA\delta L/L = EA(u_2{}^* - u_1{}^*)/L \quad \textbf{5.14}$$

where P^* is the reactive axial load. We remind the reader, that it is positive if tensile and that, at the ends of the element, we have $F_{u2}{}^* = P^*$, $F_{u1}{}^* = -P^*$. When these expressions are included, we obtain, after rearrangement, the relationship

$$\begin{bmatrix} F_{u1}{}^* \\ F_{v1}{}^* \\ M_1{}^* \\ F_{u2}{}^* \\ F_{v2}{}^* \\ M_2{}^* \end{bmatrix} = \begin{bmatrix} a & 0 & 0 & -a & 0 & 0 \\ 0 & V & S & 0 & -V & S \\ 0 & S & M & 0 & -S & M' \\ -a & 0 & 0 & a & 0 & 0 \\ 0 & -V & -S & 0 & V & -S \\ 0 & S & M' & 0 & -S & M \end{bmatrix} \begin{bmatrix} u_1{}^* \\ v_1{}^* \\ \theta_1{}^* \\ u_2{}^* \\ v_2{}^* \\ \theta_2{}^* \end{bmatrix} - \begin{bmatrix} 0 \\ p^*L/2 \\ p^*L^2/12 \\ 0 \\ p^*L/2 \\ -p^*L^2/12 \end{bmatrix}$$

or

$$\{q^*\} = k^*\{d^*\} - \{q_f{}^*\} \quad \textbf{5.15}$$

where $a = EA/L$, $V = 12EI/L^3$, $S = 6EI/L^2$, $M = 4EI/L$, $M' = 2EI/L$ and $\{q_f{}^*\}$ are the fixed end actions produced by the beam loads on the end supports.

Equation 5.15 applies only to a horizontal beam but can be transformed so that it applies to a beam inclined to the global axes. Before describing the details, however, we shall derive the stiffness matrix using the theorem of minimum total potential energy.

5.2   Energy formulation of the beam element stiffness matrix

To determine the 4×4 stiffness matrix of equation 5.13, using the energy method, we assume, for convenience, that the local x^* and global x axes coincide and use a cubic interpolation of the transverse displacement v^*, viz

$$v^* = c_1 + c_2 x + c_3 x^2 + c_4 x^3 = \{M\}^t \{c\} \quad \textbf{5.16}$$

where $\{M\}^t = \langle 1 \; x \; x^2 \; x^3 \rangle$ is the modal matrix
$\{c\} = \{c_1 \; c_2 \; c_3 \; c_4\}$ is a vector of modal
amplitudes written row-wise for convenience.
It follows from equation 5.16 that

$$\theta^* = dv^*/dx = c_2 + 2c_3x + 3c_4x^2 \qquad \textbf{5.17}$$

Selecting the origin for x at midspan and substituting the nodal
freedoms v_1^*, θ_1^*, v_2^*, θ_2^* and the nodal co-ordinates $x = \pm L/2$
into equations 5.16 and 5.17, we obtain

$$\{d^*\} = \begin{bmatrix} v_1^* \\ \theta_1^* \\ v_2^* \\ \theta_2^* \end{bmatrix} = \begin{bmatrix} 1 & -L/2 & L^2/4 & -L^3/8 \\ 0 & 1 & -L & 3L^2/4 \\ 1 & L/2 & L^2/4 & L^3/8 \\ 0 & 1 & L & 3L^2/4 \end{bmatrix} \begin{bmatrix} c_1 \\ c_2 \\ c_3 \\ c_4 \end{bmatrix} = C^{-1}\{c\} \qquad \textbf{5.18}$$

By inverting the matrix C^{-1} we can express $\{c\}$ as the product
$C\{d\}$ where

$$C = \begin{bmatrix} 1/2 & L/8 & 1/2 & -L/8 \\ -3/2L & -1/4 & 3/2L & -1/4 \\ 0 & -1/2L & 0 & 1/2L \\ 2/L^3 & 1/L^2 & -2/L^3 & 1/L^2 \end{bmatrix} \qquad \textbf{5.19}$$

The bending couple is given by equation 5.1a as

$$M_b^* = EId^2v^*/dx^2 \qquad \textbf{5.20}$$

Using equation 5.20 the total potential energy of the element
can be expressed in the form

$$\Pi_e = \tfrac{1}{2}\int M_b^*(d^2v^*/dx^2)dx - \{d^*\}^t\{q^*\} - \int v^*p^*dx \qquad \textbf{5.21}$$

in which the last term is the work done by the distributed load on
the beam. The curvature d^2v^*/dx^2 is obtained from equation 5.16
as

$$d^2v^*/dx^2 = 2c_3 + 6c_4x = [0 \; 0 \; 2 \; 6x]\{c\}$$
$$= S\{c\} = SC\{d^*\} = B\{d^*\} \qquad \textbf{5.22}$$

where B is the strain interpolation matrix for the generalised
strain, d^2v^*/dx^2, and v^* is obtained from equations 5.16 and 5.19
as

$$v^* = \{1 \; x \; x^2 \; x^3\}^t\{c\} = \{M\}^tC\{d^*\} \qquad \textbf{5.23}$$

Substituting equations 5.22 and 5.23 into equation 5.21 we obtain the final expression for element total potential energy

$$\Pi_e = \tfrac{1}{2}\{d^*\}^t C^t \left(\int S^t(EI)Sdx \right) C\{d^*\}$$

$$-\{d^*\}^t\{q^*\} - \{d^*\}^t(p^*)C^t \int \{M\}dx \qquad \textbf{5.24}$$

in which equations 5.20 and 5.22 have been combined.
Minimising equation 5.24 with respect to each displacement in turn we obtain

$$\partial\Pi_e/\partial\{d^*\} = k^*\{d^*\} - \{d^*\}^t\{q^*\} - (p^*)C^t \int \{M\}dx = \{0\} \qquad \textbf{5.25}$$

Stiffness matrix The element stiffness matrix is given by

$$k^* = C^t \left(\int_{-L/2}^{L/2} S^t(EI)Sdx \right) C = C^t k C \qquad \textbf{5.26}$$

where k is called the kernel stiffness matrix. For a homogenous (E constant) and prismatic (I constant) beam, k is obtained by substituting for S, giving

$$\int S^t(EI)Sdx = EI \int_{-L/2}^{L/2} \begin{bmatrix} 0 & 0 & 0 & 0 \\ 0 & 0 & 0 & 0 \\ 0 & 0 & 4 & 12x \\ 0 & 0 & 12x & 36x^2 \end{bmatrix} dx$$

$$= EI \begin{bmatrix} 0 & 0 & 0 & 0 \\ 0 & 0 & 0 & 0 \\ 0 & 0 & 4L & 0 \\ 0 & 0 & 0 & 3L^2 \end{bmatrix} \qquad \textbf{5.27}$$

Before substituting this result into equation 5.26 the zero rows and columns may be removed, as these correspond to the rigid body modes and make no contribution to the element stiffness matrix. Finally we obtain

$$k^* = \begin{bmatrix} 0 & 2/L^3 \\ -1/2L & 1/L^2 \\ 0 & -2/L^3 \\ 1/2L & 1/L^2 \end{bmatrix} \begin{bmatrix} 4EIL & 0 \\ 0 & 3EIL^3 \end{bmatrix} \begin{bmatrix} 0 & -1/2L & 0 & 1/2L \\ 2/L^3 & 1/L^2 & -2/L^3 & 1/L^2 \end{bmatrix}$$

$$\textbf{5.28}$$

which yields the same 4 × 4 stiffness matrix as equation 5.13.

Load matrix   The term involving the transverse surface traction p in equation 5.25 yields the consistent load matrix. Denoting this as $\{q_f^*\}$, we obtain

$$\{q_f^*\} = (p^*)C^t \int_{-L/2}^{L/2} \{1 \quad x \quad x^2 \quad x^3\} dx$$

$$= \{p^*L/2 \quad p^*L^2/12 \quad p^*L/2 \quad -p^*L^2/12\} \qquad \textbf{5.29}$$

which corresponds with the values on the RHS of equation 5.15.

We further illustrate the present approach by way of an example involving a beam under a point load P^* positioned at a distance x from the left hand end. We obtain the load vector by replacing $\int p^* dx$ in equation 5.29 by P^* and substituting the value of x. This leads to

$$\{q_f^*\} = C^t(P^*)(1 \quad x \quad x^2 \quad x^3\}$$

$$= P^* \begin{bmatrix} 0.5 - 3x/2L + 2x^3/L^3 \\ L/8 - x/4 - x^2/2L + x^3/L^2 \\ 0.5 + 3x/2L - 2x^3/L^3 \\ -L/8 - x/4 + x^2/2L + x^3/L^2 \end{bmatrix} = P^*\{f\} \qquad \textbf{5.30}$$

If x = 0, for example, then

$$\{q_f^*\} = \{P^*/2 \quad P^*L/8 \quad P^*/2 \quad -P^*L/8\} \qquad \textbf{5.31}$$

as the consistent loads for a point load at midspan.

Finally, for the general distributed load case, the consistent loads are calculated using

$$\{q_f^*\} = p^* \int \{f\} dx \qquad \textbf{5.32}$$

in which numerical integration procedures, described later, are used to compute the integral $\{f\}$ are the dimensionless interpolation functions of equation 5.30.

5.3   Co-ordinate transformation of frame elements

Co-ordinate transformation for the 6 freedom frame element with freedoms u, v, and θ at each node follows the same scheme as shown in Fig 4.2. As the local rotation θ* equals the global value

θ the transformation required is only a simple extension of equation 4.10, viz

$$\{d^*\} = \begin{bmatrix} u_1^* \\ v_1^* \\ \theta_1^* \\ u_2^* \\ v_2^* \\ \theta_2^* \end{bmatrix} = \begin{bmatrix} c & s & 0 & 0 & 0 & 0 \\ -s & c & 0 & 0 & 0 & 0 \\ 0 & 0 & 1 & 0 & 0 & 0 \\ 0 & 0 & 0 & c & s & 0 \\ 0 & 0 & 0 & -s & c & 0 \\ 0 & 0 & 0 & 0 & 0 & 1 \end{bmatrix} \begin{bmatrix} u_1 \\ v_1 \\ \theta_1 \\ u_2 \\ v_2 \\ \theta_2 \end{bmatrix} = T\{d\}$$

5.33

where $c = \cos\alpha$ and $s = \sin\alpha$.

Using equation 5.33 and equation 4.15, (ie $k = T^t k^* T$ where k^* is given by equation 5.15) the global element stiffness matrix is finally given by

$$k = \begin{bmatrix} k_{uv} & \begin{matrix} -Ss \\ Sc \end{matrix} & -k_{uv} & \begin{matrix} -Ss \\ Sc \end{matrix} \\ -Ss \quad Sc & M & Ss \quad -Sc & M' \\ -k_{uv}{}^t & \begin{matrix} Ss \\ -Sc \end{matrix} & k_{uv} & \begin{matrix} Ss \\ -Sc \end{matrix} \\ -Ss \quad Sc & M' & Ss \quad -Sc & M \end{bmatrix}$$

5.34

where

$$k_{uv} = \begin{bmatrix} ac^2 + Vs^2 & acs - Vsc \\ acs - Vcs & as^2 + Vc^2 \end{bmatrix}$$

The global element load matrices are given by

$$\{q\} = T^t\{q^*\}$$

$$\{q_f\} = T^t\{q_f^*\}$$

Using equation 5.34, the element stiffness matrix (ESM) for each element of rigid frames can be computed and assembled as described in Chapter 4 to form the structure stiffness matrix. Imposing the boundary conditions as also described previously the system equations can be solved to determine the displacement vector $\{D\}$.

A special note is required concerning the assembly procedure for loads. Reference to equations 5.15 indicates that the element equation has the form $\{q^*\} = k^*\{d^*\} - \{q_f^*\}$ which, after transformation to global coordinates, becomes

$$\{q\} = k\{d\} - \{q_f\}$$

5.35

After assembly we arrive at the structure equations

$$\{Q\} = K\{D\} - \{Q_f\} \qquad\qquad \textbf{5.36}$$

where $\{Q\} = \Sigma\{q\}$
$\qquad\qquad$ = vector of loads applied directly to nodes,
$\qquad \{Q_f\} = \Sigma\{q_f\}$
and Σ indicates summation over all nodes or elements.

The term $\{Q_f\}$ is now transposed to the LHS of equation 5.36 and combined with $\{Q\}$ to form the final system equations, ie

$$\{Q\} = \{Q\} + \{Q_f\} = K\{D\} \qquad\qquad \textbf{5.37}$$

We now solve equation 5.37 for the nodal displacements $\{D\}$. Once these are known, the local element displacements $\{d^*\}$ are calculated using the expression $\{d^*\} = T\{d\}$. The local displacements are then used to compute the element axial loads, shears and bending moments. In computing these quantities it is necessary to use equation 5.15, which involves subtracting $\{q_f^*\}$ from $k^*\{d^*\}$.

5.4 BASIC program for frame analysis

The BASIC program given below uses equation 5.34 to calculate the ESMs for a frame and the consistent loads of equation 5.29 to deal with loads distributed along the elements and also in the calculation of the element forces. Summation of the element matrices to form the structure stiffness matrix (SSM) and setting of boundary conditions is accomplished in the same way as in the truss program of Chapter 4 and again a very short Gauss–Jordan reduction solution routine is used.

Data input requirements are

Lines	Data
1	#nodes, #elements, #suppressed displacement, (NP) (NE) (NB) #loaded nodes #property sets(PS) (NL) (NS)
NS lines	E, A, I_x, PY and PN for each property set (PS(I,1 − 5) where I = PS number)
NP lines	x co-ordinate(CO(I,1)), y co-ordinate(CO(I,2))
NE lines	PS number(P(I)), 1st node#(NO(N,1)), 2nd node#(NO(I,1))
NL lines	node number (N), horizontal load (QU), vertical load(QV), moment load(QM)
NB lines	node number (N) and freedoms (NF = 1,2,3 if u,v,θ = 0 respectively for boundary nodes)

A new property set must be defined where different intensities of gravity load PY (vertical) and normal load PN (perpendicular to the element)are specified on elements.

Listing of program *FRAME*

```
10 READ M$,N$,O$:DATA u,v,rotation
20 LPRINT"#############################################
###################################":LPRINT:LPRINT
30 READ B$:LPRINT B$
40 LPRINT:LPRINT:LPRINT
50 LPRINT"#############################################
##################################"
60 LPRINT:LPRINT:LPRINT
70 DIM ES(6,6),SS(30,30),Q(30),P(20)
80 DIM NO(20,2),CO(10,2),PS(8,5)
90 LPRINT"*** PROBLEM PARAMETERS":LPRINT:LPRINT
100 REM      np = number of nodes
110 REM      ne = number of elements
120 REM      nb = number of boundary conditions
130 REM      nl = number of loaded nodes
140 REM      ns = number of properties
150 READ NP,NE,NB,NL,NS
160 LPRINT NP," nodes":LPRINT NE," elements":LPRINT NB
," boundary conditions"
170 LPRINT NL," nodes have loads acting on them":LPRIN
T NS," property sets"
180 LPRINT:LPRINT
190 NN= 3*NP
200 FOR I=1 TO NN
210 Q(I)=0
220 FOR J=1 TO NN
230 SS(I,J)=0
240 NEXT J
250 NEXT I
260 REM     input e a i py pn
270 REM     py = gravity load per unit length
280 REM     pn = applied load per unit length
290 FOR I= 1 TO NS
300 LPRINT "FOR PROPERTY SET ";:LPRINT I
310 LPRINT"*** ELEMENT PROPERTIES":LPRINT:LPRINT
320 LPRINT"     E          A          I          P
y         Pn":PRINT
330 READ  PS(I,1),PS(I,2),PS(I,3),PS(I,4),PS(I,5)
340 LPRINT PS(I,1),PS(I,2),PS(I,3),PS(I,4),PS(I,5):LPR
INT:NEXT I
350 LPRINT"*** NODAL COORDINATES":LPRINT:LPRINT
360 LPRINT:LPRINT
370 LPRINT " x coord      y coord":LPRINT
380 FOR I= 1 TO NP
390 READ CO(I,1),CO(I,2)
400 LPRINT CO(I,1),CO(I,2)
410 NEXT I
420 LPRINT:LPRINT
430 LPRINT "Property No  Node I         Node J":LPRINT
```

```
440 FOR I=1 TO NE
450 READ P(I),NO(I,1),NO(I,2)
460 LPRINT P(I),NO(I,1),NO(I,2)
470 NEXT I
480 FOR N=1 TO NE
490 NI=NO(N,1)
500 NJ=NO(N,2)
510 DX=CO(NJ,1)-CO(NI,1)
520 DY=CO(NJ,2)-CO(NI,2)
530 EL =SQR(DX*DX+DY*DY)
540 CA=DX/EL:SA=DY/EL:K=P(N)
550 E= PS(K,1):A=E*PS(K,2)/EL
560 M=4*E*PS(K,3)/EL:S=1.5*M/EL
570 ES(1,1)=A*CA*CA+2*S*SA*SA/EL
580 ES(1,2)=A*CA*SA-2*S*SA*CA/EL
590 ES(2,1)=ES(1,2)
600 ES(2,2)=A*SA*SA+2*S*CA*CA/EL
610 FOR I=1 TO 2:FOR J=1 TO 2
620 ES(I,J+3)=-ES(I,J)
630 ES(I+3,J)=-ES(I,J)
640 ES(I+3,J+3)=ES(I,J)
650 NEXT J:NEXT I
660 ES(3,1)=-S*SA:ES(3,2)=S*CA
670 ES(3,3)=M:ES(3,4)=S*SA
680 ES(3,5)=-S*CA:ES(3,6)=M/2
690 FOR I=1 TO 6
700 ES(I,3)=ES(3,I):ES(I,6)=ES(3,I)
710 ES(6,I)=ES(3,I):NEXT I
720 ES(6,6)=M:ES(3,6)=M/2:ES(6,3)=M/2
730 FM=PS(K,4)+CA*PS(K,5)
740 Q(3*NI-1)=Q(3*NI-1)+FM*EL/2
750 Q(3*NJ-1)=Q(3*NJ-1)+FM*EL/2
760 FM=CA*PS(K,4)+PS(K,5)
770 Q(3*NI)=Q(3*NI)+FM*EL*EL/12
780 Q(3*NJ)=Q(3*NJ)-FM*EL*EL/12
790 FM=SA*PS(K,5)*EL/2
800 Q(3*NI-2)=Q(3*NI-2)-FM
810 Q(3*NJ-2)=Q(3*NJ-2)-FM
820 FOR I=1 TO 2
830 FOR J=1 TO 2
840 FOR IL=1 TO 3
850 IE=3*(I-1)+IL:NR=3*NO(N,I)-3+IL
860 FOR JL=1 TO 3
870 JE=3*(J-1)+JL:NC=3*NO(N,J)-3+JL
880 SS(NR,NC)=SS(NR,NC)+ES(IE,JE)
890 NEXT JL:NEXT IL
900 NEXT J:NEXT I
910 NEXT N
920 IF NL=0 GOTO 1010
930 LPRINT:LPRINT
940 LPRINT "Node No          Fx              Fy
Mz":LPRINT
950 FOR I=1 TO NL
960 READ N,QU,QV,QM
970 LPRINT N,QU,QV,QM
980 Q(3*N-2)=Q(3*N-2)+QU
```

```
990  Q(3*N-1)=Q(3*N-1)+QV
1000 Q(3*N)=Q(3*N)+QM:NEXT I
1010 LPRINT:LPRINT
1020 LPRINT"*** FREEDOMS AT BOUNDARY NODES":LPRINT:LPR
INT
1030 FOR I = 1 TO NB
1040 READ N,NF
1050 L$=M$:IF NF=2 THEN L$=N$
1060 IF NF=3 THEN L$=O$
1070 LPRINT"node ";:LPRINT N;:LPRINT L$
1080 NF =3*N-3+NF
1090 FOR J=1 TO NN
1100 SS(NF,J)=0:SS(J,NF)=0:NEXT J
1110 SS(NF,NF)=1:Q(NF)=0:NEXT I
1120 FOR I=1 TO NN
1130 X=SS(I,I):Q(I)=Q(I)/X
1140 FOR J=I+1 TO NN
1150 SS(I,J)=SS(I,J)/X:NEXT J
1160 FOR K=1 TO NN
1170 IF K=I GOTO 1210
1180 X=SS(K,I):Q(K)=Q(K)-X*Q(I)
1190 FOR J=I+1 TO NN
1200 SS(K,J)=SS(K,J)-X*SS(I,J):NEXT J
1210 NEXT K
1220 NEXT I
1230 A$="## +#.###^^^^ +#.###^^^^ +#.###^^^^"
1240 LPRINT"##################################################
##################################################":LPRINT:LPRINT:L
PRINT"                    OUTPUT":LPRINT:LPRINT
1250 LPRINT"##################################################
##################################################":LPRINT:LPRINT
1260 LPRINT "Nodal displacements":LPRINT
1270 LPRINT" Node      u        v        rot":LPRINT
1280 FOR I=1 TO NP
1290 LPRINT USING A$;I,Q(3*I-2),Q(3*I-1),Q(3*I)
1300 NEXT I
1310 LPRINT:LPRINT
1320 FOR N=1 TO NE
1330 NI=NO(N,1):NJ=NO(N,2):K=P(N)
1340 DX=CO(NJ,1)-CO(NI,1)
1350 DY=CO(NJ,2)-CO(NI,2)
1360 EL=SQR(DX*DX+DY*DY)
1370 CA=DX/EL:SA=DY/EL
1380 UI=Q(3*NI-2)*CA+Q(3*NI-1)*SA
1390 VI=-Q(3*NI-2)*SA+Q(3*NI-1)*CA
1400 UJ=Q(3*NJ-2)*CA+Q(3*NJ-1)*SA
1410 VJ=-Q(3*NJ-2)*SA+Q(3*NJ-1)*CA
1420 RI=Q(3*NI):RJ=Q(3*NJ)
1430 FM=PS(K,4)*CA+PS(K,5)
1440 T=PS(K,1)*PS(K,2)*(UJ-UI)/EL
1450 M=4*PS(K,1)*PS(K,3)/EL
1460 S=1.5*M/EL:V=2*S/EL
1470 VL=V*(VI-VJ)+S*(RI+RJ)-FM*EL/2
1480 VR=-V*(VI-VJ)-S*(RI+RJ)-FM*EL/2
1490 FM=FM*EL*EL/12
1500 ML=S*(VI-VJ)+M*(RI+RJ/2)-FM
```

```
1510 MR=S*(VI-VJ)+M*(RI/2+RJ)+FM
1520 LPRINT"Element   ";N:LPRINT:LPRINT
1530 LPRINT"Node     Axial          Shear         Mome
nt":LPRINT"         load":LPRINT
1540 A$=" +#.####^^^^    +#.####^^^^    +#.####^^^^"
1550 LPRINT"I ";:LPRINT NI;:LPRINT USING A$;T,VL,ML
1560 LPRINT"J ";:LPRINT NJ;:LPRINT USING A$;T,VR,MR
1570 LPRINT:LPRINT
1580 NEXT N
1590 END
```

Notes

1 As in program *TRUSS* a few lines of code could have been saved by storing the direction cosines for each element, when calculated for the ESM, for reuse in the element force calculation loop.

2 The global ESM is obtained directly from equation 5.34 because computing the co-ordinate transformation by matrix multiplication is time consuming.

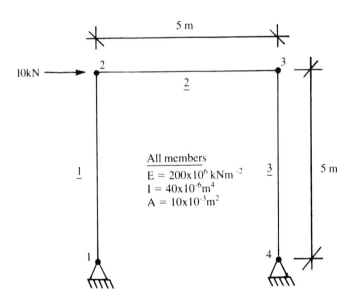

Figure 5.2 Rigid jointed frame

The data required for the analysis of the frame of Fig 5.2 is therefore

4,3,4,1,1	NP,NE,NB,NL,NS
1,0.2E9,0.1E–1,0.4E–4,0,0	Prop. Data N,E,A,I,PY,PN

Co-ordinate data	CO(I,1),	CO(I,2)	
	x	y	
	0.0,	0.0	
	0.0,	5.0	
	5.0,	5.0	
	5.0,	0.0	

Element data	P(I), Property Number	NO(I,1), Node i	NO(I,2) Node j
	1,	1,	2
	1,	2,	3
	1,	3,	4

Nodal loads	N, Node No.	QU x load	QV y load	M Moment
	2,	10.0,	0.0,	0.0

Boundary conditions		N,	NF
		1,	1
		1,	2
		4,	1
		4,	2

The foregoing problem does not involve distributed loads within elements. When a distributed gravity load p_y is present the consistent loads for this are

$$\{q_c\} = \{0,\ p_y L/2,\ p_y L^2 c/12,\ 0,\ p_y L/2,\ -p_y L^2 c/12\} \quad \textbf{5.35}$$

while for a normal pressure loading of intensity p_n

$$\{q_c\} = \{-s p_n L/2,\ c p_n L/2,\ p_n L^2/12,\ -s p_n L/2,\ c p_n L/2,\ -p_n L^2/12\}$$
$$\textbf{5.36}$$

where p_n is taken positive if it acts anticlockwise about the first node number for the element; $c = \cos\alpha$, $s = \sin\alpha$.

The contributions from both equations 5.35 and 5.36 are added to the structure vector $\{Q\}$ in lines 740–810 of the program. Then in lines 1430–1510 the end effects of these consistent loads are also included in the calculations of the shears and moments at each end of the element. For the shears this is achieved by computing $p^* = c p_y + p_n$, as the total pressure transverse to the element, and then subtracting $p^* L/2$ from the shears at each end. An analogous process is applied to the moments.

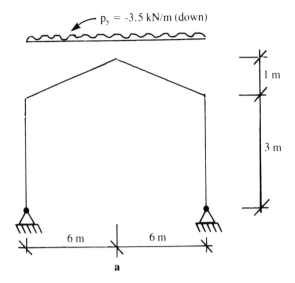

$E = 200 \times 10^6 \, \text{kN/m}^2$, $A = 4 \times 10^{-3} \, \text{m}^2$ and $I = 50 \times 10^{-6} \, \text{m}^4$ for all members.

Figure 5.3a

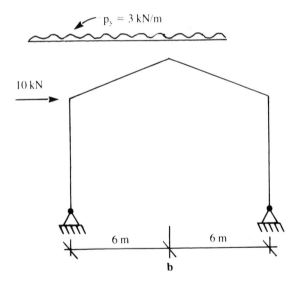

$E = 200 \times 10^6 \, \text{kN/m}^2$, $A = 4 \times 10^{-3} \, \text{m}^2$ and $I = 50 \times 10^{-6} \, \text{m}^4$ for all members.

Figure 5.3b

5.5   Exercises

1   Work through the steps of Section 5.2 to ensure that you follow the energy formulation of the 4 freedom beam stiffness matrix. This involves equations 5.16 to 5.28; complete the multiplications.

2   Work through the derivations of the consistent load calculations of equations 5.29 to 5.31.

3   Type in the program of Section 5.4 and test it on simple cantilever and beam problems with E,A,I = 1. Try:
   a a cantilever with a unit load on the end,
   b a simply supported beam with distributed load,
   c a simply supported beam with unit load at midspan.

4   Analyse the problem of Fig 5.2. You should obtain u = 0.0391 at the left eave and shears and thrusts of magnitude 5 and 10 throughout. Rerun the problem with E,A,I = 1 and note that the results are different from those expected with realistic without realistic ratios of A/I.

5   Analyse the problems shown in Fig 5.3.

Your results should conform the following:

	First loading	Second loading
u at LH eave	−0.00364	0.0171
v at RH eave	0.00364	0.0102
v at ridge	−0.0225	0.0209
M at LH eave	±33.5	±45.7
M at RH eave	±33.5	±15.71
M at ridge	±19.3	±18.8
P in LH column	−21.3	20.7
P in RH column	−21.3	15.7
P in LH rafter	−12.8	7.10
P in RH rafter	−12.8	6.25
Shear in LH column (bottom)	−11.2	15.2
Shear in RH column (top)	11.2	−5.2
Shear in LH rafter (left)	19.2	−19.6
Shear in RH rafter (right)	−19.2	−0.33

Reference

1 P G Lowe, *Classical Theory of Structures*, Cambridge University Press, Cambridge, 1971.

CHAPTER 6

Finite Element Analysis of Vibrations

In this chapter the beam stiffness matrix developed in Chapter 5 is used to analyse the vibrations of frames. We consider the use of both numerical time stepping techniques, in which finite difference approximations in time are used for the velocity and acceleration terms, and modal analysis techniques.

The modal analysis method involves an initial determination of those natural vibration modes (or eigenvectors) which have the most significant effect on the dynamic behaviour of the structure. These are used to diagonalise the stiffness and mass matrices and thereby transform the problem to one of analysing a system of equivalent and independent one degree of freedom systems, involving a set of artificial variables. The analysis of these independent systems may be readily undertaken by such methods as numerical time stepping techniques and Fourier type analyses. Finally, modal analysis involves summing appropriate multiples of the various natural modes and a transformation back to the original variables.

6.1 Dynamic problem types

There is a variety of forces under which structural response will vary with time. Wind and earthquake loading are obvious natural forces and dynamic forces from machinery are obvious man-made forces. Structural behaviour is influenced by the structure's stiffness, mass and damping characteristics and the nature of the forces. However, visco–elastic creep under static loading is also a dynamical problem but, because displacements develop slowly, inertial effects may be regarded as insignificant. Their omission simplifies the analysis considerably and we can regard it as a special case of the more general problem.

The general equation governing the dynamic behaviour of a structural system is

$$M\partial^2\{D\}/\partial t^2 + C\partial\{D\}/\partial t + K\{D\} = \{Q(t)\} \qquad \textbf{6.1}$$

In equation 6.1 the mass matrix M is multiplied by the vector of accelerations and the damping matrix C is multiplied into the vector of velocities. Mass and damping matrices are considered later and, in this introductory text, we restrict discussion to lumped mass systems. K is the usual structure stiffness matrix and $\{Q(t)\}$ is the vector of, in general, time dependent loads.

6.2 Finite difference expressions used for time stepping

The most common method of modelling the variation of time is through the use of finite difference techniques. We consider a variety of the more common approximations.

Inertial effects not significant

In problems involving creep inertial effects associated with the mass matrix are not significant; we require finite difference expressions only for the velocities. In the Crank–Nicolson scheme

$$\{D\} = (\{D\}_{n+1} + \{D\}_n)/2 \qquad \textbf{6.2}$$

$$\partial\{D\}/\partial t = (\{D\}_{n+1} - \{D\}_n)/\delta t \qquad \textbf{6.3}$$

is used where δt is the time step length. The time stepping is centralised about $t_{n+1/2}$. Substituting equations 6.2 and 6.3 into equation 6.1 leads to the recurrence relation

$$[K + (2/\delta t)C]\{D\}_{n+1} = \{Q\}_{n+1/2} + [(2/\delta t)C - K]\{D\}_n \quad \textbf{6.4}$$

which is used to compute $\{D\}_{n+1}$ from $\{D\}_n$. In using equation 6.4, Irons and Ahmad[1] recommend that, for consistency, an equation similar to equation 6.2 should also be used for the loads $\{Q\}_{n+1/2}$.

A second scheme involves using the $(n + 1)^{th}$ time instant as a reference point, ie we write $\{D\} = \{D\}_{n+1}$ instead of equation 6.2 and continue to use equation 6.3. This approximation is referred to as a backward difference and leads to the recurrence relationship

$$[K + (1/\delta t)]C\{D\}_{n+1} = \{Q\}_{n+1} + (1/\delta t)C\{D\}_n \qquad \textbf{6.5}$$

This formula has been used extensively in transient heat flow analysis but seems to have little advantage over the Crank–Nicolson scheme.

A further, very similar, alternative is to use the nth time point as the reference, ie we write $\{D\}_n = \{D\}_n$ instead of equation 6.2.

This approximation is referred to as a forward difference approximation and leads to the recurrence relation

$$(1/\delta t)C\{D\}_{n+1} = \{Q\}_n + [(1/\delta t)C - K]\{D\}_n \qquad \textbf{6.6}$$

If the damping matrix, C, is diagonalised by lumping the damping constants at the nodes by intuition, the recurrence relationships, equations 6.6, become explicit because only a trivial inversion of diagonal coefficients is required to invert the C matrix and enable the time stepping to proceed. Although such lumping minimises computational effort, the approach is not particularly accurate unless small time steps are used. It can be shown that such approximations involve a truncation error of $0(\delta t)$ and are equivalent to using linear interpolation in time. On the other hand, the Crank–Nicolson method involves a truncation error of $0(\delta^2 t)$ and is equivalent to using quadratic interpolation in the time domain. It tends to have superior accuracy and is to be preferred.

Inertial effects significant

The inclusion of inertial effects involves the use of finite difference approximations for the accelerations and values of $\{D\}$ at three points in time. It is now natural to use the central difference method centred about the nth time point. Considering the two time intervals, $t_{n+1} \geq t \geq t_n$ and $t_n \geq t \geq t_{n-1}$, the velocities at the centre of these are approximated using equation 6.3 giving

$$(\partial\{D\}/\partial t)_{n-1/2} = (\{D\}_n - \{D\}_{n-1})/\delta t \qquad \textbf{6.7}$$

$$(\partial\{D\}/\partial t)_{n+1/2} = (\{D\}_{n+1} - \{D\}_n)/\delta t \qquad \textbf{6.8}$$

and the accelerations at time t_n are then estimated as

$$\partial^2\{D\}/\partial t^2 = ((\partial\{D\}/\partial t)_{n+1/2} - (\partial\{D\}/\partial t)_{n-1/2})/\delta t$$
$$= (\{D\}_{n+1} - 2\{D\}_n + \{D\}_{n-1})/(\delta t)^2 \qquad \textbf{6.9}$$

The velocity expression used within equation 6.1 is not obtained from either of equations 6.7 or 6.8. Rather, we use the centre point, t_n, as the point of reference giving

$$\partial\{D\}/\partial t = (\{D\}_{n+1} - \{D\}_{n-1})/2\delta t \qquad \textbf{6.10}$$

Substituting equations 6.9 and 6.10 into equation 6.1 we obtain the following recurrence relation

$$[M + \tfrac{1}{2}\delta t C]\{D\}_{n+1}$$
$$= (\delta t)^2\{Q\}_n + [2M - (\delta t)^2 K]\{D\}_n + [\tfrac{1}{2}\delta t C - M]\{D\}_{n-1}$$

$$\textbf{6.11}$$

This process is often referred to as one of time integration but, in fact, it can be viewed as one of extrapolation as all the finite difference approximations used above can be obtained from linear or quadratic interpolations. Equation 6.9, for example, can be obtained from equation 2.8 by replacing L by $2\delta t$.

6.3 Time stepping analysis of structural oscillations

The structure of Fig 6.1 is subject to impressed boundary displacements, such as might arise under earthquake loading, in which the ground displacement u_3 is a specified function of time. It is not unusual to study such oscillations by taking into account only the horizontal displacements of the nodes at each floor level. This implies that the bending stiffness of the floor beams is infinite by comparison with the columns. We also neglect the compression in the floor and roof, so that only a single displacement freedom is needed at each level. The stiffness matrix for each column is thus a contraction of equation 5.15 in which only the shearing entries V are required. We sum the pair of column stiffness matrices at each level, giving

$$k_{ij} = 2(12EI/L^3)\begin{bmatrix} 1 & -1 \\ -1 & 1 \end{bmatrix}$$

$$\textbf{6.12}$$

Furthermore, to simplify the analysis, we neglect damping and assume the entire mass of the building is concentrated at the first

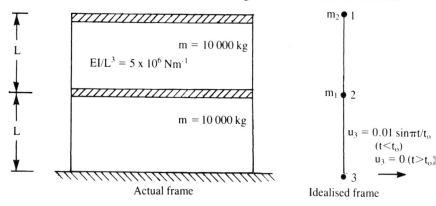

Figure 6.1 Two storey frame with lumped masses

floor and roof levels. The concentration of mass in this intuitive
fashion is referred to as lumping the masses.

Assembling the element matrices for each floor level and partitioning equation 6.11 to distinguish the specified boundary displacements (subscript b) and the free displacements (subscript f),
we obtain the recurrence relation

$$
\begin{bmatrix} M_{ff} & M_{fb} \\ M_{fb}{}^t & M_{bb} \end{bmatrix} \begin{bmatrix} D_f \\ D_b \end{bmatrix}_{n+1} =
$$

$$
\begin{bmatrix} 2M_{ff} - (\delta t)^2 K_{ff} & 2M_{fb} - (\delta t)^2 K_{fb} \\ 2M_{fb}{}^t - (\delta t)^2 K_{fb}{}^t & 2M_{bb} - (\delta t)^2 K_{bb} \end{bmatrix} \begin{bmatrix} D_f \\ D_b \end{bmatrix}_n - \begin{bmatrix} M_{ff} & M_{fb} \\ M_{fb}{}^t & M_{bb} \end{bmatrix} \begin{bmatrix} D_f \\ D_b \end{bmatrix}_{n-1}
$$

$$\textbf{6.13}$$

As $\{D\}_b$ is specified the first row of equation 6.13 is all that is
required to determine $\{D\}_f$ at each time step. Further, we can
neglect the masses of the columns or alternatively lump them
together with the naturally lumped floor masses shown in Fig 6.1.
In this case the system mass matrix is diagonalised so that M_{fb} is
null and both M_{ff} and M_{bb} are diagonal matrices. This leads to
the simplified expression

$$
M_{ff}\{D_f\}_{n+1}
$$
$$
= -(\delta t)^2 K_{fb}\{D_b\}_n + (2M_{ff} - (\delta t)^2 K_{ff})\{D_f\}_n - M_{ff}\{D_f\}_{n-1}
$$

$$\textbf{6.14}$$

where the first term on the right hand side gives the loading effect
of the specified boundary displacements upon the rest of the
system. The matrices in equation 6.14 are given by

$$
K_{ff} = 10^7 \begin{bmatrix} 1 & -1 \\ -1 & 1 \end{bmatrix} \quad K_{fb} = 10^7 \begin{bmatrix} 0 \\ -1 \end{bmatrix}
$$

$$
M_{ff} = 10^4 \begin{bmatrix} 1 & 0 \\ 0 & 1 \end{bmatrix}
$$

$$\textbf{6.15}$$

Substituting these into equation 6.14 and dividing through by a
common factor of 10^4 we obtain

$$
\begin{bmatrix} u_1 \\ u_2 \end{bmatrix}_{n+1} = \beta \begin{bmatrix} 0 \\ 1 \end{bmatrix} (u_3)_n + \begin{bmatrix} 2-\beta & \beta \\ \beta & 2-2\beta \end{bmatrix} \begin{bmatrix} u_1 \\ u_2 \end{bmatrix}_n - \begin{bmatrix} u_1 \\ u_2 \end{bmatrix}_{n-1}
$$

$$\textbf{6.16}$$

where the constant $\beta = (\delta t)^2 \times 10^3$.

The transient boundary excitation at ground level is taken to
be given by

$$u_3 = 0.01 \sin \pi t/t_0 \quad t \le t_0 \qquad \textbf{6.17a}$$

$$u_3 = 0 \qquad\qquad t > t_0 \qquad \textbf{6.17b}$$

with $t_0 = 0.2$ secs. As we use a time step length of $\delta t = 0.02$ secs we would expect this to give reasonably accurate results. It follows

$$\beta = (\delta t)^2 \times 10^3 = (0.02)^2 \times 10^3 = 0.4 \qquad \textbf{6.18}$$

Substituting this value of β and the specified value of u_3 for $t \le t_0$ into equation 6.16 we obtain the two recurrence relations

$$(u_1)_{n+1} = (1.6u_1 + 0.4u_2)_n - (u_1)_{n-1} \qquad \textbf{6.19}$$

$$(u_2)_{n+1} = 0.004 \sin (5\pi t_n) + (0.4u_1 + 1.2u_2)_n - (u_2)_{n-1} \quad \textbf{6.20}$$

Using these results we obtain results close to the exact solution produced using the techniques outlined in Section 6.4.

Once the recurrence relations have been established it is straightforward to code the time stepping solution. This is undertaken for equations 6.19 and 6.20 in Section 6.5.

6.4   Modal superposition methods

Free undamped vibrations

Modal superposition methods are based on solutions of a simplified version of equation 6.1, viz

$$M\partial^2\{D\}/\partial t^2 + K\{D\} = 0 \qquad \textbf{6.21}$$

Equation 6.21 describes unforced and undamped vibrations of an oscillating system having n degrees of freedom. We view the system as excited by some initial disturbance, which causes it to oscillate freely and indefinitely, in one of its n natural modes after the initial disturbance is removed.

In each of these natural modes, the displacements of each node are in phase, ie these all reach a maximum value at the same time. It is assumed that the displacements, associated with a natural mode, can be expressed in the form

$$\{D\} = \{e_i\} \sin (\omega_i t + \phi_i) \qquad \textbf{6.22}$$

where ω_i, ϕ_i and $\{e_i\}$ are respectively the angular frequency (in radians/second), phase angle and vector of amplitudes or eigenvector of the ith natural mode. On substitution of equation 6.22 into equation 6.21, we obtain

$$(K - \omega_i^2 M)\{e_i\} \sin(\omega_i t + \phi_i) = 0$$

which must be true for all t values so that

$$(K - \omega_i^2 M)\{e_i\} = 0 \qquad \mathbf{6.23}$$

Equation 6.23 is a statement of an eigenproblem described in Appendix A. Computer routines are given there to extract the eigenvalues, which are the square of the frequencies, and the eigenvectors or natural mode shapes.

We should note the following additional points:

1 the unit of frequency is Hertz (or cycles per second) and this is related to the angular frequency by

$$f = \omega/2\pi \qquad \mathbf{6.24}$$

2 the period to complete one cycle of oscillation is given by

$$T = 2\pi/\omega = 1/f \qquad \mathbf{6.25}$$

Orthogonality and related properties

One of the important properties of eigenvectors is their orthogonality with respect to the K and M matrices. Suppose we have two eigenpairs ω_i, $\{e_i\}$ and ω_j, $\{e_j\}$ then

$$K\{e_i\} = \omega_i^2 M\{e_i\} \qquad \mathbf{6.26a}$$

$$K\{e_j\} = \omega_j^2 M\{e_j\} \qquad \mathbf{6.26b}$$

Premultiply equation 6.26a by $\{e_j\}^t$ and equation 6.26b by $\{e_i\}^t$ and subtract the two expressions. Noting that K and M are symmetric and $\{e_i\}^t K\{e_j\}^t = \{e_j\}^t K\{e_i\}^t$, it follows that

$$0 = (\omega_i^2 - \omega_j^2)\{e_i\}^t M\{e_j\}^t \qquad \mathbf{6.27}$$

Since the eigenvalues are, in general, different it follows that

$$\{e_i\}^t M\{e_j\} = 0 \qquad \text{for } i \neq j \qquad \mathbf{6.28a}$$

and it is supposed that, by suitably scaling $\{e_i\}^t$,

$$\{e_i\}^t M\{e_j\} = 1 \qquad \text{for } i = j \qquad \mathbf{6.28b}$$

We conclude from equations 6.28 that

$$\{e_i\}^t K\{e_j\} = 0 \qquad \text{for } i \neq j \qquad \textbf{6.29a}$$

$$= \omega_i^2 \qquad \text{for } i = j \qquad \textbf{6.29b}$$

If the eigenvectors are scaled to satisfy equation 6.28b, they are said to be normalised with respect to the M matrix; both computer routines given in Appendix A normalise and output the eigenvectors in this form.

Assume also that a square matrix E is constructed, the columns of which are the eigenvectors $\{e_i\}$. If I represents the unit matrix then

$$E^t M E = I \qquad \textbf{6.30a}$$

and $$E^t K E = \Omega^2 \qquad \textbf{6.30b}$$

where Ω^2 is a diagonal matrix with values ω_i^2 on the leading diagonal.

Forced undamped vibrations

When an undamped structure is subjected to the influence of disturbing forces which are maintained, equation 6.1 becomes

$$M\partial^2\{D\}/\partial t^2 + K\{D\} = \{Q(t)\} \qquad \textbf{6.31}$$

It is assumed that, for an arbitrary $\{Q(t)\}$, the displacements may be expressed as a linear combination of the eigenvectors or natural modes. Let this linear combination be represented as

$$\{D\} = E\{\delta\} \qquad \textbf{6.32}$$

where $\{\delta\}$ represents the various multiples of the eigenvectors to be taken. Substituting equation 6.32 into 6.31 leads to

$$ME\partial^2\{\delta\}/\partial t^2 + KE\{\delta\} = \{Q(t)\}$$

which, on premultiplication by E^t and the use of equations 6.30, gives

$$\partial^2\{\delta\}/\partial t^2 + \Omega^2\{\delta\} = E^t\{Q(t)\} \qquad \textbf{6.33}$$

In equation 6.33 the various equations are decoupled, ie these can be separated into n single degree of freedom systems each having the form

$$\partial^2 \delta_i / \partial t^2 + \omega_i^2 \delta_i = q_i(t) \qquad \qquad \textbf{6.34}$$

where $q_i(t) = \{e_i\}^t\{Q(t)\}$. To solve equation 6.31 we can now undertake the simpler exercise of solving the individual decoupled equations, 6.34, by time stepping or other techniques. The final solution is obtained by substituting the δ_i values back into equation 6.32 to obtain the real nodal displacements $\{D\}$.

In actual analyses, the problem is simpler than just outlined in that only a few of the natural modes contribute significantly to the dynamic behaviour, viz those having frequencies close to the dominant frequencies in the disturbance. For example, in the well known gust factor method for wind disturbance, only the eigenvector corresponding to the lowest mode is taken into account.

Damped forced vibrations

The introduction of arbitrary damping matrices does not allow the decoupling (described above) to take place. This means that the modal superposition method cannot be applied in general. In practice, special forms of damping are used in which the damping matrix is a linear combination of the mass and stiffness matrix. For uniform viscous damping, it is assumed that $C = 2\gamma K$ which leads to the decoupled system

$$\partial^2 \{\delta\}/\partial t^2 + 2\gamma \Omega^2 \partial \{\delta\}/\partial t + \Omega^2 \{\delta\} = E^t \{Q(t)\} \qquad \textbf{6.35}$$

Individual systems can be separated from this equation in the same manner as for undamped systems and have the form

$$\begin{aligned} d^2\delta_i/dt^2 + (2\gamma\omega_i^2)d\delta/dt + \omega_i^2\delta &= \{e_i\}^t\{Q(t)\} \\ &= q_i \end{aligned} \qquad \textbf{6.36}$$

If the damping is expressed in terms of the mass matrix then the damping is described as uniform mass damping and, if it is a linear combination of the K and M matrices, it is known as Rayleigh damping.

Behaviour of single freedom systems

The behaviour of a single freedom damped system is governed by the equation

$$md^2\delta_i/dt^2 + cd\delta_i/dt + k\delta = q_i(t) \qquad \qquad \textbf{6.37}$$

where $q_i(t)$ represents a general disturbance.

Equation 6.37 can also be written in the form

$$d^2\delta_i/dt^2 + (c/m)d\delta_i/dt + (k/m)\delta_i = q_i/m$$

or $\qquad d^2\delta_i/dt^2 + (2\gamma\omega_i^2)d\delta_i/dt + \omega_i^2\delta = q_i \qquad$ **6.38**

where

$\omega_i^2 = k/m$
$\gamma = c/c_i$ damping ratio
c = damping ratio
c_i = critical damping constant for the nth mode
    $= k/\pi f_i = 2k/\omega_i = 2m\omega_i = 4\pi mf_i$

Comparing equation 6.36 with equation 6.38 we observe that, provided we view q_i in equation 6.38 as equal to $\{e_i\}'\{Q(t)\}$ in equation 6.36, all statements made about equation 6.38 are also true of equation 6.36. If we solve equation 6.35 in the form of equations 6.36 and 6.38 we can recover the final displacements using

$$\{D\} = E'\{\delta\} \qquad \textbf{6.39}$$

Sinusoidal Disturbance

Assume that a structure is subject to a disturbance $\{Q\}\cos(\omega_0 t - \alpha)$ implying that the disturbing forces at all nodes are synchronous. Equation 6.38 therefore takes the form

$$q_i(t) = \bar{q}_i + q_{fi}\cos(2\pi\omega_0 t - \alpha) = e\{e_i\}'\{Q\} \qquad \textbf{6.40}$$

where

$\bar{q}_i$ = average value of the disturbing force
ω_0 = frequency of the disturbing force
q_{fi} = value of the fluctuating component of the disturbing force
α = phase angle

Ignoring transients, equation 6.38, with equation 6.39 substituted on the right hand side, has the solution

$$\delta_i = \bar{q}_i/k + \chi(\omega_0)(q_i/m\omega_i^2)\cos(2\pi\omega_0 t - \alpha - \theta_i) \qquad \textbf{6.41}$$

where

$\chi(\omega_0) = [(1 - \omega_0^2/\omega_i^2)^2 + (2\gamma\omega_0/\omega_i)^2]^{-1/2}$
    = dynamic load factor
θ_i = atan $[(2\gamma\omega_0/\omega_i)/(1 - \{\omega_0/\omega_i\}^2)]$

Solution of equation 6.38 in practice

In practice, equations 6.37 and 6.38 are solved by numerical methods as described in Section 6.3 or by decomposing q(t) into its Fourier series components. However, when a well defined forcing function is available, it is preferable to use the numerical techniques described in Section 6.2 in conjunction with modal decomposition. The procedure follows.

1 Form the stiffness and mass matrices and extract the eigenpairs of significance; usually those corresponding to the 3 to 5 smallest values (except in small systems or ones where the forcing frequencies are high).

2 Determine the decoupled vector using $q = E^t\{q(t)\}$ where E has 3 to 5 columns corresponding to those eigenvectors taken into account.

3 Select the damping constant and analyse the individual decoupled systems, computing the displacements for each of the decoupled systems. Combine these using equation 6.39.

Example

Consider the frame shown in Fig. 6.2. For simplicity, we assume the forcing function is given by $\{Q(t)\} = 30\,000\,\{0.50\quad 0.75\quad 1.00\}\cos(2\pi t/0.1 - \pi/2)$. Thus we avoid the use of numerical time stepping. We take damping to be 2 percent of critical.

Following the same procedure outlined in Section 6.3 we treat the floor and roof beams as infinitely rigid. The reduced stiffness matrix for the frame is

$$K = \begin{bmatrix} 14016 & -5491.2 & 0 \\ -5491.2 & 9868.8 & -4377.6 \\ 0 & -4377.6 & 4377.6 \end{bmatrix}$$

and the mass matrix is given by

$$M = \begin{bmatrix} 20.456 & 0 & 0 \\ 0 & 20.456 & 0 \\ 0 & 0 & 10.456 \end{bmatrix}$$

After processing through the determinant search program of Section A.11 the following eigenpairs are obtained.

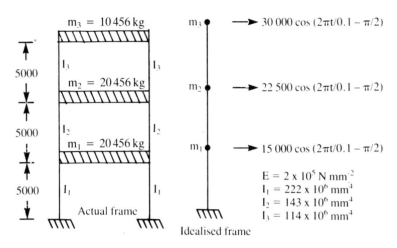

Figure 6.2   Frame analysis by modal method

After processing through the determinant search program of Section A-11 the following eigenpairs are obtained.

ω^2	ω	$\{e\}^t$		
89.393	9.455	0.06993	0.15520	0.19734
558.087	23.624	0.14716	0.06967	-0.20922
938.808	30.640	0.14946	-0.14121	0.11366

We shall include only the two lowest eigenpairs in the analysis so that the matrix E is given by

$$E = \begin{bmatrix} 0.06993 & 0.14716 \\ 0.15520 & 0.06967 \\ 0.19734 & -0.20922 \end{bmatrix}$$

and

$$E^t\{Q(t)\} = 30\,000 \begin{bmatrix} 0.34871 \\ -0.08339 \end{bmatrix} \cos\,(2\pi t/0.1 - \pi/2)$$

$$= \begin{bmatrix} 10\,461.4 \\ -2501.7 \end{bmatrix} \cos\,(2\pi t/0.1 - \pi/2)$$

The decoupled equations are

$$d^2\delta_1/dt^2 + 0.04 \times 89.39 d\delta_1/dt + 89.39\delta_1$$
$$= 10\,461.4 \cos\,(2\pi t/0.1 - \pi/2)$$

or for mode 1

$$d^2\delta_1/dt^2 + 3.5756d\delta_1/dt + 89.39\delta_1$$
$$= 10\,461.4\cos(2\pi t/0.1 - \pi/2) \qquad \textbf{6.42}$$

and for mode 2

$$d^2\delta_2/dt^2 + 22.324d\delta_2/dt + 558.1\delta_2$$
$$= -2501.7\cos(2\pi t/0.1 - \pi/2) \qquad \textbf{6.43}$$

The solutions of equations 6.42 and 6.43 would often be obtained numerically but, for this particular driving force, we have a closed form solution, equation 6.41, which leads to

$$\delta_1 = X_1(10\,461.4/89.39)\cos(2\pi t/0.1 - \pi/2 + 0.34262)$$
$$= X_1(117.03)\cos(2\pi t/0.1 - \pi/2 + 0.34262)$$
$$\delta_2 = X_2(-4.4825)\cos(2\pi t/0.1 - \pi/2 - 0.02062)$$

where

$$X_1 = [(1 - \{10/9.45\}^2)^2 + (2 \times 0.02 \times 10/9.45)^2]^{-1/2}$$
$$= 7.94125$$
$$X_2 = [(1 - \{10/23.62\}^2)^2 + (2 \times 0.02 \times 10/23.62)^2]^{-1/2}$$
$$= 1.21804$$

Finally the displacements in the structure are given by

$$\{D\} = E\{\delta\}$$

which leads to the values below.

t secs	d_1 mm	d_2 mm	d_3 mm
0	21.9	48.5	61.6
0.01	53.2	118.5	152.0
0.02	64.2	143.8	184.4
0.03	50.7	113.9	146.3

6.5 BASIC program for earthquake oscillation

The BASIC program below is based on the time stepping recurrence relations, equation 6.19 and 6.20, for the two storey frame shown in Fig 6.1. It plots the results in a straightforward fashion.

In the program the values of u, which are given by Y, appear at lines 170 (top floor), 190 (bottom floor) and 210 (ground movement). The values have been multiplied by 2500 and then divided by a scale factor S. The +100 added causes the plot to start at the left-middle of the screen on an IBM PC when in medium resolution graphics mode.

Listing for program *QUAKE*

```
10  N=5:A$="##.##":P=ATN(1)*4
20  T=0:A1=0:A2=0:B1=0:B2=0
30  D=.02:E=.2:PRINT "Input M,K,S"
40  INPUT M,K,S:F=1000*D*D:L=F*K*.01:SCREEN 1:CLS
50  PRINT:PRINT:PRINT "Horiz line = ground"
60  PRINT "M = ";:PRINT USING A$;M
70  PRINT "K = ";:PRINT USING A$;K
80  PRINT "S = ";:PRINT USING A$;S
90  X1=0:Y1=100:Y2=100:Y3=100
100 FOR I=1 TO 6:PRINT:NEXT I
110 PRINT"                                  Time"
120 FOR I=1 TO 60:T=T+D:IF T>E THEN L=0
130 A3=(2*M-F*K)*A2+F*K*B2-M*A1:A3=A3/M
140 B3=L*SIN(P*T/E)+F*K*A2+(2*M-2*F*K)*B2-M*B1:B3=B3/M
150 X=4*I+10:Y=2500*A3/S:Y=Y/N+100
160 LINE (X1,Y1) - (X,Y):Y1=Y
170 Y=2500*B3/S:Y=Y/N+100
180 LINE (X1,Y2) - (X,Y):Y2=Y
190 Y=2500*L*SIN(P*T/E)/(S*F*K):Y=Y/N+100
200 LINE (X1,Y3) - (X,Y):X1=X:Y3=Y
210 B1=B2:A1=A2:B2=B3:A2=A3
220 NEXT I
230 FOR I=1 TO 4:PRINT:NEXT I:END
```

Notes:

1 Values of M and K are multiples of the values for the problem given in Section 6.3 in which $M = 10^4$ kg, $K = 10^7$ N/m. High values of the K/M ratio give the two floors nearly in phase and a high frequency of vibration. Low values of the K/M ratio give a pudding like response with small displacement and almost no oscillation. Excessively high K/M ratios will result in breakdown of the time stepping calculation in which case smaller time steps are required.

2 $A1 = (u_1)_{n-1}$, $A2 = (u_1)_n$, $A3 = (u_1)_{n+1}$
  $B1 = (u_2)_{n-1}$, $B2 = (u_2)_n$, $B3 = (u_2)_{n+1}$
  D = time stepping increment
  E = length of the half sine wave shock, see equation 6.17a

6.6 Exercises

1 Carefully check the working in Section 6.3 leading to equations 6.19 and 6.20 and make sure that you understand how they were obtained.

2 Type in the program given in Section 6.5.

3 Run the program with M = K = S = 1. You should get the first four peaks in u_1 of magnitude close to 0.02 m, the first peak in u_2 should be about 0.0137 m and, the three following, about 0.012 m in magnitude.

4 Rerun the program with M = 1, K = 0.1 and S = 1 and observe that there is now a much greater phase lag between the movements of the two floors and that the peaks are much further apart.

5 Rerun the program with M = 100, K = 1 and S = 0.2 and observe that, with a low stiffness, the response is pudding like with the building displacing slowly in the direction of the shock and then back again.

6 Rerun the program with a high stiffness, taking care to select the scaling factor appropriately. You should observe that the frequency of vibration is increased as, in general, these values are proportional to the square root of the stiffness/mass ratio.[2]

7 Combine the frame program of Chapter 5 and the Jacobi eigensolver of the Appendix to develop your own program to extract the natural frequencies of vibration of a rigid jointed frame. Use a lumped mass approach in which the user must input the masses as data.

References

1 B M Irons and S Ahmad, *Techniques of Finite Elements*, Ellis–Horwood, Chichester, 1980.

2 G B Warburton, *The Dynamical Behaviour of Structures*, 2nd edn, Pergamon, Oxford, 1976.

CHAPTER **7**

TWO DIMENSIONAL ISOPARAMETRIC ELEMENTS: PSEUDO–HARMONIC FIELD APPLICATIONS

In this chapter we encounter, for the first time, two dimensional problems. We describe a range of elements which can be used in their solution, including straight sided elements and isoparametric elements having, in general, curved sides. We illustrate the application of these elements in the solution of pseudo-harmonic field problems.

In Section 2.1 we encountered Laplace's equation in connection with heat flow. Problems governed by this equation are said to be harmonic while those governed by equations involving the Laplacian operator, together with a constant, are said to be pseudo-harmonic. In this chapter we also introduce the problem of potential fluid flow, ie inviscid, irrotational, incompressible, steady state fluid flow, and plane torsion. The former problem is harmonic and the latter is pseudo–harmonic. A simple BASIC program, which analyses Laplace's equation, is given towards the end of the chapter.

7.1 Simple two dimensional interpolations for finite elements

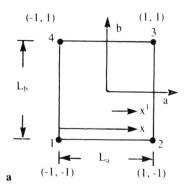

Figure 7.1 Some simple two dimensional Langrangian elements

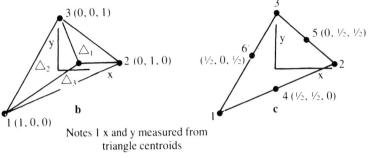

Notes 1 x and y measured from
triangle centroids

2 Node area co-ordinates in brackets

Figure 7.1 *Continued*

In Section 2.1, see Fig 2.2, we encountered one dimensional linear and quadratic elements, in which the nodal freedoms involved the field variables only. Such elements are known as Lagrangian elements. In dealing with beam elements we also encountered one dimensional cubic elements in which the nodal freedoms included both the field variable and its derivative. Such elements are known as Hermitian elements.

Two dimensional Lagrangian elements

We now consider the simple two dimensional Lagrangian finite elements, shown in Fig 7.1, which, we assume, have a single degree of freedom, u, at each node.

Bilinear rectangle The bilinear rectangle is shown in Fig 7.1a. It has four freedoms and an interpolation based on the displacement function

$$u = c_1 + c_2x + c_3y + c_4xy \qquad 7.1$$

The interpolation functions for this can be derived, using the inversion procedure of Section 5.2, by substituting the nodal values and corresponding co-ordinates into equation 7.1. It is possible to proceed more directly, however, by noting that equation 7.1 can also be obtained by multiplying together two linear functions in x and y, viz,

$$u = (c_1 + c_2x)(c_3 + c_4y)$$
$$= c_1c_3 + c_2c_3x + c_1c_4y + c_2c_4xy \qquad 7.2$$

Because the functions in x and y can be separated by factorising, the interpolation can be written as the product of the one dimensional linear interpolations introduced in Chapter 2. For the x direction, we have $f_1 = (1 - x/L)$ and $f_2 = x/L$ with the origin for x at the left end of the element. In the rectangle, it is convenient to take the origin at the centroid and to replace x with x', where $x' = x - \frac{1}{2}L_a$. We write the interpolations as $f_1 = \frac{1}{2}(1 - x'/2L_a) = \frac{1}{2}(1 - a)$ and $f_2 = \frac{1}{2}(1 + x'/2L_a) = \frac{1}{2}(1 + a)$ where $a = x'/2L_a$. Using similar functions for the 'b' direction the complete bilinear interpolation takes the form

$$u = f_1u_1 + f_2u_2 + f_3u_3 + f_4u_4 = \{f\}^t\{u\} \qquad 7.3$$

where $\qquad\qquad f_i = (1 + a_ia)(1 + b_ib)/4 \qquad 7.4$

A particular advantage of using dimensionless co-ordinates a and b is that the same interpolation can be used for quadrilateral elements, as demonstrated in Section 7.2.

Linear triangle   The three node triangular element shown in Fig 7.1b is the most fundamental two dimensional element, ie it has the minimum number of sides and, as such, is termed a two dimensional simplex. Its interpolation functions can be obtained by writing a displacement function, initially, in the form,

$$u = c_1 + c_2x + c_3y = \{c\}^t\{M\} \qquad 7.5$$

We then substitute the nodal values on both sides of equation 7.5, use the inversion procedure described in Section 5.2 and obtain the interpolation from $\{f\} = C^t\{M\}$ where the matrix C is given by

$$\begin{bmatrix} u_1 \\ u_2 \\ u_3 \end{bmatrix} = \begin{bmatrix} 1 & x_1 & y_1 \\ 1 & x_2 & y_2 \\ 1 & x_3 & y_3 \end{bmatrix}\begin{bmatrix} c_1 \\ c_2 \\ c_3 \end{bmatrix} = C^{-1}\{c\} \qquad 7.6$$

Sparing the reader some tedious algebra, this results in the interpolation

$$u = L_1u_1 + L_2u_2 + L_3u_3 \qquad 7.7$$

where $\qquad\qquad L_1 = (a - y_{32}x + x_{32}y)/2\Delta \qquad 7.8$

$$L_2 = (a - y_{13}x + x_{13}y)/2\Delta \qquad 7.9$$

$$L_3 = (a - y_{21}x + x_{21}y)/2\Delta \qquad 7.10$$

and $\qquad$ $y_{32} = y_3 - y_2$ etc.

$$\Delta = \text{area of the triangle}$$

$$= (x_{21}y_{32} - x_{32}y_{21})/2$$

$$a = 2\Delta/3. \qquad\qquad \textbf{7.11}$$

L_1, L_2 and L_3 are called the area co-ordinates because, for any point within the triangle, the three areas shown in Fig 7.1b are related to the area co-ordinates by

$$L_1 = \Delta_1/\Delta, \quad L_2 = \Delta_2/\Delta, \quad L_3 = \Delta_3/\Delta \qquad \textbf{7.12}$$

from which the identity

$$L_1 + L_2 + L_3 = 1 \qquad\qquad \textbf{7.13}$$

follows immediately.

In triangular elements the area co-ordinates enable the interpolations to be written in a particularly simple algebraic form. Although area co-ordinates cannot be used directly for numerical computation, this is not a disadvantage as these can be readily transformed to Cartesian co-ordinates using equations 7.8 to 7.10.

Six node quadratic triangle Finally, consider the six node triangle shown in Fig 7.1c and suppose its interpolation is given by

$$u = c_1L_1{}^2 + c_2L_2{}^2 + c_3L_3{}^2 + c_4L_1L_2 + c_5L_2L_3 + c_6L_3L_1 \quad \textbf{7.14}$$

As nodes 4, 5 and 6 are the midpoints of the sides it follows that these have the area co-ordinates shown in Fig 7.1c. Substituting these and their corresponding freedoms u_4, u_5 and u_6 into equation 7.14 we obtain

$$u_1 = c_1, \quad u_2 = c_2, \quad u_3 = c_3 \qquad\qquad \textbf{7.15}$$

$$u_4 = (c_1 + c_2 + c_4)/4 \qquad\qquad \textbf{7.16}$$

$$u_5 = (c_2 + c_3 + c_5)/4 \qquad\qquad \textbf{7.17}$$

$$u_6 = (c_1 + c_3 + c_6)/4 \qquad\qquad \textbf{7.18}$$

which may be solved for the coefficients $\{c\}$.

Substituting these coefficients into equation 7.14 we obtain, after some rearrangement,

$$u = f_1u_1 + f_2u_2 + f_3u_3 + f_4u_4 + f_5u_5 + f_6u_6 \qquad \textbf{7.19}$$

where

$$f_1 = L_1(2L_1 - 1), \quad f_2 = L_2(2L_2 - 1), \quad f_3 = L_3(2L_3 - 1)$$
$$f_4 = 4L_1L_2, \qquad\quad f_5 = 4L_2L_3, \qquad\quad f_6 = 4L_3L_1$$

are the required interpolation functions.

These expressions can be transformed to Cartesian expressions using equations 7.8–7.10 but much simpler finite element formulations are obtained, using isoparametric mapping, as described in Section 7.2.

7.2   Isoparametric mapping for finite elements

The derivation of equations for elements of arbitrary quadrilateral shape and for high order elements, such as the quadratic triangle of Fig 7.1c, is very laborious if undertaken directly in terms of Cartesian co-ordinates. It is easier to map such elements into a more convenient co-ordinate system, eg the bilinear quadrilateral element shown in Fig 7.2a can be mapped into the simplified rectangular shape shown in Fig 7.2b. We choose reference axes which appear, in the Cartesian reference frame, as a system of non-parallel lines intersecting, in general, at angles other than 90°. The origin is still taken at the midpoint of the lines bisecting the two sides of the quadrilateral. Along these axes the dimensionless co-ordinates still vary between ±1 in a linear manner as we proceed from one side to the other of the quadrilateral. The process is even more complex in elements with curved boundaries where the grid lines of the reference frame appear as a series of curved lines. However, the general approach remains the same.

The most common method of defining the local co-ordinate system is known as isoparametric mapping, referred to above, in which the axes have their shape defined by the same interpolation functions as the problem variables. For the quadrilateral element of Fig 7.2a the interpolation functions of the mapped rectangular element, shown in Fig 7.2b, are given by

$$u = \{f\}^t\{u\} \quad \text{where } f_i = (1 + a_ia)(1 + b_ib)/4 \qquad \textbf{7.20}$$

and $\{u\}$ is the vector of nodal freedoms. The mapping itself is defined by the relationships

$$x = \{f\}^t\{x\} \quad y = \{f\}^t\{y\} \qquad \textbf{7.21}$$

where $\{x\}$ and $\{y\}$ are the vectors of the Cartesian nodal co-ordinates i.e. equation 7.21 expresses the mapping illustrated in Fig 7.2.

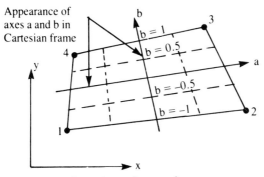

a Global element in Cartesian reference frame

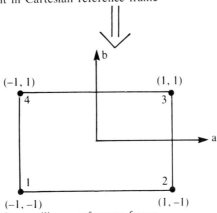

b Local element in curvilinear reference frame

Figure 7.2 Isoparametric mapping of a quadrilateral element into a rectangular shape

We also need to be able to transform those derivates, which occur in the element equations, from one co-ordinate system to the other. If the problem to be analysed is governed by Laplace's equation, $\partial^2 u/\partial x^2 + \partial^2 u/\partial y^2 = 0$, for example, then we transform the problem to one involving first derivatives by using integration by parts (as shown in Chapter 2 for a one dimensional element). As an analogous procedure applies in two dimensions we need to know the values $\partial u/\partial x$ and $\partial u/\partial y$ at any point in the element. We obtain these by first calculating the values of $\partial u/\partial a$ and $\partial u/\partial b$ at any point using the interpolation of equation 7.20, viz

$$\partial u/\partial a = (\partial \{f\}^t/\partial a)\{u\} \quad \text{and} \quad \partial u/\partial b = (\partial \{f\}^t/\partial b)\{u\} \qquad \textbf{7.22}$$

In matrix form this yields

$$\begin{bmatrix} \partial u/\partial a \\ \partial u/\partial b \end{bmatrix} = \frac{1}{4}\begin{bmatrix} -(1-b) & (1-b) & (1+b) & -(1+b) \\ -(1-a) & -(1+a) & (1+a) & (1-a) \end{bmatrix}\{u\} = S\{u\}$$

$$\textbf{7.23}$$

The transformation to Cartesian derivatives is then obtained by using

$$\begin{bmatrix} \partial u/\partial a \\ \partial u/\partial b \end{bmatrix} = \begin{bmatrix} \partial x/\partial a & \partial y/\partial a \\ \partial x/\partial b & \partial y/\partial b \end{bmatrix}\begin{bmatrix} \partial u/\partial x \\ \partial u/\partial y \end{bmatrix} = J\begin{bmatrix} \partial u/\partial x \\ \partial u/\partial y \end{bmatrix} \qquad \textbf{7.24}$$

The connecting 2×2 matrix, J, is known as a Jacobian matrix. This can be evaluated numerically at any point in the quadrilateral element using the matrix S of equation 7.23 and equation 7.21 ie

$$J = \begin{bmatrix} \partial \{f\}^t/\partial a \\ \partial \{f\}^t/\partial b \end{bmatrix}[\{x\} \quad \{y\}] = S[\{x\} \quad \{y\}] \qquad \textbf{7.25}$$

where $[\{x\} \quad \{y\}]$ denotes a 4×2 matrix with the nodal x co-ordinates in the first column and the y co-ordinates in the second column.

The Cartesian derivatives required in the finite element formulation are obtained by inverting J in equation 7.24 followed by use of the expression

$$\begin{bmatrix} \partial u/\partial x \\ \partial u/\partial y \end{bmatrix} = J^{-1}\begin{bmatrix} \partial u/\partial a \\ \partial u/\partial b \end{bmatrix} = J^{-1}S\{u\} = T\{u\} \qquad \textbf{7.26}$$

Equation 7.23 is used subsequently to evaluate the local derivatives $\partial u/\partial a$ and $\partial u/\partial b$.

Once we have expressions for the Cartesian derivatives at any point we are able to calculate the strains, velocities etc. needed to obtain the finite element equations. Because $[\{x\} \quad \{y\}]$ varies for every element so too will J and hence T in equation 7.26. Thus it becomes a massive undertaking to obtain explicit algebraic expressions for the derivatives in Cartesian co-ordinates. Fortunately it is possible to avoid this difficulty by the use of numerical integration.

The procedure described above can also be applied to triangular elements and three dimensional elements. With the triangular element of Fig 7.1c, for example, we use equations 7.19 to evaluate the matrix S but otherwise the procedure is the same.

7.3 Application of isoparametric elements to potential flow problems: numerical integration

Potential flow approach

Potential flow refers to inviscid, incompressible, irrotational flow which can be described in terms of a potential function ϕ. the velocities in the two dimensions are given by

$$u = -\partial\phi/\partial x \qquad v = -\partial\phi/\partial y \qquad\qquad \textbf{7.27}$$

For conservation of mass, the amount of material in a given control volume remains the same. Mathematically this requirement is expressed in the form

$$\partial u/\partial x + \partial v/\partial y = 0 \qquad\qquad \textbf{7.28}$$

which is referred to as the continuity condition.

Substituting equations 7.27 into equation 7.28 we obtain Laplace's equation, ie

$$\nabla^2\phi = \partial^2\phi/\partial x^2 + \partial^2\phi/\partial y^2 = 0 \qquad\qquad \textbf{7.29}$$

Equations 7.27 also identically satisfy the irrotationality condition

$$\omega = \partial v/\partial x - \partial u/\partial y = 0 \qquad\qquad \textbf{7.30}$$

ie the vorticity, ω, is zero.

Stream function approach

An alternative approach is to use a stream function ψ defined by

$$u = \partial\psi/\partial y \quad v = -\partial\psi/\partial x \qquad\qquad \textbf{7.31}$$

Substituting this into the irrotationality condition, equation 7.30, we obtain Laplace's equation again

$$\nabla^2\psi = \partial^2\psi/\partial x^2 + \partial^2\psi/\partial y^2 = 0 \qquad\qquad \textbf{7.32}$$

and equations 7.31 also identically satisfy the continuity condition.

We choose the stream function approach here as, in most cases,[1] it involves simpler boundary conditions. Substituting the interpolation $\psi = \{f\}'\{\psi\}$ into equation 7.32 leads to a residual R.

Multiplying this residual by the interpolation functions $\{f\}^t$ and integrating over the element area, we obtain

$$\int \{f\} R \, dA = \int \{f\} (\partial^2 \{f\}^t / \partial x^2 + \partial^2 \{f\}^t / \partial y^2) \, dA \{\psi\} = 0 \quad \textbf{7.33}$$

where $\int dA$ denotes integration over a finite element.

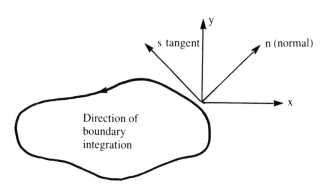

Figure 7.3   Normal and tangent at a boundary point

Use of Green's theorem

Now we apply integration by parts to equation 7.33 to reduce the second derivatives to first derivatives. For the first and second terms in equation 7.33 we can write, for an element of unit thickness,

$$\int_A \{f\}\{f_{xx}\}^t dx dy = \int_S \{f\}\{f_x\}^t dy - \int_A \{f_x\}\{f_x\}^t dx dy \quad \textbf{7.34}$$

$$\int_A \{f\}\{f_{yy}\}^t dx dy = -\int_S \{f\}\{f_y\}^t dx - \int_A \{f_y\}\{f_y\}^t dx dy \quad \textbf{7.35}$$

where $\{f_x\} = \partial\{f\}/\partial x$ and $\{f_{xx}\} = \partial^2\{f\}/\partial x^2$ etc. The reason for the differing signs attached to the first terms on the right hand sides of equations 7.34 and 7.35 is associated with taking the line integral in an anticlockwise direction and the effect this has on the integration limits. Full explanations are given in many texts in discussions of Green's theorem.

The first terms on the right hand sides of equations 7.34 and 7.35 apply to the element boundary. These terms represent boundary fluxes (flows across a boundary) or interelement fluxes at the interfaces between elements. Provided the elements are compatible, the interelement fluxes are self cancelling, ie what flows out of one element across a common boundary must flow into its neighbouring element. However, the boundary fluxes are not self cancelling.

Fig 7.3 indicates a typical boundary point where we denote n as a co-ordinate in the outward normal direction and s as a tangential co-ordinate in the anticlockwise direction. If c_x and c_y are the direction cosines of the normal and tangential axes at the point we can write

$$dx/dn = c_x \quad dy/dn = c_y \qquad \textbf{7.36}$$

$$dx/ds = -c_y \quad dy/ds = c_x \qquad \textbf{7.37}$$

Substituting equations 7.34 and 7.35 into equation 7.33 and using equations 7.36 and 7.37 to modify the boundary integral terms we obtain

$$\int_A (\{f_x\}\{f_x\}^t + \{f_y\}\{f_y\}^t)dxdy\{\psi\}$$

$$= \int_S \{f\}(\{f_x\}^t dy - \{f_y\}^t dx)\{\psi\}$$

$$= \int_S \{f\}(\{f_x\}^t c_x + \{f_y\}^t c_y)ds\{\psi\}$$

or
$$k\{\psi\} = \int_S \{f\}(uc_y - vc_x)ds = \{q\} \qquad \textbf{7.39}$$

where $\{f_x\}^t\{\psi\} = -v$ and $\{f_y\}^t\{\psi\} = u$ from the definitions of equations 7.31.

Equation 7.39 gives the required finite element equations in which the boundary flux terms $\{q\}$ vanish when the resultant velocity $V (= (u^2 + v^2)^{1/2})$ is perpendicular to the boundary ie when $u = c_x V$ and $v = c_y V$. Typically, as shown in Fig 7.4, we choose the control volume as rectangular and the velocities, at inlet and outlet, are indeed perpendicular to the boundary.[2]

If the potential function approach is used instead we obtain the same element matrix k but now the fluxes are given by

$$\{q\} = -\int_S \{f\}(uc_x + vc_y)ds \qquad \textbf{7.40}$$

and this does not vanish at the boundaries in Fig 7.4.

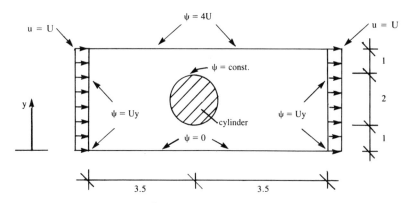

Figure 7.4   Stream function boundary conditions for potential flow over a cylinder

As an exercise in the choice of the correct boundary conditions, consider the problem of Fig 7.4 in which the stream function approach is being used. The values at inlet, outlet and the top are deduced using the first of equations 7.31. The zero value at the bottom is an arbitrary datum value and ψ is constant on the surface of the cylinder because the velocity normal to it is zero. Thus $\partial\psi/\partial s = 0$ around the cylinder.

Numerical integration

Except for very simple elements, such as rectangles and three node triangles, numerical integration is the only practical means of obtaining the element matrix k. Moreover, in most cases, this leads to simpler coding if the isoparametric mapping approach described in Section 7.2 is used.

For the stream function formulation, the element matrix is given by writing the integration as the summation

$$k = \sum_{i=1}^{4} (\{f_x\}\{f_x\}^t + \{f_y\}\{f_y\}^t)|J|_{abs}\omega_i \qquad \textbf{7.41}$$

$|J|_{abs}$ gives that part of the element volume associated with the integration point and ω_i is the weight associated with the point. In Simpson's rule, for example, for one dimensional integration, the weights are 1/6, 4/6, 1/6.

In the finite element method, it is usual to use Gauss quadrature as it requires fewer points than Simpson's rule and other quadrature rules to integrate a polynomial of given order exactly.[3]

The simplest of these is the two point Gauss rule for which the integration point co-ordinates in a one dimensional domain, $-1 \leq x \leq +1$, are $x = \pm 1/\sqrt{3}$ and the weights are both $\frac{1}{2}$. This integrates exactly a cubic polynomial $f(x)$ (= $c_1 + c_2 x + c_3 x^2 + c_4 x^3$) as $I = \frac{1}{2}f(1/\sqrt{3}) + \frac{1}{2}f(-1/\sqrt{3})$.

For integration in a rectangular domain, such as shown in Fig 7.1a, we use a 2×2 Gauss rule with $a = \pm 1/\sqrt{3}$, $b = \pm 1/\sqrt{3}$ and weights $\omega_i = 1$. For the 4 freedom element, bilinear interpolation yields only quadratic terms which 2×2 Gauss quadrature integrates exactly; in fact, it can integrate cubic terms such as x^3, $x^2 y$, etc exactly.

Within a computer program numerical integration is usually carried out within a loop and often as a subroutine. At the start of this routine, we provide the co-ordinates a_i and b_i of the integration points and the corresponding weights ω_i. We then proceed as follows.

1   The values a_i and b_i for the integration point are selected and the elements of matrix S of equation 7.23 are evaluated numerically.

2   The J matrix is calculated from equation 7.25.

3   J^{-1} is calculated from J by inversion.

4   The 2×4 Cartesian derivative matrix of equation 7.26 is calculated using $T = J^{-1}S$.

5   The rows of matrix T are, in fact, f_x and f_y which are used to evaluate
$$(\{f_x\}\{f_x\}^t + \{f_y\}\{f_y\}^t)|J|_{abs}\omega_i$$
which is the integration point's contribution to the element matrix k. It is added to any existing contributions.

The BASIC program given in Section 7.5 carries out these computations for the bilinear element. In order to obtain the solution for the stream function value at each node, we follow the same general procedures used in the programs of previous chapters. After computing the stream function values, the flow velocities may be obtained from equations 7.31. Although this feature is not included in the computer program at present, it can be added, with little effort, by the interested reader.

7.4   Plane torsion

The problem of plane torsion is very similar to the flow problem of Section 7.3. It can be shown that any plane torsion problem can be reduced to the form

$$\partial^2\phi/\partial x^2 + \partial^2\phi/\partial y^2 + 2G\theta = 0 \qquad \textbf{7.42}$$

where G is the shear modulus, θ the angle of twist per unit length and ϕ is the Prandtl stress function. The shear stresses are related this function by $\sigma_{xz} = \partial\phi/\partial y$ and $\sigma_{yz} -\partial\phi/\partial x$. The boundary conditions are especially simple, viz $\phi = 0$. After computing the stress function the torsion moment is given by

$$m_t = \int_A \phi dxdy = GJ\theta \qquad 7.43$$

where J = St Venant's torsion constant.

To obtain the solution to this problem, we note, firstly, that we need to incorporate the additional term $2G\theta$ in equation 7.33. By analogy with equation 7.39, this leads to

$$k\{\phi\} = \int_S \{f\}(\{f_x\}^t c_x + \{f_y\}^t c_y)ds\{\phi\} + 2G\theta \int_A \{f\}dxdy \qquad 7.44$$

and, provided all f_i in $\{f\}$ are zero on the boundary, the first term on the RHS vanishes, leaving

$$k\{\phi\} = 2G\theta \int \{f\}dxdy \qquad 7.45$$

as the element expression. After solution for ϕ, we compute the torsion moment and J using equation 7.43.

7.5   BASIC program for potential flow

The following program for potential flow analysis uses the bilinear quadrilateral element of Fig 7.2 and is principally based upon equations 7.23, 7.39 and 7.41. Once more Gauss–Jordan reduction is used to solve the final system equations but a more efficient routine, which takes account of banding, is given in Chapter 8.

Data input requirements are

Lines	Data
1	#nodes(NP), #elements(NE), #boundary conditions(NB)
NP	x co-ordinate(CO(N,1)), y co-ordinate(CO(N,2))
NE	the four node numbers for each element(NN(1–4)
NB	node number(N), stream function value (F)

Flux loadings are not included as data but, if required, are calculated by application of equation 7.39, read as data and added to the system load vector $\{Q\}$. Alternatively, this calculation can be added to the numerical integration loop but manual input is sometimes simpler, particularly if we assume, in calculating $\{q\}$ for an element with a side on the boundary, that u and v are constant. The computation involved is

$$\{q\} = (uc_y - vc_x)\int \{f\}dS = (uc_y - vc_x)\{L/2 \quad L/2\} \quad \textbf{7.46}$$

The two terms are easily obtained and added at the appropriate place in the vector $\{Q\}$.

For ease of reference the data for the problem of Fig 7.4 is included in DATA type statements. Owing to the symmetry of the problem, only one quadrant needs to be analysed. The mesh used is shown in Fig 7.5.

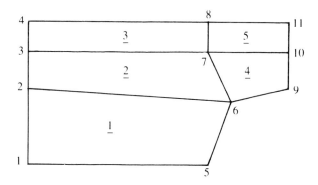

Figure 7.5 Mesh of Quadrilateral elements for the problem of Figure 7.4

Listing of program *POTFLW*

```
10 DIM X(41),Y(41),XM(40),YM(40),G(40,40),F1(40),DF(40)
20 DIM XC(4),YC(4),GI(4),OM(4)
30 DIM KO(40),CX(40),CY(40),SO(40),H(40,40)
40 NX=40
50 GOSUB 140
60 GOSUB 300
70 GOSUB 490
80 GOSUB 660
90 GOSUB 770
100 END
110 REM
120 REM **********SUB INPUT**********
130 REM
```

```
5 A$="  ##     +#.####^^^^"
10 DIM CO(25,2),EM(4,4),S(25,25),Q(25)
20 DIM XY(4,2),NN(4),DL(2,4),TJ(2,2)
30 DIM T(2,4):R3=SQR(1/3)
40 READ NP,NE,NB
50 FOR I=1 TO NP
60 Q(I)=0
70 FOR J=1 TO NP
80 S(I,J)=0:NEXT J:NEXT I
90 FOR I=1 TO NP
100 READ CO(I,1),CO(I,2):NEXT I
110 FOR N=1 TO NE
120 READ NN(1),NN(2),NN(3),NN(4)
130 FOR I=1 TO 4
140 K=NN(I)
150 XY(I,1)=CO(K,1):XY(I,2)=CO(K,2)
160 FOR J=1 TO 4:EM(I,J)=0:NEXT J
170 NEXT I
180 FOR IX=1 TO 2:FOR IY=1 TO 2
190 A=R3^IX:B=R3^IY
200 DL(1,1)=(B-1)/4:DL(1,2)=(1-B)/4
210 DL(1,3)=(1+B)/4:DL(1,4)=-(1+B)/4
220 DL(2,1)=(A-1)/4:DL(2,2)=-(1+A)/4
230 DL(2,3)=(1+A)/4:DL(2,4)=(1-A)/4
240 FOR I=1 TO 2:FOR J=1 TO 2
250 TJ(I,J)=0:FOR K=1 TO 4
260 TJ(I,J)=TJ(I,J)+DL(I,K)*XY(K,J)
270 NEXT K:NEXT J:NEXT I
280 DJ=TJ(1,1)*TJ(2,2)-TJ(1,2)*TJ(2,1)
290 DD=TJ(1,1):TJ(1,1)=TJ(2,2)/DJ
300 TJ(2,2)=DD/DJ:TJ(1,2)=-TJ(1,2)/DJ
310 TJ(2,1)=-TJ(2,1)/DJ
320 FOR I=1 TO 2:FOR J=1 TO 4
330 T(I,J)=0:FOR K=1 TO 2
340 T(I,J)=T(I,J)+TJ(I,K)*DL(K,J)
350 NEXT K:NEXT J:NEXT I
360 F=ABS(DJ)
370 FOR I=1 TO 4:FOR J=1 TO 4
380 EM(I,J)=EM(I,J)+F*T(1,I)*T(1,J)
390 EM(I,J)=EM(I,J)+F*T(2,I)*T(2,J)
400 NEXT J:NEXT I
410 NEXT IY:NEXT IX
420 FOR I=1 TO 4:NR=NN(I)
430 FOR J=1 TO 4:NC=NN(J)
440 S(NR,NC)=S(NR,NC)+EM(I,J)
450 NEXT J:NEXT I
460 NEXT N
470 FOR I=1 TO NB
480 READ N,F
490 FOR J=1 TO NP:Q(J)=Q(J)-F*S(J,N)
500 S(J,N)=0:S(N,J)=0:NEXT J
510 S(N,N)=1:Q(N)=F:NEXT I
520 FOR I=1 TO NP
530 X=S(I,I):Q(I)=Q(I)/X
540 FOR J=I+1 TO NP
550 S(I,J)=S(I,J)/X:NEXT J
```

```
560 FOR K=1 TO NP
570 IF K=I GOTO 610
580 X=S(K,I):Q(K)=Q(K)-X*Q(I)
590 FOR J=I+1 TO NP
600 S(K,J)=S(K,J)-X*S(I,J):NEXT J
610 NEXT K
620 NEXT I
630 PRINT "SOLUTIONS"
650 FOR I=1 TO NP
660 PRINT USING A$;I,Q(I):NEXT I
800 DATA 11,5,9
801 DATA 0,0
802 DATA 0,1
803 DATA 0,1.5
804 DATA 0,2
805 DATA 2.5,0
806 DATA 2.79289,0.70711
807 DATA 2.5,1.5
808 DATA 2.5,2
809 DATA 3.5,1
810 DATA 3.5,1.5
811 DATA 3.5,2
812 DATA 1,5,6,2
813 DATA 2,6,7,3
814 DATA 3,7,8,4
815 DATA 6,9,10,7
816 DATA 7,10,11,8
817 DATA 1,0
818 DATA 2,1
819 DATA 3,1.5
820 DATA 4,2
821 DATA 5,0
822 DATA 6,0
823 DATA 8,2
824 DATA 9,0
825 DATA 11,2
830 END
```

Notes

1 Data given is for a quadrant of the flow past a cylinder problem shown in Figs 7.4 and 7.5. With this data the value of the stream function obtained at node 10 is 1.0883.

2 This potential flow program can also be modified for the analysis of plane torsion. In the torsion problem the Prandtl torsion stress function takes the place of the stream function.[3]

3 The program can also be used for heat flow and electromagnetic wave problems. In the former, realistic modelling requires the inclusion of surface convection effects which is beyond the scope of the present book.[3]

4 Again the program can be used to model other inviscid fluid flow problems, eg those of flow in a harbour when a steady inviscid approximation of the flow pattern is obtained. Often these problems involve time stepping and require the application techniques such as those used for the earthquake problem of Chapter 6.

5 As stated above, the value of the stream function at node 10 should be 1.0883. The velocities above the crest can then be calculated as

$$u_{10-11} = (\psi_{11} - \psi_{10})/(y_{11} - y_{10}) = (2 - 1.0883)/0.5 = 1.8234$$
$$u_{9-10} = (\psi_{10} - \psi_9)/(y_{10} - y_9) = (1.0883 - 0)/0.5 = 2.1766$$

which are reasonable results with such a coarse mesh and low order element; the exact solution is 1.1025.[4]

Sometimes the flow velocities are of little interest and instead we may wish to determine the pressure on the cylinder, as in the case of a bridge pier. In such a case we use Bernoulli's theorem

$$\tfrac{1}{2}V^2 + q + p/\rho = \text{const.} \qquad\qquad \textbf{7.47}$$

where q the body force potential, ρ the mass density and V is the resultant velocity given by

$$V^2 = u^2 + v^2 = (\partial\psi/\partial y)^2 + (\partial\psi/\partial x)^2 \qquad\qquad \textbf{7.48}$$

The total pressure exerted on the cylinder in the horizontal direction is obtained finally from the expression $\int pc_x dS$.

7.6 Exercises

1 Check that the interpolation functions of equation 7.4 give the correct values at the nodes, ie zero or unity. Do likewise for the functions of equation 7.19.

2 Verify that the matrix S of equation 7.23 is correct by differentiating the functions of equation 7.4.

3 Choosing simple nodal co-ordinates for a rectangular element verify, using equation 7.25, that $\Sigma|J|_{abs}$ does indeed yield the element area.

4 Type in the program given in Section 7.5 and run it with the given data. Check whether the value of ψ_{10} cited above is obtained and whether the other values are reasonable.

5 Rerun the same problem with some alternative meshes, eg shift node 6 to the co-ordinates (2.5,1) and observe the difference in results.

6 Use the program to solve a plane torsion problem. Add the additional code to compute the St Venant's torsion constant.

References

1 J J Connor and C A Brebbia, *Finite Element Techniques for Fluid Flow*, Butterworths, London, 1977.

2 K A Heubner, *Finite Element Techniques for Engineers*, Wiley, New York, 1975.

3 O C Zienkiewicz and R L Taylor, *The Finite Element Method*, 4th edn, McGraw–Hill, New York, 1984.

4 T J Chung, *Finite Elements in Fluid Dynamics*, McGraw–Hill, New York, 1979.

CHAPTER 8

Plane Stress and Plane Strain

Plane stress and plane strain analysis of solids is an important area of application of the finite element method. In this chapter we introduce relevant details of the theory of elasticity and concentrate on the application of the bilinear isoparametric element to such problems. Near the end we give a BASIC program for plane stress analysis. The solution routine differs from that of previous chapters in that only half of the stiffness band is stored.

8.1 Two dimensional stress systems: stress transformations

Fig 8.1 shows an element within a two dimensional plate of unit thickness in which positive direct stresses σ_x, σ_y and a shear stress σ_{xy} act. Such a stress state is said to be one of plane stress.

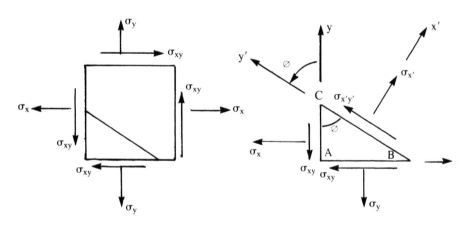

Figure 8.1 Plane stress system

In the solution of plane stress problems it is often desirable to determine a statically equivalent set of stresses $\sigma_{x'}$, $\sigma_{y'}$, $\sigma_{x'y'}$, within a reference frame x'y', which is inclined at an anticlockwise angle, ϕ, to the xy reference frame; see Fig 8.1b. These statically equivalent stresses are determined by equating the resolved parts in the x' and y' directions of the forces acting on the faces AB and AC of the small triangular prism ABC. For the x' direction we have

force on face BC in the positive x' direction
$$= \sigma_{x'} BC \qquad \textbf{8.1a}$$

force on face AC in the negative x' direction
$$= \sigma_x AC \cos\phi + \sigma_{xy} AC \sin\phi \qquad \textbf{8.1b}$$

force on face BC in the negative x' direction
$$= \sigma_y AB \sin\phi + \sigma_{xy} AB \cos\phi \qquad \textbf{8.1c}$$

Substituting $AC = BC\cos\phi$, $AB = BC\sin\phi$ and equating the positive and negative forces leads to

$$\sigma_{x'} = \sigma_x \cos^2\phi + \sigma_y \sin^2\phi + 2\sigma_{xy}\cos\phi\sin\phi \qquad \textbf{8.2a}$$

Applying a similar process to the y' direction leads to

$$\sigma_{x'y'} = \sigma_x \cos\phi\sin\phi - \sigma_y\cos\phi\sin\phi + \sigma_{xy}\cos 2\phi \qquad \textbf{8.2b}$$

To obtain the transformation for $\sigma_{y'}$, we need only to replace ϕ with $(\phi + \pi/2)$ in equation 8.2a which gives

$$\sigma_{y'} = \sigma_x \cos^2\phi + \sigma_y \sin^2\phi - 2\sigma_{xy}\sin\phi\cos\phi \qquad \textbf{8.2c}$$

Equations 8.2 provide the necessary transformations between the stress components in the two reference frames. However, we also often wish to have values of the maximum and minimum direct stresses, known as the principal stresses σ_1 and σ_2, which are given by

$$\sigma_1, \sigma_2 = \tfrac{1}{2}(\sigma_x + \sigma_y) \pm \sqrt{[(\sigma_x - \sigma_y)^2/4 + \sigma_{xy}^2]} \qquad \textbf{8.3}$$

These stresses act on the element shown in Fig 8.2a inclined at an angle ϕ_1 to the x axis where

$$\tan 2\phi_1 = 2\sigma_{xy}/(\sigma_x - \sigma_y) \qquad \textbf{8.4}$$

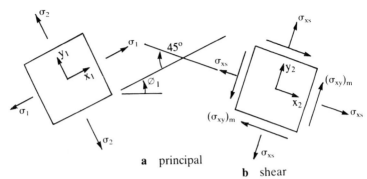

Figure 8.2   Maximum stresses

The maximum shear stresses are also of interest in some situations and these are given by

$$(\sigma_{xy})_m = \sqrt{[(\sigma_x - \sigma_y)^2/4 + \sigma_{xy}^2]} \qquad \textbf{8.5a}$$

They are accompanied by direct stresses

$$\sigma_{xz} = \sigma_{yz} = \tfrac{1}{2}(\sigma_x + \sigma_y) \qquad \textbf{8.5b}$$

and occur on the element shown in Fig 8.2b.

8.2   Strain-displacement and stress–strain relationships

In an infinitesimal element undergoing small displacements it can be shown that the direct strain is equal to the first derivative of the displacement in that direction, ie

$$\varepsilon_x = \lim_{\delta x \to 0} \delta u/\delta x = \partial u/\partial x \qquad \textbf{8.6}$$

and similarly for the y direction

$$\varepsilon_y = \partial v/\partial y \qquad \textbf{8.7}$$

The above definitions, which conform to the elementary definitions of change in length per unit length, are interpreted geometrically in Fig 8.3a. Referring to Fig 8.3b, shear strain produces a change in shape of the element which is calculated as the angular deformation given by

$$\varepsilon_{xy} = \phi_2 + (-\phi_1) = \delta u/\delta y + \delta v/\delta x \qquad \textbf{8.8}$$

For an infinitesimal element

$$\varepsilon_{xy} = \partial u/\partial y + \partial v/\partial x \qquad \textbf{8.9}$$

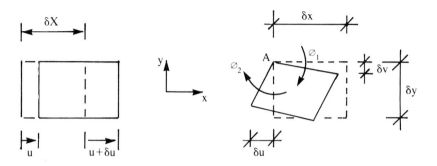

Figure 8.3 Definitions of direct and shear strain

Extension to three dimensions is simple but six strains must now be defined, namely

$$\varepsilon_x = \partial u/\partial x, \ \varepsilon_y = \partial v/\partial y, \ \varepsilon_z = \partial w/\partial z$$
$$\varepsilon_{xy} = \partial u/\partial y + \partial v/\partial x$$
$$\varepsilon_{yz} = \partial v/\partial z + \partial w/\partial y$$
$$\varepsilon_{zx} = \partial w/\partial x + \partial u/\partial z \qquad \textbf{8.10}$$

For the purposes of analysis we also need relationships between stresses and strains. These are provided by the generalised Hooke's laws

for direct stress

$$\varepsilon_x = \sigma_x/E - \nu\sigma_y/E - \nu\sigma_z/E$$
$$\varepsilon_y = \sigma_y/E - \nu\sigma_z/E - \nu\sigma_x/E$$
$$\varepsilon_z = \sigma_z/E - \nu\sigma_x/E - \nu\sigma_y/E \qquad \textbf{8.11}$$

for shear stress

$$\varepsilon_{xy} = \sigma_{xy}/G, \ \varepsilon_{yz} = \sigma_{yz}/G, \ \varepsilon_{zx} = \sigma_{zx}/G \qquad \textbf{8.12}$$

where E is Young's modulus, ν is Poisson's ratio and $G = E/2(1 + \nu)$.

Inverting equations 8.11 and 8.12 we obtain the three dimensional stress–strain relationships which, written in matrix notation, have the form

$$
\begin{bmatrix} \sigma_x \\ \sigma_y \\ \sigma_z \\ \sigma_{xy} \\ \sigma_{yz} \\ \sigma_{zx} \end{bmatrix}
=
\frac{E}{1-v-2v^2}
\begin{bmatrix}
1-v & v & v & 0 & 0 & 0 \\
v & 1-v & v & 0 & 0 & 0 \\
v & v & 1-v & 0 & 0 & 0 \\
0 & 0 & 0 & \dfrac{1-2v}{2} & 0 & 0 \\
0 & 0 & 0 & 0 & \dfrac{1-2v}{2} & 0 \\
0 & 0 & 0 & 0 & 0 & \dfrac{1-2v}{2}
\end{bmatrix}
\begin{bmatrix} \varepsilon_x \\ \varepsilon_y \\ \varepsilon_z \\ \varepsilon_{xy} \\ \varepsilon_{yz} \\ \varepsilon_{zx} \end{bmatrix}
$$

$$\textbf{8.13}$$

For two dimensional problems two cases are usually distinguished. In *plane strain* problems the strains ε_z, ε_{yz}, and ε_{zx}, are assumed to be zero. Typically this is appropriate in the analysis of retaining walls where it is assumed the ends of the walls are prevented from moving. Putting ε_z, ε_{yz}, $\varepsilon_{zx} = 0$ in equation 8.13 leads to

$$
\{\sigma\} = \begin{bmatrix} \sigma_x \\ \sigma_y \\ \sigma_{xy} \end{bmatrix}
= \frac{E}{1-v-2v^2}
\begin{bmatrix}
1-v & v & 0 \\
v & 1-v & 0 \\
0 & 0 & \dfrac{1-v}{2}
\end{bmatrix}
\begin{bmatrix} \varepsilon_x \\ \varepsilon_y \\ \varepsilon_{xy} \end{bmatrix}
= D\{\varepsilon\}
$$

$$\textbf{8.14}$$

where D is called the modulus matrix.

In *plane stress* problems the stresses σ_z, σ_{yz} and σ_{zx} are assumed to be zero. This assumption is appropriate in the analysis of thin plates subject to in-plane loads. Substituting $\sigma_z = 0$ in equations 8.12, we obtain with the inclusion of shear stress term

$$
\{\sigma\} = \begin{bmatrix} \sigma_x \\ \sigma_y \\ \sigma_{xy} \end{bmatrix}
= \frac{E}{1-v^2}
\begin{bmatrix}
1 & v & 0 \\
v & 1 & 0 \\
0 & 0 & \dfrac{1-v}{2}
\end{bmatrix}
\begin{bmatrix} \varepsilon_x \\ \varepsilon_y \\ \varepsilon_{xy} \end{bmatrix}
= D\{\varepsilon\}
$$

$$\textbf{8.15}$$

8.3 Bilinear quadrilateral element for plane stress and strain

Among the first continuum finite elements developed by researchers for plane stress and strain problems were the six freedom constant strain triangle and the eight freedom bilinear rectangle. These elements are shown in Figs 7.1a and 7.1b respectively.

The bilinear quadrilateral is an isoparametric element developed from the bilinear rectangle. It uses the interpolation functions given in Section 7.1 for both the u and v displacements. Because the eight freedom rectangular element converges more rapidly than the six triangular freedom element, we concentrate on the former herein. However, in recognition of the limited applicabilty of rectangular elements, we shall develop an eight freedom quadrilateral element from it using the isoparametric mapping technique introduced in Section 7.2.

Applying the interpolation of equation 7.3 to both the displacements and Cartesian co-ordinates leads to

$$u = \Sigma f_i u_i = \{f\}^t \{u\}, \quad v = \Sigma f_i v_i = \{f\}^t \{v\} \quad i = 1 \rightarrow 4 \qquad \textbf{8.16}$$

$$x = \Sigma f_i x_i = \{f\}^t \{x\}, \quad y = \Sigma f_i y_i = \{f\}^t \{y\} \quad i = 1 \rightarrow 4 \qquad \textbf{8.17}$$

$$\text{where } f_i = (1 + a_i a)(1 + b_i b)/4 \qquad \textbf{8.18}$$

As described in Section 7.2 we now form a matrix S, which we restate for convenience, given by

$$S = \begin{bmatrix} \partial\{f\}^t/\partial a \\ \partial\{f\}^t/\partial b \end{bmatrix} = \frac{1}{4}\begin{bmatrix} -(1-b) & (1-b) & (1+b) & -(1+b) \\ -(1-a) & -(1+a) & (1+a) & (1-a) \end{bmatrix}$$

$$\textbf{8.19}$$

The Jacobian matrix is determined using

$$J = \begin{bmatrix} \partial x/\partial a & \partial y/\partial a \\ \partial x/\partial b & \partial y/\partial b \end{bmatrix} = \begin{bmatrix} \partial\{f\}^t/\partial a \\ \partial\{f\}^t/\partial b \end{bmatrix}[\{x\} \quad \{y\}] = S[\{x\} \quad \{y\}]$$

$$\textbf{8.20}$$

where $[\{x\} \quad \{y\}]$ denotes a 4×2 mixtrix with the nodal x co-ordinates in the first column and the y co-ordinates in the second column.

The Cartesian derivatives required to calculate the strains in the element are obtained by inverting J. For strains associated with u displacements, we use

$$\begin{bmatrix} \partial u/\partial x \\ \partial u/\partial y \end{bmatrix} = J^{-1}\begin{bmatrix} \partial u/\partial a \\ \partial u/\partial b \end{bmatrix} = J^{-1}S\{u\} = T\{u\} \qquad \textbf{8.21}$$

and a similar expression is used for the displacements $\{v\}$.

If the matrix T is denoted as

$$T = \begin{bmatrix} t_{11} & t_{12} & t_{13} & t_{14} \\ t_{21} & t_{22} & t_{23} & t_{24} \end{bmatrix} \qquad \textbf{8.22}$$

and we note that the element displacement vector is ordered such that

$$\{d\} = \{u_1 \quad v_1 \quad u_2 \quad v_2 \quad u_3 \quad v_3 \quad u_4 \quad v_4\} \qquad \textbf{8.23}$$

then the strain–displacement matrix B at any point within the element is given by

$$\begin{aligned}
\{\varepsilon\} &= \begin{bmatrix} \partial u/\partial x \\ \partial v/\partial y \\ \partial u/\partial y + \partial v/\partial x \end{bmatrix} \\
&= \begin{bmatrix} t_{11} & 0 & t_{12} & 0 & t_{13} & 0 & t_{14} & 0 \\ 0 & t_{21} & 0 & t_{22} & 0 & t_{23} & 0 & t_{24} \\ t_{21} & t_{11} & t_{22} & t_{12} & t_{23} & t_{13} & t_{24} & t_{14} \end{bmatrix}\{d\} \\
&= B\{d\}
\end{aligned}$$

$$\textbf{8.24}$$

The energy principles introduced in Section. 2.1 can now be used, by analogy, to provide a general formula for evaluating the stiffness matrix. Because there are now three stresses and strains involved, the 3×3 modulus matrix D of equation 8.14 or 8.15, as appropriate, replaces the scalar E in equation 2.23. The stiffness matrix is obtained by the expression

$$k = \int B^t DB dV \qquad \textbf{8.25a}$$

If numerical integration is employed equation 8.25 takes the alternative form

$$k = \Sigma B^t DB(\omega_i t|J|_{abs}) \qquad \textbf{8.25b}$$

where t is the element thickness.

As the matrix product of equations 8.25a and 8.25b involves terms of highest order a^2, ab etc. the four point Gaussian quadrature introduced in Chapter 7 is again used; this exactly integrates a cubic polynomial. When using equation 8.25b we compute B numerically by selecting the integration point values of a and b (ie $a_i = \pm 1/\sqrt{3}$, $b_i = \pm 1/\sqrt{3}$, with $\omega_i = 1$), form the matrix product $B^t DB$ and substitute in the equation.

The solution of the problem follows the same procedure as other finite element analyses. The element matrices are assembled to form the structure stiffness matrix K, the applied loads are read into the load vector $\{Q\}$ and the equations solved to determine the nodal displacement vector $\{D\}$. Loads must be applied directly to the nodes in the formulation given herein. This is also true of the computer program given in Section 8.4.

Once $\{D\}$ has been determined, we return to each element in turn to select the appropriate values from $\{D\}$ to form the element displacement vector $\{d\}$. The element stresses are finally given by

$$\{\sigma\} = DB\{d\} \qquad \textbf{8.26}$$

The element stresses can be calculated at the nodes, the integration points or at the centroid as required. Integration point stress sampling is popular with this type of element as experience indicates that the stresses are most accurate there. Some programs, however, also average the nodal values from all the adjoining elements. In the program of Section 8.4 centroidal stresses are used for the sake of simplicity.

8.4 BASIC program for plane stress and plane strain analysis

The following program for plane stress or strain analysis uses the bilinear quadrilateral element described in Section 8.3. To reduce storage requirements and computation times a Gauss reduction solution routine, which stores and operates on the upper half band of the stiffness matrix, is used. The width of this band is calculated in lines 280–300 and is given by

NW = (maximum node number difference in an element)NDF + NDF

where NDF is the number degrees of freedom per node. It is equal to 2 for plane stress and strain problems.

Data input requirements are

	Data

1 line   #nodes(NP), #elements(NE), #property sets(NS),
                #nodes involving boundary conditions(NB),
                #loaded nodes(NL)

[NS must equal 1 in the current version; see Note 2 below.]

1 line   Young's modulus (E), Poisson's ratio (P), thickness (TH)

NP lines   x co-ordinate(CO(I,1)), y co-ordinate(CO(I,2))

NE lines   four element node numbers (NN(I,1 → 4). These must be
                given in a counter-clockwise order.

NL lines   node number (N), x load (Q(2*N−1)), y load (Q(2*N))

NB lines   node number (N), two boundary flags NU and NV;
                NU = 1 if u = 0, NV = 1 if v = 0.

The data is read from DATA statements and is that required
to solve the problem of Fig 8.4. This is one half of a simply
supported beam with a load of 4200 kN uniformly distributed
through the depth at midspan.

Listing of program *PLNSTR*

```
5 CLS
6 READ B$:LPRINT B$:LPRINT:LPRINT:LPRINT
10 S3=SQR(1/3):PF=10000
20 DIM S(100,20),Q(100),CO(50,2)
30 DIM RM(20),D(3,3),NN(50,4)
40 DIM EM(8,8),XY(4,2),T(3,8),ED(8)
50 DIM TJ(2,2),DL(2,4),C(3,8),ES(3)
60 READ NP,NE,NS,NB,NL:NT=2*NP
70 READ E,P,TH
80 LPRINT "NUMBER OF NODES = ";:LPRINT NP:LPRINT
90 LPRINT"NUMBER OF ELEMENTS = ";:LPRINT NE:LPRINT
100 LPRINT"NUMBER OF PROPERTY SETS = ";:LPRINT NS
110 LPRINT:LPRINT"NUMBER OF BOUNDARY NODES = ";:LPRINT
 NB:LPRINT
120 LPRINT"NUMBER OF NODES WITH LOADS APPLIED = ";
130 LPRINT NL:LPRINT
140 LPRINT"YOUNG'S MODULUS = ";:LPRINT E:LPRINT
150 LPRINT"POISSONS RATIO = ";:LPRINT P:LPRINT
160 LPRINT"THICHNESS = ";:LPRINT TH:LPRINT:LPRINT:LPRINT
170 LPRINT"NODAL COORDINATES":LPRINT:LPRINT
180 LPRINT "NODE           X                Y":LPRINT
190 FOR I=1 TO NP
200 READ CO(I,1),CO(I,2) :LPRINT I,CO(I,1),CO(I,2):NEXT
210 LPRINT:LPRINT
220 LPRINT"ELEMENT NODE NUMBERS":LPRINT:LPRINT
230 LPRINT"ELE           NI              NJ
NK              NL"
240 LPRINT
```

```
250 NW=0:FOR I=1 TO NE
260 READ NN(I,1),NN(I,2),NN(I,3),NN(I,4)
270 LPRINT I,NN(I,1),NN(I,2),NN(I,3),NN(I,4)
280 FOR J1=1 TO 4:FOR J2=J1 TO 4
290 NW1=ABS(NN(I,J1)-NN(I,J2)):IF NW1>NW THEN NW=NW1
300 NEXT J2:NEXT J1
310 NEXT I:NW=NW*2+2:LPRINT:LPRINT
320 D(1,1)=E*TH/(1-P*P):D(2,2)=D(1,1)
330 D(1,2)=P*D(1,1):D(2,1)=D(1,2)
340 D(3,3)=.5*(1-P)*D(1,1):D(3,2)=0
350 D(1,3)=0:D(2,3)=0:D(3,1)=0
360 FOR I=1 TO NT:Q(I)=0:FOR J=1 TO 20
370 S(I,J)=0:NEXT J:NEXT I
380 FOR N=1 TO NE
390 FOR I=1 TO 8:FOR J=1 TO 8
400 EM(I,J)=0:NEXT J:NEXT I
410 FOR II=1 TO 4:A=S3:B=S3
420 IF II=1 THEN A=-A:B=-B
430 IF II=2 THEN B=-B
440 IF II=4 THEN A=-A
450 GOSUB 1280
460 DJ=ABS(DJ)
470 FOR I=1 TO 8:FOR J=1 TO 8
480 FOR K=1 TO 3
490 EM(I,J)=EM(I,J)+C(K,I)*T(K,J)*DJ
500 NEXT K
510 NEXT J:NEXT I
520 NEXT II
530 FOR I=1 TO 4:IN=NN(N,I)
540 FOR J=1 TO 4:JN=NN(N,J)
550 FOR IL=1 TO 2
560 IE=(I-1)*2+IL:NR=(IN-1)*2+IL
570 FOR JL=1 TO 2
580 JE=(J-1)*2+JL:NC=(JN-1)*2+JL
590 NCB=NC-NR+1
600 IF NCB<=0 GOTO 620
610 S(NR,NCB)=S(NR,NCB)+EM(IE,JE)

630 NEXT JL:NEXT IL
640 NEXT J:NEXT I
650 PRINT"ELEMENT",N:NEXT N
660 LPRINT:LPRINT:LPRINT"NODAL LOADS":LPRINT:LPRINT
670 LPRINT"NODE            QX                QY":LPRINT
680 FOR I=1 TO NL
690 READ N,Q(2*N-1),Q(2*N):LPRINT I,Q(2*N-1),Q(2*N):NEXT I
700 LPRINT:LPRINT:LPRINT"BOUNDARY CONDITIONS":LPRINT:L
PRINT
710 LPRINT"NODE          U CONDN.          V CONDN.":LPRINT
720 FOR I=1 TO NB
730 READ N,NU,NV
740 LPRINT N,NU,NV
750 K=2*N-1
760 IF NU=1 THEN S(K,1)=S(K,1)*PF
770 IF NV=1 THEN S(K+1,1)=S(K+1,1)*PF
780 NEXT I
```

```
790 FOR L=1 TO NP
800 ND=(NP-L+1)*2
810 IF ND>(NW-2) THEN LM=NW
820 FOR I=1 TO 2
830 LM=LM-1:IP=2*(L-1)+I
840 X=S(IP,1):Q(IP)=Q(IP)/X
850 FOR J=1 TO LM
860 RM(J)=S(IP,J+1):NEXT J
870 FOR J=1 TO LM+1
880 S(IP,J)=S(IP,J)/X:NEXT J
890 FOR K=1 TO LM
900 NR=IP+K:NC=LM-K+1
910 X=RM(K):Q(NR)=Q(NR)-X*Q(IP)
920 FOR J=1 TO NC:JP=J+K
930 S(NR,J)=S(NR,J)-X*S(IP,JP):NEXT J
940 NEXT K
950 NEXT I
960 NEXT L
970 I=NT:Q(NT)=Q(NT)/S(NT,1)
980 I=I-1
990 IF LM<(NW-1) THEN LM=LM+1
1000 FOR J=1 TO LM
1010 Q(I)=Q(I)-S(I,J+1)*Q(I+J):NEXT J
1020 IF I>1 GOTO 980
1030 LPRINT"NODAL DISPLACEMENTS"
1040 LPRINT:LPRINT:LPRINT"ELE          U              V"
1050 LPRINT"NUM":LPRINT
1060 A$="##   +#.####^^^^   +#.####^^^^"
1070 FOR I=1 TO NP
1080 LPRINT USING A$;I,Q(2*I-1),Q(2*I)
1090 NEXT I
1100 PRINT"PRESS RETRN FOR STRESS"
1110 INPUT B$
1120 LPRINT:LPRINT"ELEMENT STRESSES"
1130 LPRINT:LPRINT:LPRINT"ELE   SIGMA-X      SIGMA-Y
    SIGMA-XY"
1140 LPRINT"NUM":LPRINT
1150 A$="##   +#.###^^^^   +#.###^^^^   +#.###^^^^"
1160 FOR N=1 TO NE:A=0:B=0
1170 GOSUB 1280
1180 FOR I=1 TO 4:K=NN(N,I)
1190 ED(2*I-1)=Q(2*K-1)
1200 ED(2*I)=Q(2*K):NEXT I
1210 FOR I=1 TO 3:ES(I)=0
1220 FOR J =1 TO 8
1230 ES(I)=ES(I)+T(I,J)*ED(J)
1240 NEXT J:NEXT I
1250 LPRINT USING A$;N,ES(1),ES(2),ES(3)
1260 NEXT N
1270 END
1280 FOR I=1 TO 4:K=NN(N,I)
1290 XY(I,1)=CO(K,1):XY(I,2)=CO(K,2)
1300 NEXT I
1310 DL(1,1)=(B-1)/4:DL(1,2)=(1-B)/4
```

```
1320 DL(1,3)=(1+B)/4:DL(1,4)=-(1+B)/4
1330 DL(2,1)=(A-1)/4:DL(2,2)=-(1+A)/4
1340 DL(2,3)=(1+A)/4:DL(2,4)=(1-A)/4
1350 FOR I=1 TO 2:FOR J=1 TO 2
1360 TJ(I,J)=0:FOR K=1 TO 4
1370 TJ(I,J)=TJ(I,J)+DL(I,K)*XY(K,J)
1380 NEXT K:NEXT J:NEXT I
1390 DJ=TJ(1,1)*TJ(2,2)-TJ(1,2)*TJ(2,1)
1400 DD=TJ(1,1):TJ(1,1)=TJ(2,2)/DJ
1410 TJ(2,2)=DD/DJ:TJ(1,2)=-TJ(1,2)/DJ
1420 TJ(2,1)=-TJ(2,1)/DJ
1430 FOR I=1 TO 2:FOR J =1 TO 4
1440 T(I,J)=0:FOR K=1 TO 2
1450 T(I,J)=T(I,J)+TJ(I,K)*DL(K,J)
1460 NEXT K:NEXT J:NEXT I
1470 FOR I=1 TO 3:FOR J=1 TO 8
1480 C(I,J)=0:NEXT J:NEXT I
1490 FOR J=1 TO 4
1500 C(1,2*J-1)=T(1,J):C(3,2*J)=T(1,J)
1510 C(2,2*J)=T(2,J):C(3,2*J-1)=T(2,J)
1520 NEXT J
1530 FOR I= 1 TO 3:FOR J=1 TO 8
1540 T(I,J)=0:FOR K=1 TO 3
1550 T(I,J)=T(I,J)+D(I,K)*C(K,J):NEXT K
1560 NEXT J: NEXT I
1570 RETURN
1580 DATA                 TEST PLANE STRESS PROBLEM
1590 DATA 9,4,1,6,3
1600 DATA .2E8,.2,.5
1610 DATA 0,0
1620 DATA 0,.5
1630 DATA 0,1
1640 DATA 1,0
1650 DATA 1,.5
1660 DATA 1,1
1670 DATA 2,0
1680 DATA 2,.5
1690 DATA 2,1
1700 DATA 1,4,5,2
1710 DATA 2,5,6,3
1720 DATA 4,7,8,5
1730 DATA 5,8,9,6
1740 DATA 7,0,-700
1750 DATA 8,0,-700
1760 DATA 9,0,-700
1770 DATA 1,0,1
1780 DATA 2,0,1
1790 DATA 3,0,1
1800 DATA 7,1,0
1810 DATA 8,1,0
1820 DATA 9,1,0
```

Notes

1 The program uses the bilinear quadrilateral plane stress element. To deal with plane strain the modulus matrix must be altered in lines 320–350.

2 The program assumes all elements have the same E, v and t values, ie the material is homogenous. Nonhomogeneity can be dealt with quite easily by varying the properties between elements using the property set concept used in the frame program of Chapter 5.

3 A subroutine, lines 1280–1570, computes the strain interpolation matrix B, which is used to form the stress matrix DB and compute the element stresses (line 1230). The element stiffness matrices are calculated as $k = \Sigma B^t DB dV$ (line 490).

4 Stresses are printed only at the element centroids. A further loop on the stress segment of the program (lines 1160–1260) is needed to calculate integration point or averaged nodal values.

5 The bilinear plane stress element performs better if selective reduced integration is used. It is preferable to take the shear strain contributions to the stiffness matrix at the centroid only but four point integration should be retained for the direct stress terms.[1,2]

6 In this problem the four element stiffness matrices are identical. The program can be made to execute much faster if coding is added to take advantage of this common feature, as in the program of Chapter 9.

7 No provision has been made for distributed loads or body forces. The program can be easily extended to deal with these within the integration loop but, for uniform loadings such as self-weight, the present program can be employed by intuitively lumping the distributed loads at nodes and reading these as input data. The contributions from individual elements have to be summed manually by the user but this is not difficult.

8 The program above requires about 15 Kb of core and, if more core is available, then larger problems can be tackled by extending the dimensions of the array S(,). The first is the number of problem freedoms and the second the half band width. It is also possible to write equation solvers which use disks to store the structure stiffness matrix and the size of problem is then effectively unlimited. In these the only part of the stiffness matrix in core is a triangular block lying above the pivot row. Such programs execute too slowly on microcomputers fitted with floppy disks, to be practical.

9 The above program can be made to compute principal stresses by the addition of some simple code. This is left as an exercise.

10 Note that this program suppresses displacements by the simple expedient of multiplying the corresponding diagonal entry by a large number PF (lines 10, 760 and 770).

Comments on example of Fig 8.4

Table 8.1 shows the results obtained using a varying number of elements to solve the problem of Fig 8.4. These indicate satisfactory convergence of displacements towards the correct solutions. The stress values cited are averaged nodal values and have also converged to provide satisfactory results.[2]

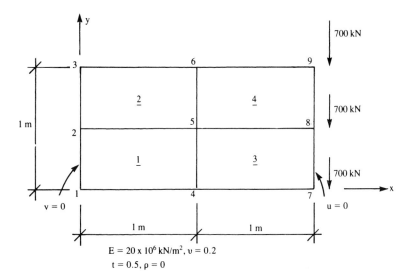

Figure 8.4 One half of a simply supported beam with four bilinear finite elements

Table 8.1 Numerical results with the bilinear plane stress element for the analysis of the problem of Fig 8.4

Elements	Total freedoms	$-v_8$ (mm)	$(\sigma_x)_6$(MPa)	$(\sigma_{xy})_5$(MPa)
2 × 2	18	5.43	17.9	0.67
3 × 3	32	6.55	21.5	2.70
4 × 4	50	7.08	23.0	3.40
5 × 5	72	7.37	23.8	4.89
6 × 6	98	7.54	24.4	5.48
Analytical solution		7.93	25.2	6.30

8.5 Exercises

1 Solve equations 8.11 to check the first three rows of equation 8.13.

2 Carry out exercises 1, 2 and 3 in Section 7.6 if you have not already done so.

3 Type in the program given in Section 8.4 and run the problem shown in Fig 8.4. Check the results against those of Table 8.1.

4 Solve the problem of Fig 8.4 using the other meshes used in Table 8.1 and examine the convergence of your solutions.

5 Selecting one or two meshes use one point integration in forming the shear strain energy of the ESMs. (Hint: Use a fifth pass through the numerical integration loop using a = 0 and b = 0. In the first four passes use 480 FOR K = 1 TO 2.)

6 Modify the program to compute nodal stresses, (ie using a = −1, b = −1 etc. in the stress calculation loop), with a reasonably fine mesh. Note the stress discontinuities indicated and average the results at nodes. Compare the results with those of Table 8.1.

7 The program does not calculate the consistent loads. Using equation 5.32 include provision for gravity loadings in the integration loop. These are given by

$$\{q\} = \iint \{f\}q(x,y)dxdy$$

References

1 C A Brebbia and J J Connor, *Finite Element Techniques for Structural Engineers*, Butterworths, London, 1973.

2 G A Mohr, 'A simple rectangular membrane element including the drilling freedom', *Computers and Structures*, vol 13, 1981, p 483.

CHAPTER 9

Bending of Thin Plates

This chapter takes us into the realm of plate bending analysis which is a more difficult area of study than plane strain analysis. It should not be beyond the comprehension of serious undergraduate students, however. The subject is introduced, along with some more advanced topics, in a manner which is different to that of previous chapters and deliberately designed to extend students' horizons.

The nodal freedoms usually used are w, $\partial w/\partial x$ and $\partial w/\partial y$ and this means that there are normally three freedoms per node. If we restrict attention to elements of triangular and quadrilateral shapes there will be either nine or twelve freedoms per element. In this introductory book, we restrict attention to triangular elements and conclude this chapter with a useful triangular element plate bending program written in BASIC.

9.1 Generalised stresses and strains in thin plates

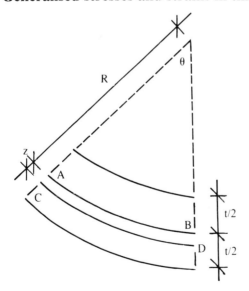

Figure 9.1 Deformed section of a plate in bending

In plate bending analysis, it is customary to assume the plate lies in the xy plane. We consider a short section of a plate along the x axis, as shown in Fig 9.1, and assume that it is subjected to bending in the xz plane only. If plane sections remain plane during bending, the strain in the filament CD shown in Fig 9.1, height z below the neutral surface, is given by

$$\varepsilon_x = (R_x\theta + z\theta - R_x\theta)/R_x\theta = z/R_x \qquad 9.1$$

where R_x is the radius of curvature of plate surface in the zx plane and θ is the angle subtended at the centre of curvature 0.

If the section taken in Fig 9.1 is of unit width, we can integrate the stress σ_x over the thickness of the plate to obtain the moment per unit width, m_x, given by

$$m_x = \int_{-t/2}^{t/2} \sigma_x z dz \qquad 9.2$$

The quantity m_x is referred to as a generalised stress.

In plate (and beam) bending problems, corresponding to a generalised stress such as m_x, we also need to define a generalised strain for the purpose of analysis. The appropriate quantity to select in this case is the curvature $1/R_x$. This generalised strain is related to displacements by

$$\Phi_x = 1/R_x = \partial^2 w/\partial x^2/[1 + (\partial w/\partial x)^2]^{3/2}$$
$$\approx \partial^2 w/\partial x^2 \qquad 9.3$$

By following a similar procedure for direct stresses σ_y and shear stresses σ_{xy} we arrive at the complete set of corresponding generalised stresses and strains for plate bending

Generalised stresses

$$m_x \quad m_y \quad m_{xy}$$

Generalised strains

$$\Phi_x = \partial^2 w/\partial x^2 \quad \Phi_y = \partial^2 w/\partial y^2 \quad \Phi_{xy} = 2\partial^2 w/\partial x \partial y \qquad 9.4$$

The generalised stresses and strains are chosen in such a way that the expression, $\frac{1}{2}[m_x\Phi_x + m_y\Phi_y + m_{xy}\Phi_{xy}]$, for strain energy per unit area, when *integrated over the plate area*, produces the same value as the expression, $\frac{1}{2}[\sigma_x\varepsilon_x + \sigma_y\varepsilon_y + \sigma_{xy}\varepsilon_{xy}]$, for strain energy per unit volume, *integrated over the plate volume*. The factor 2 associated with the generalised strain Φ_{xy} arises because there are two complementary shear stresses acting on any plate lamina of which each contributes to the strain energy.[1]

The link between the generalised stresses and strains is provided, as usual, by a modulus matrix. This is derived by observing that, as stated above, each lamina is in a state of plane stress. From equations 9.1 and 8.15

$$
\begin{aligned}
m_x &= \int_{-t/2}^{t/2} \sigma_x z \, dz \\
&= \frac{E}{(1 - v^2)} \int_{-t/2}^{t/2} (\varepsilon_x + v\varepsilon_y) z \, dz \\
&= \frac{E}{(1 - v^2)} (1/R_x + v/R_y) \int_{-t/2}^{t/2} z^2 \, dz \\
&= Et^3 (\Phi_x + v\Phi_y)/12(1 - v^2)
\end{aligned}
\qquad 9.5
$$

The generalised stresses m_y and m_{xy} are related to the generalised strains by following a similar procedure. Thus the modulus matrix is obtained by multiplying the plane stress modulus matrix of equation 8.15 by the scalar $t^3/12$. This leads to

$$
\begin{bmatrix} m_x \\ m_y \\ m_{xy} \end{bmatrix} = \frac{Et^3}{12(1 - v^2)} \begin{bmatrix} 1 & v & 0 \\ v & 1 & 0 \\ 0 & 0 & \dfrac{1-v}{2} \end{bmatrix} \begin{bmatrix} \Phi_x \\ \Phi_y \\ \Phi_{xy} \end{bmatrix} = D\{\Phi\}
\qquad 9.6
$$

It follows from the discussion above that the total potential energy of a bent thin plate is given by

$$
\begin{aligned}
\Pi &= \tfrac{1}{2} \int (\{\Phi_x \quad \Phi_y \quad \Phi_{xy}\}^t \{m_x \quad m_y \quad m_{xy}\} - 2qw) \, dx \, dy \\
&= \tfrac{1}{2} \int (\{\Phi\}^t D\{\Phi\} - 2qw) \, dx \, dy
\end{aligned}
\qquad 9.7
$$

where $q \ (= q(x,y))$ is the load per unit area acting on the surface of the plate.

If we form an interpolation $w = \{f\}^t \{d\}$ and differentiate this according to equations 9.4 to form a curvature interpolation matrix B, then the curvatures at any point are given by $\{\Phi\} = B\{d\}$ so that the total potential energy of a finite element finally can be expressed as[2]

$$
\begin{aligned}
\Pi_d &= \tfrac{1}{2}\{d\}^t \left(\int B^t D B \, dx \, dy \right) \{d\} - \{d\}^t \int \{f\}^t q \, dx \, dy \\
&= \tfrac{1}{2}\{d\}^t k\{d\} - \{d\}^t \{q\}
\end{aligned}
\qquad 9.8
$$

Equation 9.8 indicates that the element stiffness matrix is given by integrating the matrix product B^tDB over the element area.

In Section 9.5 we use equations 9.4, 9.6 and 9.8 to form the stiffness matrix for a nine freedom triangular thin plate element. This is undertaken by the use of Lagrangian area co-ordinate interpolation, natural strains parallel to the sides of triangular elements and basis transformation. While the use of Lagrangian interpolation is unusual in thin plate bending analysis, it is an excellent starting point, since we are already familiar with it from plane stress analysis and the algebra is less cumbersome.

9.2   Lagrangian area co-ordinate interpolation in triangles

We have already shown in Section 7.1 that the interpolation for the six freedom element shown in Fig 7.1b can be expressed as

$$w = L_1w_1 + L_2w_2 + L_3w_3 \qquad\qquad 9.9$$

where the area co-ordinates are defined as

$$L_1 = (a - y_{32}x + x_{32}y)/2\Delta \qquad\qquad 9.10$$

$$L_2 = (a - y_{13}x + x_{13}y)/2\Delta \qquad\qquad 9.11$$

$$L_3 = (a - y_{21}x + x_{21}y)/2\Delta \qquad\qquad 9.12$$

and $\qquad a = 2\Delta/3, \; \Delta = \text{area of triangle}, \qquad\qquad 9.13$

$$y_{32} = y_3 - y_2, \; y_{13} = y_1 - y_3, \; y_{21} = y_2 - y_1 \qquad 9.14a$$

$$x_{32} = x_3 - x_2, \; x_{13} = x_1 - x_3, \; x_{21} = x_2 - x_1 \qquad 9.14b$$

Also, as shown in Chapter 7, the identity

$$L_1 + L_2 + L_3 = 1 \qquad\qquad 9.15$$

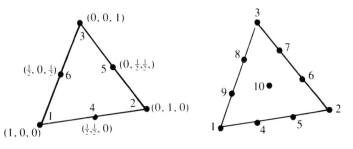

Figure 9.2   Quadratic and cubic Lagrangian triangular elements

applies so that only two of the area co-ordinates are independent.
We also need to be able to relate the area and Cartesian
co-ordinates which involves the relationships

$$x = L_1x_1 + L_2x_2 + L_3x_3 \qquad\qquad \textbf{9.16}$$

$$y = L_1y_1 + L_2y_2 + L_3y_3 \qquad\qquad \textbf{9.17}$$

where (x_1,y_1), (x_2,y_2) and (x_3,y_3) are the Cartesian co-ordinates
of the vertices.

Interpolation in triangles for plate bending problems

In plate bending problems, the generalised strains are curvatures,
that is, second derivatives of the basic field variable, the displacement w. The lowest order element which can be used for plate
bending is quadratic and it models constant curvatures. Such
elements are simple to derive but converge too slowly for practical purposes. Cubic elements, which model linear curvature and
are used much more commonly in practice, are of the minimum
order which should be used.

Quadratic triangle by matrix inversion

In Section 7.1 we dealt with the six node Lagrangian quadratic
triangle of Fig 9.2a in connection with plane stress problems,
where its use is quite common. As an introduction to area co-
ordinate interpolation formulation by inversion, we commence
with the quadratic polynomial

$$w = c_1L_1{}^2 + c_2L_2{}^2 + c_3L_3{}^2 + c_4L_1L_2 + c_5L_2L_3 + c_6L_3L_1$$
$$= \{M\}^t\{c\} \qquad\qquad \textbf{9.18}$$

where $c_1, \ldots c_6$ are a set of constants. Equation 9.18 contains all
terms of up to order 2, ie x^0, y^0, x^1, y^1, x^2, y^2, xy, which readers
can verify by expanding equation 9.18 using the area co-ordinate
definitions of equations 9.10–9.12.

Writing the nodal values for w on the left side of equation 9.18
with the corresponding nodal co-ordinates substituted on the
right hand side, six simultaneous equations are obtained

$$
\begin{bmatrix} w_1 \\ w_2 \\ w_3 \\ w_4 \\ w_5 \\ w_6 \end{bmatrix}
=
\begin{bmatrix}
1 & 0 & 0 & 0 & 0 & 0 \\
0 & 1 & 0 & 0 & 0 & 0 \\
0 & 0 & 1 & 0 & 0 & 0 \\
\frac{1}{4} & \frac{1}{4} & 0 & \frac{1}{4} & 0 & 0 \\
0 & \frac{1}{4} & \frac{1}{4} & 0 & \frac{1}{4} & 0 \\
\frac{1}{4} & 0 & \frac{1}{4} & 0 & 0 & \frac{1}{4}
\end{bmatrix}
\begin{bmatrix} c_1 \\ c_2 \\ c_3 \\ c_4 \\ c_5 \\ c_6 \end{bmatrix}
= C^{-1}\{c\}
\qquad\qquad \textbf{9.19}
$$

After inversion, the interpolation functions are obtained as

$$\{f\}^t = \{M\}^t C = \{M\}^t \begin{bmatrix} 1 & 0 & 0 & 0 & 0 & 0 \\ 0 & 1 & 0 & 0 & 0 & 0 \\ 0 & 0 & 1 & 0 & 0 & 0 \\ -1 & -1 & 0 & 4 & 0 & 0 \\ 0 & -1 & -1 & 0 & 4 & 0 \\ -1 & 0 & -1 & 0 & 0 & 4 \end{bmatrix} \qquad \textbf{9.20}$$

or
$$\begin{aligned}
f_1 &= L_1^2 - L_1 L_2 - L_3 L_1 = L_1^2 - L_1(L_2 + L_3) \\
&= L_1^2 - L_1(1 - L_1) = L_1(2L_1 - 1) \\
f_2 &= L_2(2L_2 - 1), \quad f_3 = L_3(2L_3 - 1) \\
f_4 &= 4L_1 L_2, \quad f_5 = 4L_2 L_3, \quad f_6 = 4L_3 L_1
\end{aligned} \qquad \textbf{9.21}$$

These functions can written more compactly for triangular Lagrangian elements using the formula[3]

$$f_{abc}(L_1, L_2, L_3) = f_a(L_1) f_b(L_2) f_c(L_3) \qquad \textbf{9.22}$$

where
$$\begin{aligned}
f_a(L_1) &= \prod_{i=1}^{a} (nL_1 - i + 1)/i, \quad a \geq 1 \\
&= 1 \qquad\qquad\qquad\qquad a = 0
\end{aligned}$$

In equation 9.22, a $(= nL_1)$, b $(= nL_2)$, c $(= nL_3)$ are given by the nodal co-ordinates of the point where the freedom occurs and 'n' is the order of the interpolation (n = 1 for linear interpolation, n = 2 for quadratic interpolation etc).

For f_1, for example, we have
$$(a, b, c) = (2, 0, 0)$$
giving $f_1 = \{(2L_1 - 1 + 1)/1\}\{(2L_1 - 2 + 1)/2\}$
$$= L_1(2L_1 - 1) \qquad \textbf{9.23}$$

Cubic triangle

For the ten node cubic Lagrangian triangle shown in Fig 9.2b the area co-ordinate modes are

$$\begin{aligned}
\{M\} = \{&L_1^3, L_2^3, L_3^3, L_1^2 L_2, L_1^2 L_3, L_2^2 L_3, L_2^2 L_1, \\
&L_3^2 L_1, L_3^2 L_2, L_1 L_2 L_3\}
\end{aligned} \qquad \textbf{9.24}$$

and following the procedures used for the quadratic triangle the interpolation functions are given by $\{f\}^t = \{M\}^t C$ which, written out in detail, are

$$f_i = L_i(3L_i - 1)(3L_i - 2)/2 \qquad i = 1,2,3$$
$$f_n = 4.5L_iL_j(3L_i - 1) \quad n = 4,6,8 \quad i = 1,2,3 \quad j = 2,3,1$$
$$f_n = 4.5L_iL_j(3L_j - 1) \quad n = 5,7,9 \quad i = 1,2,3 \quad j = 2,3,1$$
$$f_{10} = 27L_1L_2L_3 \qquad\qquad\qquad\qquad\qquad\qquad\quad \textbf{9.25}$$

9.3   Natural slopes and curvatures in triangular elements

In the preceding section, we have seen that area co-ordinates yield simple and elegant interpolations for Lagrangian triangular elements. However, we cannot use area co-ordinates directly in the curvature definitions of equations 9.4, since these expressions involve Cartesian derivatives. It is found that the algebra needed to derive the element equations has a simpler form if we use three natural co-ordinates a, b, c parallel to the three sides of the triangular elements; see Fig 9.3.

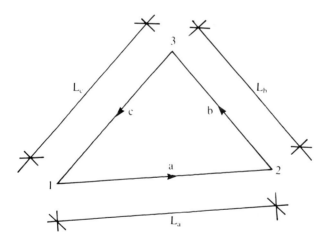

Figure 9.3   Natural co-ordinates in a triangle

Natural slopes and curvatures in terms of Cartesian slopes and curvatures

By definition the natural slopes are taken to mean slopes parallel to the sides, eg for side 12

$$\phi_a = \partial w/\partial a = (\partial w/\partial x)(\partial x/\partial a) + (\partial w/\partial y)(\partial y/\partial a)$$
$$= c_{ax}(\partial w/\partial x) + c_{ay}(\partial w/\partial y) \qquad \textbf{9.26}$$

where $\quad c_{ax} = (x_2 - x_1)/L_a = x_{21}/L_a, \; c_{ay} = y_{21}/L_a$

The terms c_{ax} and c_{ay} are the direction cosines of the side with respect to the Cartesian axes. The natural slopes ϕ_b and ϕ_c, parallel to the other two sides, follow from equation 9.26 by appropriate changes in subscripts, yielding

$$\phi_b = c_{bx}(\partial \omega/\partial x) + c_{by}(\partial \omega/\partial y)$$
$$\phi_c = c_{cx}(\partial \omega/\partial x) + c_{cy}(\partial \omega/\partial y) \qquad \textbf{9.27}$$

The natural curvature parallel to a side is obtained by differentiating the natural slope with respect the natural co-ordinate parallel to that side, eg for side 12 $\partial\phi_a/\partial a$ ($= \partial^2 w/\partial a^2$) is given by differentiating equation 9.26 with respect to 'a' ie

$$\Phi_a = \partial^2 w/\partial a^2 = c_{ax}\partial(\partial w/\partial x)/\partial a + c_{ay}\partial(\partial w/\partial y)/\partial a$$
$$= c_{ax}[(\partial w_x/\partial x)(\partial x/\partial a) + (\partial w_x/\partial y)(\partial y/\partial a)]$$
$$+ c_{ay}[(\partial w_y/\partial x)(\partial x/\partial a) + (\partial w_y/\partial y)(\partial y/\partial a)]$$
$$= c_{ax}^2\partial^2 w/\partial x^2 + c_{ay}^2\partial^2 w/\partial y^2 + 2c_{ax}c_{ay}\partial^2 w/\partial x\partial y \qquad \textbf{9.28}$$

in which $w_x = \partial w/\partial x$ and $w_y = \partial w/\partial y$.

The expressions for the natural curvatures parallel to the other two sides take the same form. Expressing the transformation from Cartesian to natural curvatures in matrix form we obtain

$$\begin{bmatrix} \Phi_a \\ \Phi_b \\ \Phi_c \end{bmatrix} = \begin{bmatrix} c_{ax}^2 & c_{ay}^2 & \sqrt{2}c_{ax}c_{ay} \\ c_{bx}^2 & c_{by}^2 & \sqrt{2}c_{bx}c_{by} \\ c_{cx}^2 & c_{cy}^2 & \sqrt{2}c_{cx}c_{cy} \end{bmatrix} \begin{bmatrix} \Phi_x \\ \Phi_y \\ \Phi_{xy} \end{bmatrix} \qquad \textbf{9.29}$$

Note that factors $\sqrt{2}$ are used in the transformation matrix of equation 9.29. This equates with the original transformation used by Argyris.[4] Correspondingly, the twist curvature is now defined as $\Phi_{xy} = \sqrt{2}\partial^2 w/\partial x\partial y$ and the twist modulus of equation 9.6, ie the entry in row three and column three must be doubled to calculate the strain energy of a finite element correctly.[5]

If readers are perplexed by the notion of natural curvatures, perhaps reference to the familiar process of experimental stress analysis will assist them to understand. Engineers will be aware that, with the strain rosette, we measure linear strains in three directions and convert these to two direct and one shear strain in Cartesian axes. The same concept is simply applied to curvatures, which are generalised strains, in dealing with plate bending.

Inversion of the matrix of equation 9.29 yields the transformation from natural to Cartesian curvatures which allows us to calculate natural curvatures directly from the area co-ordinate interpolations.

Natural slopes and curvatures in terms of area co-ordinate derivatives

We also need to relate the natural slopes and curvatures to the area co-ordinate derivatives. For side 12, the natural slope is given by

$$\phi_a = \partial w/\partial a$$
$$= (\partial w/\partial L_1)(\partial L_1/\partial a) + (\partial w/\partial L_2)(\partial L_2/\partial a) + (\partial w/\partial L_3)(\partial L_3/\partial a)$$
$$= (\partial w/\partial L_2 - \partial w/\partial L_1)/L_a \qquad \mathbf{9.30}$$

in which we have used the fact that L_3 is zero on this side and L_1 and L_2 vary between zero and unity along the side.

Differentiating equation 9.30, the natural curvature Φ_a is given by

$$\Phi_a = \partial \phi_a/\partial a = (\partial \phi_a/\partial L_2 - \partial \phi_a/\partial L_1)/L_a$$
$$= [\partial(\partial w/\partial L_2 - \partial w/\partial L_1)/\partial L_2 - \partial(\partial w/\partial L_2 - \partial w/\partial L_1)/\partial L_1]/L_a{}^2$$
$$= [\partial^2 w/\partial L_1{}^2 + \partial^2 w/\partial L_2{}^2 - 2\partial^2 w/\partial L_1 \partial L_2]/L_a{}^2 \qquad \mathbf{9.31}$$

The corresponding expressions for Φ_b and Φ_c follow by cyclic progression of subscripts. Φ_a, Φ_b, Φ_c are used in Section 9.5 to calculate natural strains from the area co-ordinate interpolation functions for an element.

9.4 Basis transformation techniques

As shown in Reference 5, nonconformity or inequality of, for example, slope across element boundaries, can prevent the convergence of finite element solutions to the exact differential equation solutions. We can increase interelement continuity by including surface traction or displacement fields along the element boundary. Hybrid stiffness, flexibility and mixed methods which do this have been the subject of much research. An alternative approach to these involves the use of basis transformation techniques.

Before considering examples of basis transformation, however, we shall clarify the term basis and related concepts.[7]

A **linear space** V contains elements which obey the usual addition and multiplication laws of algebra, examples being

1 the sets of real and complex numbers,
2 the set of infinite series,
3 a set of unit vectors, and
4 the set of polynomials.

From the point of view of polynomial interpolation, our interest lies in the set of polynomials $x^0(=1)$, $x^1(=x)$, x^2, ..., x^n.

A **subset S** of V is said to be contained in a subspace of V. Such a subset may include linear combinations of the elements of V and subsets comprising alternative linear combinations of the same elements are said to have the same linear span. For example, the pair of subsets $\{1, x, x^2\}$ and $\{1, (1 + x), (1 + x)^2\}$ span the same subspace and the set $\{1, x, x^2\}$ is a subset of $\{1, x, x^2, x^3\}$.

A **finite set S**, of variables v_i, is independent if $\Sigma c_i v_i = 0$ only if all $c_i = 0$ or all $v_i = 0$. For example, the polynomial set $v_i = x^i$, i $= 0 \rightarrow n$ is obviously independent as the sum $\Sigma c_i x^i$ cannot vanish for $x \neq 0$ unless all the coefficients c_i are zero. The set $\{1, x, x^2, (x + x^2)\}$, on the other hand, is obviously dependent since $c_1 v_1 + c_2 v_2 + c_3 v_3 + c_4 v_4 = c_1 + c_2 x + c_3 x^2 + c_4(x + x^2)$ is zero if $c_1 = 0$, $c_2 = 1$, $c_3 = 1$, $c_4 = -1$.

A finite set S in a linear space V is called a **finite basis for V** if it is independent and spans V. Also, if such a basis contains n elements, then n = dim (V) is the dimension of S. In the finite element method, for example, we use, for the four freedom beam element, a finite cubic basis $\{M\} = \{1, x, x^2, x^3\}$. Thus dim $\{M\}$ = 4 and $\{M\}$ is clearly linearly independent. When we obtain interpolation functions $\{f\}$ from the original polynomial, this is, in fact, an exercise in basis transformation as we shall show.

Changing a polynomial basis

In the finite element method, we use finite polynomial bases as approximating functions in each element. For the cubic beam element of Chapter 5, for example, we commenced with the interpolation for v in the form

$$v = c_1 + c_2 x + c_3 x^2 + c_4 x^3$$
$$= \{f^*\}^t\{d^*\} \qquad\qquad \textbf{9.32}$$

where $\{f^*\}^t (= \langle 1 \ x \ x^2 \ x^3 \rangle)$ is an initial basis, which we denoted in Chapter 5 as $\{M\}^t$, and $\{d^*\}^t$ $(= \langle c_1 \ c_2 \ c_3 \ c_4 \rangle)$ are the initial freedoms, previously denoted $\{c\}^t$. We can also express v in the form

$$v = \{f\}^t\{v_1 \ \phi_1 \ v_2 \ \phi_2\} = \{f\}^t\{d\} \qquad \textbf{9.33}$$

where

$$f_1 = 0.5 - 3x/2L + 2x^3/L^3$$
$$f_2 = L/8 - x/4 - x^2/2L + x^3/L^2$$
$$f_3 = 0.5 + 3x/L - 2x^3/L^3$$
$$f_4 = -L/8 - x/4 + x^2/2L + x^3/L^2$$

Vectors $\{f\}$ and $\{d\}$ are the final basis and freedoms. It follows from equations 9.32 and 9.33, that

$$\{f\}^t\{d\} = \{f^*\}^t\{d^*\} \qquad \textbf{9.34}$$

If $\{d^*\}$ is related to $\{d\}$ by some independent means, using the relationship

$$\{d^*\} = T\{d\} \qquad \textbf{9.35a}$$

then the final basis is related to the initial basis by

$$\{f\}^t = \{f^*\}^t T \qquad \textbf{9.35b}$$

When changing basis in this manner, we never need to discover $\{f\}$ explicitly, provided the final basis does not violate criteria necessary to ensure convergence.

The final stiffness matrix is given by

$$k = T^t k^* T \qquad \textbf{9.36}$$

where k^* is derived using the basis $\{f^*\}$ which the matrix T denoted C in Section 5.2 transforms to the basis $\{f\}$.

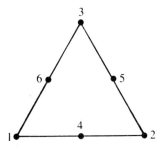

Figure 9.4 Quadratic triangular element

Applying constraints

To illustrate the use of a basis transformation in reducing the number of freedoms we consider the quadratic triangle of Fig 9.4. Suppose we wish to suppress some midside nodal displacements to allow the element to be used alongside other elements which do not possess midside nodes.

If the element possesses only a single degree of freedom ϕ at each node then, to remove initial freedoms ϕ^*_4 and ϕ^*_6, for example, we simply introduce the linear constraints $\phi^*_4 = (\phi_1 + \phi_2)/2$ and $\phi^*_6 = (\phi_1 + \phi_2)/2$ by the transformation[8]

$$\{\phi^*\} = \begin{bmatrix} \phi^*_1 \\ \phi^*_2 \\ \phi^*_3 \\ \phi^*_4 \\ \phi^*_5 \\ \phi^*_6 \end{bmatrix} = \begin{bmatrix} 1 & 0 & 0 & 0 \\ 0 & 1 & 0 & 0 \\ 0 & 0 & 1 & 0 \\ \frac{1}{2} & \frac{1}{2} & 0 & 0 \\ 0 & \frac{1}{2} & \frac{1}{2} & 0 \\ \frac{1}{2} & 0 & \frac{1}{2} & 0 \end{bmatrix} \begin{bmatrix} \phi_1 \\ \phi_2 \\ \phi_3 \\ \phi_5 \end{bmatrix} = T\{\phi\}$$

9.38

Another interesting example of basis transformation also occurs in the element of Fig 9.4. Here it is found that shifting the midside nodes on two sides, to the quarter points, provides the square root displacement variation on these sides required to model the effect of cracks. This application was first recognized as a basis transformation by Okabe et al.[9]

9.5 Nine freedom thin plate element by basis transformation

Fig 9.5a shows a nine freedom triangular thin plate element with freedoms w, $\partial w/\partial x$ and $\partial w/\partial y$ at the vertices. A complete cubic interpolation in two dimensions, however, requires ten terms. Simple expedients, such as omitting one of the higher order cubic modes, do not result in satisfactory formulations for the 'highly desirable' 9 d.f. plate element. A great deal of research has thus been directed at the problem, resulting in many elaborate formulations.[6]

One of the most elegant solutions to this difficulty is through the use of basis transformation methods[6] where the initial stiffness matrix for the element of Fig 9.5b is transformed to the final stiffness matrix for the element shown in Fig 9.5a.

First, however, it is worth summarising the steps required to carry out the necessary basis transformation and form the final element stiffness matrix.

1 An initial basis $\{f^*\}$ and set of freedoms is chosen for the element of Fig 9.5b. In this case we select $\{f^*\}$ as having

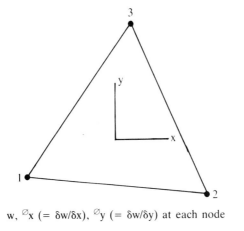

w, $^{\varnothing}x$ (= $\delta w/\delta x$), $^{\varnothing}y$ (= $\delta w/\delta y$) at each node

Figure 9.5a Nine freedom 'global' element (for which the 'natural' basis is incomplete cubic Hermitian)

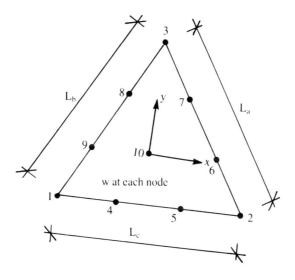

w at each node

Figure 9.5b Ten freedom 'local' element (for which the basis is complete cubic Lagrangian)

components $f_1 - f_{10}$ given in equations 9.25 and $\{d^*\}$ as having components $w_1 - w_{10}$.

2   The final set of freedoms $\{d\}$ is chosen as indicated for the element of Fig 9.5a. In this case we choose $\{d\}$ as having components w_1, ϕ_{x1}, ϕ_{y1}, w_2, ϕ_{x2}, ϕ_{y2}, w_3, ϕ_{x3}, ϕ_{y3}.

3   A basis transformation relationship is formed to relate the initial freedoms $\{d^*\}$ to the final freedoms, ie $\{d^*\} = T\{d\}$.

4   An initial stiffness matrix k^* is derived using the concept of natural curvatures to simplify the algebra.

5   The initial stiffness matrix k^* is transformed to the final stiffness matrix k using $k = T^t k^* T$.

Formation of the initial basis stiffness matrix

The 10×10 initial basis stiffness matrix relating to the freedoms shown in Fig 9.5b is obtained by using the interpolation functions of equations 9.25. Restating these for convenience the cubic Lagrangian interpolation for the lateral displacement w is expressed as the simple summation

$$w = \Sigma f^*_i w^*_i \qquad \qquad \textbf{9.39}$$

where

$$f^*_1 = (9L_1^3 - 9L_1^2 + 2L_1)/2, \quad f^*_2 = (9L_2^3 - 9L_2^2 + 2L_2)/2$$

$$f^*_3 = (9L_3^3 - 9L_3^2 + 2L_3)/2, \quad f^*_4 = 13.5L_1^2L_2 - 4.5L_1L_2,$$

$$f^*_5 = 13.5L_1L_2^2 - 4.5L_1L_2, \quad f^*_6 = 13.5L_2^2L_3 - 4.5L_2L_3,$$

$$f^*_7 = 13.5L_2L_3^2 - 4.5L_2L_3, \quad f^*_8 = 13.5L_3^2L_1 - 4.5L_3L_1,$$

$$f^*_9 = 13.5L_3L_1^2 - 4.5L_3L_1, \quad f^*_{10} = 27L_1L_2L_3 \qquad \textbf{9.40}$$

The natural curvatures used to simplify the algebra are then obtained from equation 9.31 and its two permutations as

$$\Phi_a = \partial^2w/\partial a^2 = (\partial^2w/\partial L_1^2 + \partial^2w/\partial L_2^2 - 2\partial^2w/\partial L_1\partial L_2)/L_a^2 \quad \textbf{9.41}$$

$$\Phi_b = \partial^2w/\partial b^2 = (\partial^2w/\partial L_2^2 + \partial^2w/\partial L_3^2 - 2\partial^2w/\partial L_2\partial L_3)/L_b^2 \quad \textbf{9.42}$$

$$\Phi_c = \partial^2w/\partial c^2 = (\partial^2w/\partial L_3^2 + \partial^2w/\partial L_1^2 - 2\partial^2w/\partial L_3\partial L_1)/L_c^2 \quad \textbf{9.43}$$

where a,b,c are the natural co-ordinates parallel to the element sides.

Using equations 9.41, 9.42 and 9.43 the natural curvature-displacement matrix for the element is obtained as

$$\{\Phi_a \; \Phi_b \; \Phi_c\} = B^*\{w^*_i\} \quad i = 1 \to 10 \qquad \textbf{9.44}$$

where matrix B^* is given by*

$$B^{*t} = \begin{bmatrix} 27L_1-9 & 0 & 27L_1-9 \\ 27L_2-9 & 27L_2-9 & 0 \\ 0 & 27L_3-9 & 27L_3-9 \\ 27L_2-54L_1+9 & 0 & 27L_2 \\ 27L_1-54L_2+9 & 27L_1 & 0 \\ 27L_3 & 27L_3-54L_2+9 & 0 \\ 0 & 27L_2-54L_3+9 & 27L_2 \\ 0 & 27L_1 & 27L_1-54L_3+9 \\ 27L_3 & 0 & 27L_3-54L_1+9 \\ -54L_3 & -54L_1 & -54L_2 \end{bmatrix}$$

$$\textbf{9.45}$$

The Cartesian curvatures $\Phi_x = \partial^2 w/\partial x^2$, $\Phi_y = \partial^2 w/\partial y^2$, $\Phi_{xy} = \sqrt{2}\partial^2 w/\partial x\partial y$ are given by inverting the matrix of equation 9.29

$$\{\Phi_x \; \Phi_y \; \Phi_{xy}\} = C\{\Phi_a \; \Phi_b \; \Phi_c\} \qquad \textbf{9.46}$$

where
$$C = \begin{bmatrix} c_{ax}^2 & c_{ay}^2 & \sqrt{2}c_{ax}c_{ay} \\ c_{bx}^2 & c_{by}^2 & \sqrt{2}c_{bx}c_{by} \\ c_{cx}^2 & c_{cy}^2 & \sqrt{2}c_{cx}c_{cy} \end{bmatrix}^{-1} \qquad \textbf{9.47}$$

Finally, the initial basis stiffness matrix for the element is given by numerical integration at the midpoints of the sides as

$$k^* = \sum_{i=1}^{3} B^{*t}C^{T}DCB^*(\omega_i\Delta) \qquad \textbf{9.48}$$

where Δ is the area of the element and $\omega_i = \frac{1}{3}$ are the integration point weights.

Derivation of the basis transformation matrix

To define the transformation, we note that the final basis is Hermitian, ie it involves slopes and displacements at the vertices of the triangle. Along any side the displacements are likewise given by the same Hermitian interpolation used for beams and involving the nodal displacements and slopes at the nodes on that side. On side 1–2, for example, the interpolation is

$$w = f_1w_1 + f_2(L_a\phi_{a1}) + f_3w_2 + f_4(L_a\phi_{a2}) \qquad \textbf{9.49}$$

---

* Note that the rows at B_2^* must be divided by L_a^2, L_b^2 and L_c^2.

where* $\qquad f_1 = 1 - 3s^2 + 2s^3, \qquad f_2 = s - 2s^2 + s^3$

$$f_3 = 3s^2 - 2s^3, \qquad\qquad f_4 = s^3 - s^2$$

$$\phi_{a1} = (\partial w/\partial a)_1, \qquad\qquad \phi_{a2} = (\partial w/\partial a)_2 \qquad\qquad \textbf{9.50}$$

in which $0 \leq s \leq 1$ is the dimensionless co-ordinate on this side originating at node 1 and $a = L_a s$. This implies that ϕ_{a1} and ϕ_{a2} are the natural slopes, ie slopes parallel to side 1–2, which are related to the Cartesian slopes ($\theta_x = \partial w/\partial x$, $\theta_y = \partial w/\partial y$) by

$$\phi_{a1} = c_{ax}\phi_{x1} + c_{ay}\phi_{y1}, \quad \phi_{a2} = c_{ax}\phi_{x2} + c_{ay}\phi_{y2} \qquad \textbf{9.51}$$

where c_{ax} and c_{ay} are the direction cosines of this side, given by

$$c_{ax} = (x_2 - x_1)/L_a = x_{21}/L_a$$
$$c_{ay} = (y_2 - y_1)/L_a = y_{21}/L_a \qquad\qquad \textbf{9.52}$$

At node 4 of the initial element we have $s = \frac{1}{3}$ and substitutng this value into equations 9.50 we obtain

$$f_1 = \tfrac{20}{27}, \quad f_2 = \tfrac{4}{27}, \quad f_3 = \tfrac{7}{27}, \quad f_4 = -\tfrac{2}{27} \qquad \textbf{9.53}$$

Combining these results with equations 9.49 and 9.51 we obtain the displacement at node 4 as

$$27w_4 = 20w_1 + 4x_{21}\phi_{x1} + 4y_{21}\phi_{y1} + 7w_2$$
$$- 2x_{21}\phi_{x2} - 2y_{21}\phi_{y2} \qquad\qquad \textbf{9.54}$$

At node 5 we have $s = \frac{2}{3}$ and, substituting this value into equations 9.50, we obtain

$$f_1 = \tfrac{7}{27}, \quad f_2 = \tfrac{2}{27}, \quad f_3 = \tfrac{20}{27}, \quad f_4 = -\tfrac{4}{27} \qquad \textbf{9.55}$$

Combining these results with equations 9.49 and 9.51, the displacement at node 5 is given as

$$27w_5 = 7w_1 + 2x_{21}\phi_{x1} + 2y_{21}\phi_{y1} + 20w_2 - 4x_{21}\phi_{x2} - 4y_{21}\phi_{y2}$$
$$\textbf{9.56}$$

Repeating this exercise on the other two sides, we obtain expressions for $w_6 - w_9$.

---

* These are obtained from the functions of equation 9.33 by substituting $s - \tfrac{1}{2}$ for x/L, first dividing f_2 and f_4 by L.

To obtain an expression for w_{10}, we can proceed from first principles or use the approximate nine term interpolation derived by Bazley et al[10] to satisfy the constant strain criterion (Section 2.3), viz

$$
\begin{aligned}
w = &f_1 w_1 + f_2 w_2 + f_3 w_3 + f_4 (L_a \phi_{a1}) + f_5 (L_c \phi_{c1}) \\
&+ f_6 (L_b \phi_{b2}) + f_7 (L_a \phi_{a2}) + f_8 (L_c \phi_{c3}) + f_9 (L_b \phi_{b3})
\end{aligned}
\qquad \textbf{9.57}
$$

where the interpolation functions are

$$
\begin{aligned}
f_1 &= L_1 + L_1^2 L_2 + L_1^2 L_3 - L_2^2 L_1 - L_3^2 L_1 \\
f_2 &= L_2 + L_2^2 L_3 + L_2^2 L_1 - L_1^2 L_2 - L_3^2 L_2 \\
f_3 &= L_3 + L_3^2 L_1 + L_3^2 L_2 - L_1^2 L_3 - L_2^2 L_3 \\
f_4 &= L_1^2 L_2 + L_1 L_2 L_3 / 2, \quad f_5 = -L_1^2 L_3 - L_1 L_2 L_3 / 2 \\
f_6 &= L_2^2 L_3 + L_1 L_2 L_3 / 2, \quad f_7 = -L_2^2 L_1 - L_1 L_2 L_3 / 2 \\
f_8 &= L_3^2 L_1 + L_1 L_2 L_3 / 2, \quad f_9 = -L_3^2 L_2 - L_1 L_2 L_3 / 2
\end{aligned}
\qquad \textbf{9.58}
$$

At the centroid (node 10 in Fig 9.5b) we have $L_1 = L_2 = L_3 = 1/3$. On substituting these values into equations 9.58, we obtain

$$
\begin{aligned}
f_1 &= f_2 = f_3 = \tfrac{1}{3} \\
f_4 &= f_6 = f_8 = \tfrac{1}{18} \\
f_5 &= f_7 = f_9 = -\tfrac{1}{18}
\end{aligned}
\qquad \textbf{9.59}
$$

and therefore

$$
\begin{aligned}
w_{10} = &(w_1 + w_2 + w_3)/3 + L_a(\phi_{a1} - \phi_{a2})/18 \\
&+ L_b(\phi_{b2} - \phi_{b3})/18 + L_c(\phi_{c3} - \phi_{c1})/18
\end{aligned}
\qquad \textbf{9.60}
$$

Combining equations 9.51, 9.54 and 9.56 leads to

$$
\begin{aligned}
w_4 &= (20w_1 + 4L_a\phi_{a1} + 7w_2 - 2L_a\phi_{a2})/27 \\
w_5 &= (7w_1 + 2L_a\phi_{a1} + 20w_2 - 4L_a\phi_{a2})/27
\end{aligned}
\qquad \textbf{9.61}
$$

Equations 9.61 are now transposed and added leading to

$$
L_a(\phi_{a1} - \phi_{a2}) = (27/6)(w_4 + w_5 - w_1 - w_2)
\qquad \textbf{9.62}
$$

In like fashion, we obtain, for the other two sides,

$$
L_b(\phi_{b2} - \phi_{b3}) = (27/6)(w_6 + w_7 - w_2 - w_3)
\qquad \textbf{9.63}
$$

$$L_c(\phi_{c3} - \phi_{c1}) = (27/6)(w_8 + w_9 - w_3 - w_1) \qquad \textbf{9.64}$$

Substituting equations 9.62, 9.63 and 9.64 into equation 9.59 we obtain the expression for w_{10}, viz

$$w_{10} = (w_4 + w_5 + w_6 + w_7 + w_8 + w_9)/4$$
$$- (w_1 + w_2 + w_3)/6 \qquad \textbf{9.65}$$

The final expression for the transformation is

$$\{d^*\} = T\{d\} \qquad \textbf{9.66}$$

where $\qquad \{d^*\} = \{w_1 \ w_2 \ w_3 \ \dots \ w_{10}\}$

are the initial freedoms and

$$\{d\} = \{w_1 \ \phi_{x1} \ \phi_{y1} \ \dots \ w_3 \ \phi_{x3} \ \phi_{y3}\}$$

are the final freedoms. The matrix T is therefore given by

$$T = 1/27 \begin{bmatrix} 27 & 0 & 0 & 0 & 0 & 0 & 0 & 0 & 0 \\ 0 & 0 & 0 & 27 & 0 & 0 & 0 & 0 & 0 \\ 0 & 0 & 0 & 0 & 0 & 0 & 27 & 0 & 0 \\ 20 & 2a & 2b & 7 & -a & -b & 0 & 0 & 0 \\ 7 & a & b & 20 & -2a & -2b & 0 & 0 & 0 \\ 0 & 0 & 0 & 20 & 2c & 2d & 7 & -c & -d \\ 0 & 0 & 0 & 7 & c & d & 20 & -2c & -2d \\ 7 & -e & -f & 0 & 0 & 0 & 20 & 2e & 2f \\ 20 & -2e & -2f & 0 & 0 & 0 & 7 & e & f \\ & & \Sigma\text{rows}(4 \text{ to } 9)/4 & - & \Sigma\text{rows}(1 \text{ to } 3)/6 & & & & \end{bmatrix} \qquad \textbf{9.67}$$

The constants in matrix T are given by

$$a = 2x_{21}, \quad b = 2y_{21}, \quad c = 2x_{32},$$
$$d = 2y_{32}, \quad e = 2x_{13}, \quad f = 2y_{13}$$

Final basis stiffness matrix

The final 9×9 global element stiffness matrix is then given by

$$k = T^t k^* T \qquad \textbf{9.68}$$

where the transformation matrix T is given by equation 9.67.

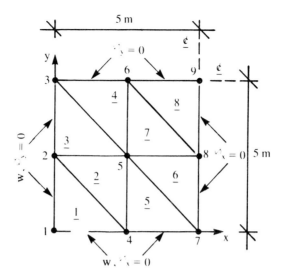

Figure 9.6 Discretisation of one quadrant of a simply supported square plate using eight elements

Fig 9.6 shows the use of the element to approximate a quadrant of a simply supported slab carrying a uniformly distributed load and Table 9.1 shows the results obtained for this and two finer meshes. Numerous other results are given in Reference 11 and compared with those of four other elements.

Table 9.1 Finite element solutions for a simply supported blanket loaded square plate (one quadrant only analysed).

Freedoms per quadrant	$10^5 w_{max} D/qL^4$	m_c/qL
27	339	0.03858
48	383	0.04585
75	396	0.04867
Exact solution[1]	406	0.04789

The present element was developed and tested on a microcomputer and is thus used in the program of Section 9.6. For practical applications, however, the more accurate element of Reference 6 is recommended and this is easily substituted into program PLATE.

9.6 BASIC program for thin plate analysis

The following program is for a small microcomputer and uses single precision computation. Computation times are reduced by assuming a domain divided into equal sized rectangular patches of two triangular elements. Thus only two element stiffness matrices need to be calculated and used repetitively for forming the structure matrix.

Dimension arrays are:

S(150,24)   banded structure stiffness matrix with maximum half band width = 24 and maximum number of nodes = 50.

Q(150)   structure load vector

CO(50,2)   nodal co-ordinates.

RM(24)   vector of 'row multipliers' used in Gauss reduction

D(3,3)   thin plate modulus matrix

NN(75,3)   element node numbers

EM(9,9)   element stiffness matrix (ESM)

ST(45,10)   stores up to 10 ESMs which can be copied if identical elements arise later

X(3), Y(3)   element co-ordinates referred to the centroid

X1(10,3)   X and Y co-ordinates of stored elements used for
Y(10,3)   copying of ESMs

T(10,9)   basis transformation matrix

ED(9)   element displacement vector

B(3,10)   local (ie for the cubic basis) interpolation matrix for the natural curvatures.

CT(3,3)   matrix for transformation from natural curvatures to Cartesian curvatures (see equation 9.47)

C(3,10)   matrix product CT and B

ES(3)   stress vector at a stress sampling point

Data input requirements are:

Line 80   Read # nodes (NP), # elements (NE), # boundary condition nodes (NB), # nodes carrying point loads (NL).

Line 90   Read Young's modulus (E), Poisson's ratio (P), element thickness (TH), intensity of uniformly distributed load (UD) — in the present version the same values are used for each element.

Line 110   Read nodal co-ordinates.

Line 130   Read node numbers for each element.

Line 710   Read concentrated loads at any nodes so loaded.

Line 730   Read flags FW, FX, FY (1 = fixed, 0 = free) for boundary condition nodes. Note that this program suppresses displacements by the simple expedient of miltiplying the corresponding diagonal entry by a large number (lines 10, 750–770).

Line 1140   Read element numbers and areal co-ordinates within elements for interactively chosen stress sampling points.

The data given in lines 2260–2530 is for the problem of Fig 9.6 (ie a simply supported slab with blanket load).

Listing of program *PLATE*

```
10  PF=1000000'
20  DIM S(150,24),Q(150),CO(50,2)
30  DIM RM(24),D(3,3),NN(75,3)
40  DIM EM(9,9),T(10,9),ED(9),EA(9,9)
50  DIM B(3,10),CT(3,3),C(3,10),ES(3)
60  DIM ST(45,10),X(10,3),Y(10,3),X1(3),Y1(3)
70  N9=0
80  READ NP,NE,NB,NL:NT=3*NP
90  READ E,P,TH,UD:TH=TH^3/12
100 FOR I=1 TO NP
110 READ CO(I,1),CO(I,2):NEXT I
120 NW=0:FOR I=1 TO NE
130 READ NN(I,1),NN(I,2),NN(I,3)
140 FOR J1=1 TO 3:FOR J2=J1 TO 3
150 NW1=ABS(NN(I,J1)-NN(I,J2))
160 IF NW1>NW THEN NW=NW1
170 NEXT J2:NEXT J1
180 NEXT I:NW=NW*3+3
190 D(1,1)=E*TH/(1-P*P):D(2,2)=D(1,1)
200 D(1,2)=P*D(1,1):D(2,1)=D(1,2)
210 D(3,3)=(1-P)*D(1,1):D(3,2)=0
220 D(1,3)=0:D(2,3)=0:D(3,1)=0
230 FOR I=1 TO NT:Q(I)=0:FOR J=1 TO 24
240 S(I,J)=0:NEXT J:NEXT I
250 FOR N=1 TO NE
260 I=NN(N,1):J=NN(N,2):K=NN(N,3)
270 XC=(CO(I,1)+CO(J,1)+CO(K,1))/3
280 YC=(CO(I,2)+CO(J,2)+CO(K,2))/3
290 FOR I1=1 TO 3:J1=NN(N,I1)
300 X1(I1)=CO(J1,1)-XC:Y1(I1)=CO(J1,2)-YC:NEXT I1
310 FOR I=1 TO 9:FOR J=1 TO 9
320 EM(I,J)=0:NEXT J:NEXT I
330 FL=0:IF N>1 THEN GOSUB 2170
340 IF FL=1 GOTO 520
350 FOR II=1 TO 3
360 IF II=1 THEN L1=.5:L2=.5
```

```
370 IF II=2 THEN L1=0:L2=.5
380 IF II=3 THEN L1=.5:L2=0
390 L3=1-L1-L2
400 GOSUB 1310
410 FOR I=1 TO 9:FOR J=1 TO 9
420 FOR K=1 TO 3
430 EM(I,J)=EM(I,J)+B(K,I)*T(K,J)*AA/6
440 NEXT K:NEXT J:NEXT I
450 NEXT II
460 IF N9=10 GOTO 510
470 N9=N9+1:N1=0:FOR I1=1 TO 9:FOR J1=I1 TO 9
480 N1=N1+1:ST(N1,N9)=EM(I1,J1):NEXT J1:NEXT I1
490 FOR I1=1 TO 3
500 X(N9,I1)=X1(I1):Y(N9,I1)=Y1(I1):NEXT I1
510 REM
520 REM
530 I=NN(N,1):J=NN(N,2):K=NN(N,3)
540 Q(3*I-2)=Q(3*I-2)+UD*AA/6
550 Q(3*J-2)=Q(3*J-2)+UD*AA/6
560 Q(3*K-2)=Q(3*K-2)+UD*AA/6
570 FOR I=1 TO 3:IN=NN(N,I)
580 FOR J=1 TO 3:JN=NN(N,J)
590 FOR IL=1 TO 3
600 IE=(I-1)*3+IL:NR=(IN-1)*3+IL
610 FOR JL=1 TO 3
620 JE=(J-1)*3+JL:NC=(JN-1)*3+JL
630 NCB=NC-NR+1
640 IF NCB<=0 GOTO 660
650 S(NR,NCB)=S(NR,NCB)+EM(IE,JE)
660 REM
670 NEXT JL:NEXT IL
680 NEXT J:NEXT I
690 PRINT "Element ",N:NEXT N
700 FOR I=1 TO NL
710 READ N,Q(3*N-2),Q(3*N-1),Q(3*N):NEXT I
720 FOR I=1 TO NB
730 READ N,FW,FX,FY
740 K=3*N-2
750 IF FW=1 THEN S(K,1)=S(K,1)*PF
760 IF FX=1 THEN S(K+1,1)=S(K+1,1)*PF
770 IF FY=1 THEN S(K+2,1)=S(K+2,1)*PF
780 NEXT I
790 FOR L=1 TO NP
800 ND=(NP-L+1)*3
810 IF ND>(NW-3) THEN LM=NW
820 FOR I=1 TO 3
830 LM=LM-1:IP=3*(L-1)+I
840 X=S(IP,1):Q(IP)=Q(IP)/X
850 FOR J=1 TO LM
860 RM(J)=S(IP,J+1):NEXT J
870 FOR J=1 TO LM+1
880 S(IP,J)=S(IP,J)/X:NEXT J
890 FOR K=1 TO LM
900 NR=IP+K:NC=LM-K+1
910 X=RM(K):Q(NR)=Q(NR)-X*Q(IP)
920 FOR J=1 TO NC:JP=J+K
```

```
930 S(NR,J)=S(NR,J)-X*S(IP,JP):NEXT J
940 NEXT K
950 NEXT I
960 PRINT "Disp",L
970 NEXT L
980 I=NT:Q(NT)=Q(NT)/S(NT,1)
990 I=I-1
1000 IF LM<(NW-1) THEN LM=LM+1
1010 FOR J=1 TO LM
1020 Q(I)=Q(I)-S(I,J+1)*Q(I+J):NEXT J
1030 IF I>1 GOTO 990
1040 LPRINT "Nodal Displacements"
1050 A$="## +#.####^^^^ +#.####^^^^ +#.####^^^^"
1060 FOR I=1 TO NP
1070 LPRINT USING A$;I,Q(3*I-2),Q(3*I-1),Q(3*I)
1080 NEXT I
1090 PRINT "PRESS Retrn FOR STRESSES"
1100 INPUT X$
1110 PRINT:PRINT"ELEMENT STRESSES"
1120 A$="## +#.###^^^^ +#.###^^^^ +#.###^^^^"
1130 PRINT "INPUT    ELEMENT NUMBER(0 TO END), L1 & L
2"
1140 INPUT N,L1,L2
1150 L3=1-L1-L2
1160 IF N=0 GOTO 1290
1170 GOSUB 1310
1180 FOR I=1 TO 3:K=NN(N,I)
1190 ED(3*I-2)=Q(3*K-2)
1200 ED(3*I-1)=Q(3*K-1)
1210 ED(3*I)=Q(3*K):NEXT I
1220 FOR I=1 TO 3:ES(I)=0
1230 FOR J=1 TO 9
1240 ES(I)=ES(I)+T(I,J)*ED(J)
1250 NEXT J:NEXT I
1260 ES(3)=ES(3)/SQR(2)
1270 PRINT USING A$;N,ES(1),ES(2),ES(3)
1280 GOTO 1130
1290 REM
1300 END
1310 I=NN(N,1):J=NN(N,2):K=NN(N,3)
1320 XA=CO(J,1)-CO(I,1)
1330 YA=CO(J,2)-CO(I,2)
1340 XB=CO(K,1)-CO(J,1)
1350 YB=CO(K,2)-CO(J,2)
1360 XC=CO(I,1)-CO(K,1)
1370 YC=CO(I,2)-CO(K,2)
1380 SA=SQR(XA*XA+YA*YA)
1390 SB=SQR(XB*XB+YB*YB)
1400 SC=SQR(XC*XC+YC*YC)
1410 AA=XA*YB-XB*YA
1420 XA=XA/SA:YA=YA/SA
1430 XB=XB/SB:YB=YB/SB
1440 XC=XC/SC:YC=YC/SC
1450 F=SQR(2)
1460 AX=XA*XA:AY=YA*YA:AZ=F*XA*YA
1470 BX=XB*XB:BY=YB*YB:BZ=F*XB*YB
```

```
1480 CX=XC*XC:CY=YC*YC:CZ=F*XC*YC
1490 DD=AX*(BY*CZ-BZ*CY)-AY*(BX*CZ-BZ*CX)+AZ*(BX*CY-BY
*CX)
1500 CT(1,1)=BY*CZ-BZ*CY
1510 CT(1,2)=-AY*CZ+AZ*CY
1520 CT(1,3)=AY*BZ-AZ*BY
1530 CT(2,1)=-BX*CZ+BZ*CX
1540 CT(2,2)=AX*CZ-AZ*CX
1550 CT(2,3)=-AX*BZ+AZ*BX
1560 CT(3,1)=BX*CY-BY*CX
1570 CT(3,2)=-AX*CY+AY*CX
1580 CT(3,3)=AX*BY-AY*BX
1590 FOR I=1 TO 3:FOR J=1 TO 10
1600 B(I,J)=0:NEXT J:NEXT I
1610 B(1,1)=27*L1-9:B(1,2)=27*L2-9
1620 B(1,4)=27*L2-54*L1+9
1630 B(1,5)=27*L1-54*L2+9:B(1,6)=27*L3
1640 B(1,9)=27*L3:B(1,10)=-54*L3
1650 B(2,2)=27*L2-9:B(2,3)=27*L3-9
1660 B(2,5)=27*L1:B(2,10)=-54*L1
1670 B(2,6)=27*L3-54*L2+9
1680 B(2,7)=27*L2-54*L3+9:B(2,8)=27*L1
1690 B(3,1)=27*L1-9:B(3,3)=27*L3-9
1700 B(3,4)=27*L2:B(3,7)=27*L2
1710 B(3,8)=27*L1-54*L3+9
1720 B(3,9)=27*L3-54*L1+9
1730 B(3,10)=-54*L2
1740 FOR J=1 TO 10
1750 B(1,J)=-B(1,J)/(SA*SA)
1760 B(2,J)=-B(2,J)/(SB*SB)
1770 B(3,J)=-B(3,J)/(SC*SC):NEXT J
1780 FOR I=1 TO 3:FOR J=1 TO 10
1790 C(I,J)=0:FOR K=1 TO 3
1800 C(I,J)=C(I,J)+CT(I,K)*B(K,J)/DD
1810 NEXT K:NEXT J:NEXT I
1820 FOR I=1 TO 10:FOR J=1 TO 9
1830 T(I,J)=0:NEXT J:NEXT I
1840 T(1,1)=27:T(2,4)=27:T(3,7)=27
1850 T(4,1)=20:T(4,2)=4*SA*XA
1860 T(4,3)=4*SA*YA:T(4,4)=7
1870 T(4,5)=-2*SA*XA:T(4,6)=-2*SA*YA
1880 T(5,1)=7:T(5,2)=2*SA*XA
1890 T(5,3)=2*SA*YA:T(5,4)=20
1900 T(5,5)=-4*SA*XA:T(5,6)=-4*SA*YA
1910 T(6,4)=20:T(6,5)=4*SB*XB
1920 T(6,6)=4*SB*YB:T(6,7)=7
1930 T(6,8)=-2*SB*XB:T(6,9)=-2*SB*YB
1940 T(7,4)=7:T(7,5)=2*SB*XB
1950 T(7,6)=2*SB*YB:T(7,7)=20
1960 T(7,8)=-4*SB*XB:T(7,9)=-4*SB*YB
1970 T(8,1)=7:T(8,2)=-2*SC*XC
1980 T(8,3)=-2*SC*YC:T(8,7)=20
1990 T(8,8)=4*SC*XC:T(8,9)=4*SC*YC
2000 T(9,1)=20:T(9,2)=-4*SC*XC
2010 T(9,3)=-4*SC*YC:T(9,7)=7
```

```
2020 T(9,8)=2*SC*XC:T(9,9)=2*SC*YC
2030 T(10,1)=-4.5:T(10,4)=-4.5
2040 T(10,7)=-4.5
2050 FOR J=1 TO 9:FOR I=4 TO 9
2060 T(10,J)=T(10,J)+T(I,J)/4
2070 NEXT I:NEXT J
2080 FOR I=1 TO 3:FOR J=1 TO 9
2090 B(I,J)=0:FOR K=1 TO 10
2100 B(I,J)=B(I,J)+C(I,K)*T(K,J)/27
2110 NEXT K:NEXT J:NEXT I
2120 FOR I=1 TO 3:FOR J=1 TO 9
2130 T(I,J)=0:FOR K=1 TO 3
2140 T(I,J)=T(I,J)+D(I,K)*B(K,J)
2150 NEXT K:NEXT J:NEXT I
2160 RETURN
2170 FOR I1=1 TO N9:F1=0:FOR J1=1 TO 3
2180 IF ABS(X(I1,J1)-X1(J1))>ABS(.00001*X1(J1)) THEN F
1=1
2190 IF ABS(Y(I1,J1)-Y1(J1))>ABS(.00001*Y1(J1)) THEN F
1=1
2200 NEXT J1
2210 IF F1=1 GOTO 2250
2220 N1=0:FOR I2=1 TO 9:FOR J2=I2 TO 9:N1=N1+1
2230 EM(I2,J2)=ST(N1,I1):EM(J2,I2)=ST(N1,I1):NEXT J2:N
EXT I2
2240 FL=1:RETURN
2250 NEXT I1:RETURN
2260 DATA 9,8,8,1
2270 DATA 0.2E+09,0.3,1.0,1.0
2280 DATA 0,0
2290 DATA 0,2.5
2300 DATA 0,5
2310 DATA 2.5,0
2320 DATA 2.5,2.5
2330 DATA 2.5,5
2340 DATA 5,0
2350 DATA 5,2.5
2360 DATA 5,5
2370 DATA 1,4,2
2380 DATA 2,4,5
2390 DATA 2,5,3
2400 DATA 3,5,6
2410 DATA 4,7,5
2420 DATA 5,7,8
2430 DATA 5,8,6
2440 DATA 6,8,9
2450 DATA 9,0,0,0
2460 DATA 1,1,1,1
2470 DATA 2,1,0,1
2480 DATA 3,1,0,1
2490 DATA 4,1,1,0
2500 DATA 6,0,0,1
2510 DATA 7,1,1,0
2520 DATA 8,0,1,0
2530 DATA 9,0,1,1
```

9.7 Exercises

1 Work through the steps in obtaining the quadratic and cubic Lagrangian interpolations in area co-ordinates described in Section 9.2.

2 Derive equation 9.28 from first principles.

3 Work through formation of equation 9.45 using equations 9.40–9.43.

4 Type the program of Section 9.6 into your microcomputer and run the problem of Fig 9.6 to check that it works (ie use the data given).

5 Use meshes with 18 and 32 elements for the problem of Fig 9.6 and check your results against those given in Table 9.1.

6 Also run your program for clamped edge conditions and with point loads with various meshes and compare results with those given in Reference 6.

References

1 S P Timoshenko and S Woinowsky–Krieger, *Theory of Plates and Shells*, 2nd edn, McGraw–Hill, New York, 1956.

2 O C Zienkiewicz and R L Taylor, *The Finite Element Method*, 4th edn, McGraw–Hill, New York, 1984.

3 P Silvester, 'Higher-order polynomial triangular elements for potential problems', *International Journal Engineering Science*, vol 7, 1971, p 849.

4 J H Argyris, 'Three dimensional anisotropic and inhomogeneous, media-matrix analysis for small and large displacements', *Ingenieur Archives*, vol 31, 1968, p 33.

5 G A Mohr and I C Medland, 'On convergence of displacement finite elements with an application to singularity problems', *Engineering Fracture Mechanics*, vol 17, 1983, p 481.

6 G A Mohr, 'Finite element formulation by nested interpolations: application to cubic elements', *Computers and Structures*, vol 14, 1981, p 211.

7 T Apostol, *Calculus*, vol 2, 2nd edn, Wiley, New York, 1972.

8 J L Meek, *Matrix Structural Analysis*, McGraw–Hill, New York, 1972.

9 M Okabe, Y Yamada and I Nishiguohi, 'Basis transformation of trial function space in Lagrangian interpolation', *Computational Methods in Applied Mechanical Engineering*, vol 23, 1980, p 85.

10 G P Bazeley, Y K Cheung, B M Irons and O C Zienkiewicz, 'Triangular plates in bending — conforming and nonconforming solu-

tions', paper delivered to conference 'Matrix Methods in Structural Mechanics', Wright–Patterson. Air Force Base, Ohio, 1965.

11 G A Mohr and R S Mohr, 'A new thin plate bending element by basis transformation', *Computers and Structures*, vol 22, 1986, p 239.

CHAPTER 10

Further Finite Element Applications

In preceding chapters our primary concern was with some of the original finite element problems; for example, those of frame analysis[1] and lumped mass analysis of vibration.[2] In this chapter we present an overview of more advanced problems which have been addressed by the finite element method and provide appropriate references. These references should assist the reader to carry out further studies.

10.1   Further applications in the mechanics of solids

Many problems of solid mechanics are now readily solvable with the aid of microcomputers and the FEM. Some are listed below.

Arches   These can be analysed directly using the frame program of Chapter 5 but the use of straight elements introduces a high measure of discontinuity at element intersections and this requires the use of double precision arithmetic if the problem is attempted in this way. The use of curved elements with three nodes improves solution accuracy considerably.[3]

Axisymmetric shells   These can be analysed by an element analogous to the frame element used in Chapter 5. It has six freedoms u,v and ϕ at each node but a third circumferential strain must now be included in the formulation.[4] An improved element can be obtained by adding a third node to the element, allowing the analysis of thick axisymmetric shells.[5]

Axisymmetric solids   These are analysed using two dimensional elements which are rotated about an axis of revolution to form a solid. Such elements are a straightforward extension of the plane stress and strain elements.[6,7]

Thin plates   Thin plate element formulations sometimes present surprising difficulties but, with basis transformation techniques, these can be developed in the same way as the plane stress and plane strain elements.[8,9,10]

Thick plates   Thick plate elements include the transverse shearing effects which become significant when the plate thickness is significant compared to the span.[7,11] With the application of *penalty factors* to suppress the shearing strains, these can also be used for the analysis of thin plates.

Shells Shell problems are most readily solved using flat triangular elements in which the stiffness matrix for flexure is augmented by the stiffness matrix for plane stress and co-ordinate transformation is used to couple the two effects.[12] This process is exactly equivalent to that used in deriving the frame element used in Chapter 5. However, usually, numerical difficulties are encountered in the analysis of deep shells, owing to the high discontinuity forces which occur[13], causing the interelement reactions to swamp the internal element actions.

. This can be overcome by the use of local co-ordinates but this is more appropriate if curved shell elements are used.[14,15,16,17] These are perhaps the most difficult FEM problems, not only because the shell equations are relatively difficult, but also because the geometry of the two dimensional curvilinear co-ordinates is quite complex.[18]

Three dimensional elements Using the isoparametric mapping technique of Chapter 7, element equations for arbitrarily shaped elements can be derived in a manner similar to that for plane strain. The interpolation functions for the *trilinear* brick element, for example, are a straightforward extension of those for the bilinear quadrilateral, ie

$$f_1 = (1 + a_1a)(1 + b_1b)(1 + c_1c)/8 \qquad \mathbf{10.1}$$

The major difficulty is the huge system stiffness matrix which develops even with relatively coarse meshes.

One solution is to extend an approach for the analysis of axisymmetric problems with non-axisymmetric loads where the problem is solved several times using a Fourier series approximation for the loading.[19] There is nothing to prevent us using axisymmetric elements with a different mesh at each load section but this is laborious and not especially advantageous.

Generally speaking three dimensional analysis is not a task for microcomputers. On the other hand, axisymmetric problems can be solved very efficiently on a microcomputer.

10.2 Further applications in the mechanics of fluids

Viscous flow Inclusion of viscosity effects in the governing equations for fluid flow leads to the *Navier–Stokes equations* which makes the mathematical steps involved in forming element matrices complicated. However, once these are derived, the element matrices are simpler than those for many problems of solid mechanics. The numerical solution of steady state slow viscous flow problems is quite economical[20,21] and amenable to solution by microcomputers.

Viscous flow including inertia effects   Inclusion of inertia effects in viscous flow analysis renders the problem nonlinear and most formulations lead to unsymmetric element matrices. It is possible, however, to obtain symmetric matrices[21] by appropriate manipulations.

Transient viscous flow   Transient viscous flow problems require the use of the time stepping techniques described in Chapter 6 but otherwise these problems are quite straightforward.[20,21]

Compressible viscous flow   These are the most difficult of the fluid problems as description of the complete *thermohydrodynamic state* of the fluid requires the inclusion of thermal energy and equations of state along with the not uncomplicated Navier–Stokes equations.[20,21]

Lubrication problems   Analysis of hydrodynamic lubrication in three dimensions can, in the case of thin film lubrication, be reduced to a two dimensional formulation. Furthermore, two dimensional problems can be reduced to one dimensional ones resulting in particularly economical finite element formulations.[22]

There are many other field problems which are similar to fluid flow problems. For example, those of *electro-magnetic vibration*, which usually have simpler solutions than compressible flow or shell problems.[23]

10.3   Further finite element techniques for nonlinear applications, discontinua and boundary effects

Large displacement problems   Where large displacements alter the geometry of a structure to a significant extent, a nonlinear problem results. For example, in trusses, the transverse displacements v_1^* and v_2^* contribute to the strains in the element which appeal to Pythagoras's theorem clearly shows. Inter alia, a nonlinear equation solution technique, usually the Newton–Raphson method, is required which progressively adjusts the displacements over a number of iterative steps.[24,25]

Large curvature problems   When large curvatures are included in bending problems the situation is even more complex. In beams, solution of the problem is not too difficult[24,25] but such effects have not yet been included in the analysis of plates and shells.

Nonlinear material problems   In plane stress and plane strain, for example, material nonlinearity adds further complexity to finite element analysis. Newton–Raphson iteration is required and the modulus matrix must be updated during iteration. Otherwise no difficulties arise.

In plates and shells the situation is more complex as these must be solved as three dimensional problems in the sense that depth integration is required to determine the influence of the non-linearities on the plate flexural stiffness.[26]

Elastic boundary conditions Elastic boundary conditions can be used to model infinite domains and approximate estimation of these is sometimes a straightforward exercise which does not increase the cost of the analysis.[6] Alternative approaches are through the use of *infinite elements*[27] or *boundary elements*[28,29] but, for the purpose of engineering approximation, the approach of Reference 6 is generally satisfactory, bearing in mind the approximate nature of the FEM itself.

Discontinua Examples of discontinua include domains with holes, which can be tackled using dummy elements[30], and cracks. Crack problems can become quite complicated but, with the use of extrapolation, quite economical solutions can be obtained to problems involving singularities with standard finite element programs.[31]

Plasticity problems These are nonlinear material problems of interest to manufacturing engineers involved in extruding processes. Problems involving ideal plasticity are of special interest and can be solved economically by applying the load in small steps.[32]

Optimisation problems With the use of optimality criteria techniques, optimisation problems can be solved, in an approximate sense, more economically than most nonlinear material problems.[12,32] This is currently an area of research.

Closure

If the time has not already arrived when all students own their own microcomputer or have easy access to one then it cannot be far away. Machines, with memory capacities of 1 Mb, are now available, at moderate cost, fitted with 32 bit microprocessors. For a somewhat higher cost, about double, a hard disk can be included to provide an extremely powerful computational system. There is little doubt that, in the very near future, large finite element problems will be solved on microcomputers if this has not already occurred.

At present commercial finite element software for micro-computers, while of reasonable cost for an engineering organisation, is beyond the level which students can afford. The programs and routines given in this book provide a useful basis for learning and a start to the development of personal systems. They require only the purchase of a BASIC compiler to be very effective.

Clearly FEM has come far quickly and microcomputers have developed even more rapidly. Together the two are revolutionising engineering analysis.

References

1 R K Livesley, 'Analysis of rigid frames by an electronic computer', *Engineering*, vol 176, 1953, p 230.

2 J S Archer, 'Consistent mass matrix for distributed systems', *Proceedings Structural Division, ASCE*, vol 89, 1963, p 161.

3 G A Mohr and R Garner, 'Reduced integration and penalty factors in an arch element', *International Journal Structures*, vol 3(1), 1983, p 9.

4 P E Grafton and D R Strome, 'Analysis of axisymmetric shells by the direct stiffness method', *Journal American Institute Aeronautics and Astronautics*, vol 1, 1963, p 2343.

5 G A Mohr, 'Application of penalty factors to a curved isoparametric axisymmetric thick shell element', *Computers and Structures*, vol 15, 1982, p 685.

6 G A Mohr and A S Power, 'Elastic boundary conditions for finite elements of infinite and semi-infinite media', *Proceedings of Institution of Civil Engineers*, part 2, vol 65, 1978, p 685.

7 O C Zienkiewicz, *The Finite Element Method*, 3rd edn, McGraw–Hill, London, 1977.

8 G A Mohr, 'Finite element formulation by nested interpolations: application to cubic elements', *Computers and Structures*, vol 14, 1981, p 211.

9 G A Mohr, 'Finite element formulation by nested interpolations: application to the drilling freedom problem', *Computers and Structures*, vol 15, 1982, p 185.

10 G A Mohr, 'Finite element formulation by nested interpolations: application to a quadrilateral thin plate bending element', *Transactions Institution of Engineers Australia*, vol CE 25(3), 1983, p 211.

11 G A Mohr, 'A triangular element for thick slabs', *Computers and Structures*, vol 9, 1978, p 595.

12 G A Mohr, 'Design of shell shape using finite elements', *Computers and Structures*, vol 10, 1979, p 745.

13 N C Knowles, A Razzaque and J B Spooner, 'Experience of finite element analysis of shell structures', in D G Ashwell and R H Gallagher (eds), *Finite Elements for Thin Shells and Curved Members*, Wiley, London, 1976.

14 C A Brebbia and J J Connor, *Finite Element Techniques for Structural Engineers*, Butterworths, London, 1973.

15 G A Mohr, 'Numerically integrated triangular element for doubly curved thin shells', *Computers and Structures*, vol 11, 1980, p 565.

16 R H Gallagher and G R Thomas, 'A triangular element based on generalised potential energy concepts', in D G Ashwell and R H Gallagher (eds), *Finite Elements for Thin Shells*, Wiley, London, 1976.

17 G A Mohr, 'Application of penalty factors to a doubly curved shell

element', *Computers and Structures*, vol 14, 1981, p 15.

18 G A Mohr and N B Patterson, 'A natural differential geometry scheme for a doubly curved shell element', *Computers and Structures*, vol 18, 1984, p 433.

19 B M Irons and S Ahmad, *Techniques of Finite Elements*, Ellis–Horwood, Chichester, 1980.

20 T J Chung, *Finite Elements in Fluid Dynamics*, McGraw–Hill, New York, 1979.

21 G A Mohr, 'Finite element analysis of viscous flow', *Computers and Fluids*, vol 12, 1984, p 217.

22 K A Heubner, *The Finite Element Method for Engineers*, Wiley, New York, 1975.

23 S H Crandall, *Engineering Analysis*, McGraw–Hill, New York, 1956.

24 G A Mohr and H R Milner, 'Finite element analysis of large displacements in flexural systems', *Computers and Structures*, vol 13, 1981, p 533.

25 H R Milner, 'Accurate analysis of large displacements in skeletal structures', *Computers and Structures*, vol 14, 1981, p 355.

26 R A Grayson and M R Horne, 'Finite element methods in the analysis of stiffened web panels', Proceedings 4th Australian International Conference on Finite Element Methods, University of Melbourne, 1982.

27 P Bettess, 'Infinite elements', *International Journal Numerical Methods Engineering*, vol 11, 1977, p 53.

28 C A Brebbia, *The Boundary Element Method for Engineers*, Pentech Press, London, 1978.

29 C A Brebbia and S Walker, 'Introduction to the boundary element method', in C A Brebbia (ed), *Recent Advances in Boundary Elements*, Pentech Press, London, 1978.

30 G A Mohr, 'Displacement of reinforcement in perforated slabs', *Transactions Institution of Engineers Australia*, vol CE 21(1), 1979, p 21.

31 G A Mohr and I C Medland, 'On convergence of displacement finite elements; with an application to singularity problems', *Engineering Fracture Mechanics*, vol 17, 1983, p 481.

32 G A Mohr, 'Elastic and plastic predictions of slab reinforcement requirement', *Transactions Institution of Engineers Australia*, vol CE21(1), 1979, p 16.

Introduction to Matrix Algebra and Algorithms

Familiarity with matrix operations and the solution of simultaneous equations are essential prerequisites in any discussion of finite element analysis. Appendix A is therefore devoted to this matter and concludes with computer programs, written in the computer language, BASIC, which provide the reader with the means of performing these operations to solve practical problems. Because many modern computer programs are written in FORTRAN, some of these programs are listed in both languages. However, later programs are given only in BASIC as this language is more universally available on microcomputers.

A.1 Matrix equations

In matrix form the simultaneous equations

$$2x_1 + 2x_2 + 2x_3 = 12$$
$$2x_1 + 3x_2 + 4x_3 = 20$$
$$2x_1 + 4x_2 + 3x_3 = 19 \qquad \textbf{A.1}$$

are written as

$$A\{x\} = \begin{bmatrix} 2 & 2 & 2 \\ 2 & 3 & 4 \\ 2 & 4 & 3 \end{bmatrix} \begin{bmatrix} x_1 \\ x_2 \\ x_3 \end{bmatrix} = \begin{bmatrix} 12 \\ 20 \\ 19 \end{bmatrix} = \{b\} \qquad \textbf{A.2}$$

where the matrix A is of dimensions 3 × 3 (3 rows and 3 columns) and the vectors $\{x\}$ and $\{b\}$ are column matrices of dimensions 3 × 1.

The inverse relationship, which provides a solution for the unknowns $\{x\}$, is written symbolically as

$$\{x\} = A^{-1}\{b\} \qquad \textbf{A.3}$$

The matrix A^{-1} is obtained by applying techniques described in Section A.4. To obtain $\{x\}$ using equation A.3, inversion must be followed by matrix multiplication of A^{-1} by $\{b\}$. Alternative, direct, approaches are described in Section A.8 which enable $\{x\}$ to be found more directly.

A.2 Simple matrix operations

Addition of two matrices A and B is accomplished by superimposing one matrix over the other and adding the superimposed elements, ie if

$$A = \begin{bmatrix} a_{11} & a_{12} & a_{13} \\ a_{21} & a_{22} & a_{23} \end{bmatrix} \quad B = \begin{bmatrix} b_{11} & b_{12} & b_{13} \\ b_{21} & b_{22} & b_{23} \end{bmatrix}$$

then

$$C = A + B = \begin{bmatrix} a_{11}+b_{11} & a_{12}+b_{12} & a_{13}+b_{13} \\ a_{21}+b_{21} & a_{22}+b_{22} & a_{23}+b_{23} \end{bmatrix} \quad \textbf{A.4}$$

Subtraction is carried out in a similar fashion with minus signs replacing the plus signs.

For addition and subtraction to be possible, matrices A and B must each have the same number of rows and columns; matrices possessing this property are said to be compatible from the point of view of addition and subtraction.

Multiplication of a matrix by a scalar involves simply multiplying each element in turn by the scalar quantity.

Differentiation or integration of a matrix consists of carrying out the operation on each element in turn, ie

if
$$A(x) = \begin{bmatrix} a_{11}(x) & a_{12}(x) & a_{13}(x) \\ a_{21}(x) & a_{22}(x) & a_{23}(x) \end{bmatrix}$$

then
$$dA/dx = \begin{bmatrix} da_{11}/dx & da_{12}/dx & da_{13}/dx \\ da_{21}/dx & da_{22}/dx & da_{23}/dx \end{bmatrix} \quad \textbf{A.5}$$

where $a_{11}(x)$ denotes that a_{11} is a function of a single independent variable x. If $a_{11}(x,y)$ is a function of two variables x and y, then partial differentiation is defined in an analogous manner.

The transpose of a matrix is obtained by interchanging the rows and columns. For example, the transpose of A of equation A.4 is given by

$$A^t = \begin{bmatrix} a_{11} & a_{21} \\ a_{12} & a_{22} \\ a_{13} & a_{23} \end{bmatrix} \quad \textbf{A.6}$$

The matrix multiplication operation C = AB is referred to as premultiplying B by A or postmultiplying A by B. It is only permissible when the number of columns of A equals the number of rows of B, in which case, the matrices are said to be compatible for the purposes of multiplication. If we denote two such matrices by $A[a_{ij}]$ (mxn) and $B[b_{ij}]$ (nxp) then their matrix product is given by $C[c_{ij}]$ (mxp) as

$$C = [c_{ij}] = \left[\sum_{k=1}^{n} a_{ik}b_{kj} \right]$$

This has the effect of summing the product of corresponding terms of row i in matrix A and those of column j in matrix B.

A.3   Determinant of a matrix

The determinant of a matrix is defined only for a square matrix. Inter alia, it indicates whether all the equations in the matrix are linearly independent; if they are not, the value of the determinant is zero. If the equations are independent then the matrix can be inverted to obtain the solution for n unknowns.

The classical method of evaluating a determinant involves the use of the Laplace expansion. If the matrix is

$$A = \begin{bmatrix} x & y & z \\ a & b & c \\ d & e & f \end{bmatrix}$$

then Laplace's expansion is

$$\det|A| = x \begin{vmatrix} b & c \\ e & f \end{vmatrix} - y \begin{vmatrix} a & c \\ d & f \end{vmatrix} + z \begin{vmatrix} a & b \\ d & e \end{vmatrix} \qquad \text{A.7}$$

The terms of the form

$$M_{11} = \begin{vmatrix} b & c \\ e & f \end{vmatrix} = bf - ce \qquad \text{A.8}$$

are called the minors and are evaluated by the cross-product $bf - ce$.

To generalise this process to larger determinants, we first define the signed minor of M_{ij} as the cofactor F_{ij} which is given by

$$F_{ij} = (-1)^{i+j}M_{ij} \qquad \text{A.9}$$

The value of the determinant is then given as

$$\det|A| = \sum_{j=1}^{n} a_{ij}F_{ij} \qquad \textbf{A.10}$$

where M_{ij} is obtained by deleting row i and column j and evaluating the remaining determinant.

The following properties of determinants should be noted:

1 the summation of equation A.10 can be made by selecting the i row anywhere, ie it is not necessary to select the first row as was done in equation A.7,

2 the value is the same irrespective of the summation row or if summation is made over any column,

3 the value of the determinant is zero if two rows are equal,

4 the value of the determinant is not altered by adding multiples of one row to another row (try to derive the proof of this yourself),

5 multiplying a row by a scalar alters the value of the determinant by that factor,

6 interchanging two rows or columns alters the sign but not the magnitude of the determinant.

A.4   Inverse of a matrix

The inverse of a square matrix may be defined as

$$A^{-1} = [F_{ij}]^t/\det|A| \qquad \textbf{A.11}$$

ie the terms of A^{-1} are the cofactors of A divided by the determinant of A. If the determinant of A is zero then the inverse of matrix A does not exist and the matrix A is said to be singular.

As an exercise the reader can verify that application of equation A.11 to the matrix A of equation A.2 yields the inverse matrix as

$$A^{-1} = \begin{bmatrix} \frac{7}{6} & -\frac{1}{3} & -\frac{1}{3} \\ -\frac{1}{3} & -\frac{1}{3} & \frac{2}{3} \\ -\frac{1}{3} & \frac{2}{3} & -\frac{1}{3} \end{bmatrix}$$

and check that $A^{-1}A = I_3$, where I_3 is a 3×3 unit matrix, ie

$$I_3 = \begin{bmatrix} 1 & 0 & 0 \\ 0 & 1 & 0 \\ 0 & 0 & 1 \end{bmatrix}$$

The identity $A^{-1}A = I$ provides a useful definition of the inverse of a matrix and is the basis of the Gauss–Jordan method discussed later. However, the classical expression for the inverse using cofactors is not computationally efficient for matrices of order greater than four; other related methods are superior.

A.5 Special matrix types

In matrix algebra special matrix types have unique names. Some of these are indicated below.

$$\begin{bmatrix} b_1 \\ b_2 \\ b_3 \end{bmatrix} \qquad [c_1 \ c_2 \ c_3] \qquad \begin{bmatrix} a_{11} & 0 & 0 \\ 0 & a_{22} & 0 \\ 0 & 0 & a_{33} \end{bmatrix} \qquad \begin{bmatrix} 0 & 0 & 0 \\ 0 & 0 & 0 \\ 0 & 0 & 0 \end{bmatrix}$$

Vector   Row matrix   Diagonal matrix   Null matrix

$$\begin{bmatrix} 1 & 0 & 0 \\ 0 & 1 & 0 \\ 0 & 0 & 1 \end{bmatrix} \qquad \begin{bmatrix} 5 & 3 & 4 \\ 3 & 6 & 5 \\ 4 & 5 & 7 \end{bmatrix} \qquad \begin{bmatrix} 5 & 3 & 4 \\ -3 & 6 & 5 \\ -4 & -5 & 7 \end{bmatrix}$$

Unit matrix   Symmetric matrix   Skew symmetric matrix
                    $A = A^t$ $a_{ij} = -a_{ji}$ for $i \neq j$

$$\begin{bmatrix} \cos \alpha & \sin \alpha \\ -\sin \alpha & \cos \alpha \end{bmatrix}$$

Orthogonal matrix
$A^t = A^{-1}$

Note that the inverse of a diagonal matrix is obtained by replacing the diagonal entries by their reciprocals.

Orthogonal matrices appear, for example, in two dimensional co-ordinate transformation between rectangular Cartesian axes x,y and x′,y′ rotated relative to one another. This transformation arises in truss and frame analysis in Chapters 4 and 5.

A.6 Some useful matrix identities

Some simple matrix rules need to be used in deriving the properties of certain finite elements. As an exercise you may wish to derive these results

$$(AB)^t = B^t A^t \qquad \qquad \text{A.12}$$

$$A(B + C) = AB + AC \qquad \qquad \text{A.13}$$

$$A^{-1}A = I \qquad \qquad \text{A.14}$$

$$(A^{-1})^t = (A^t)^{-1} \qquad \qquad \text{A.15}$$

$$(AB)^{-1} = B^{-1}A^{-1} \qquad \textbf{A.16}$$

A.7 Matrix partitioning

By partitioning a matrix we mean subdividing it into smaller submatrices. We perform partitioning because it sometimes facilitates arithmetic operations. For example, with inversion, if a matrix A is partitioned into four submatrices, the inverse matrix can be obtained in terms of the inverses of only two of the submatrices of A. Writing

$$A^{-1}A = \begin{bmatrix} B_{11} & B_{12} \\ B_{21} & B_{22} \end{bmatrix} \begin{bmatrix} A_{11} & A_{12} \\ A_{21} & A_{22} \end{bmatrix} = \begin{bmatrix} I & 0 \\ 0 & I \end{bmatrix} \qquad \textbf{A.17}$$

and expanding we easily obtain the relations

$$B_{11} = A_{11}^{-1} + XZ^{-1}Y \qquad \textbf{A.18}$$

$$B_{12} = -XZ^{-1} \qquad \textbf{A.19}$$

$$B_{21} = -Z^{-1}Y \qquad \textbf{A.20}$$

$$B_{22} = Z^{-1} \qquad \textbf{A.21}$$

where

$$X = A_{11}^{-1}A_{12} \quad Y = A_{21}A_{11}^{-1}$$
$$Z = (A_{22} - A_{21}A_{11}^{-1}A_{12})$$

When either A_{12} or A_{21} is null the inversion is much simpler and, if both are null, the reader can verify that most terms in equations A.18–A.21 vanish.

A.8 Gauss reduction

Gauss reduction, sometimes called triangular elimination, is the most widely used method of solving sets of linear equations in the finite element method. The procedure involves the following steps.

1 Eliminate the first variable x_1 from all the following equations by subtracting multiples of the first row from all following rows for all columns including the RHS vector $\{b\}$.

2 Eliminate the second variable x_2 from all equations after the second equation and repeat for all variables but the last, finishing with all entries below the leading diagonal set to zero — forward elimination is now complete.

3 Determine the last variable, x_n, from the last equation, its coefficient being the only remaining non-zero entry on the left hand side of the last equation.

4 By back substitution into the second last equation determine x_{n-1} and proceed successively back through the equations until all variables have been found.

The variables are determined in reverse order x_n, x_{n-1}, ..., x_1 by this procedure.

As an example consider the equations below

$$2x_1 + 2x_2 + 2x_3 = 12$$
$$2x_1 + 3x_2 + 4x_3 = 20$$
$$2x_1 + 4x_2 + 3x_3 = 19 \qquad \textbf{A.22}$$

First divide the first row by the coefficient for x_1 in row 1, called the pivot, giving

$$x_1 + x_2 + x_3 = 6$$
$$2x_1 + 3x_2 + 4x_3 = 20$$
$$2x_1 + 4x_2 + 3x_3 = 19 \qquad \textbf{A.23}$$

Now multiply the first equation by a_{21}, the row multiplier, in this case being 2, and subtract it from the second equation. Also multiply the first equation by a_{31} and subtract it from the third equation to obtain

$$x_1 + x_2 + x_3 = 6$$
$$0 + x_2 + 2x_3 = 8$$
$$0 + 2x_2 + x_3 = 7 \qquad \textbf{A.24}$$

The first column has now been reduced. For reduction of the second column we first divide the second row by its current pivot a_{22}, which is 1 in this instance. Next we multiply the second equation from A.24, the most recent version of it, by the row multiplier a_{23} (= 2) and subtract the result from the third equation giving

$$x_1 + x_2 + x_3 = 6$$
$$0 + x_2 + 2x_3 = 8$$
$$0 + 0 - 3x_3 = -9 \qquad \textbf{A.25}$$

Dividing row 3 by its pivot (= −3), the coefficient matrix is reduced to triangular form with unit diagonal entries.

The forward elimination is now complete and back substitution begins.

Clearly $x_3 = 3$ and, substituting back into the second reduced equation of A.25, gives

$$x_2 + 2(3) = 8 \quad \text{or} \quad x_2 = 8 - 2(3) = 2 \qquad \textbf{A.26}$$

Substitution of $x_3 = 3$ and $x_2 = 2$ into the first equation of A.25 leads to

$$x_1 = 6 - 1(2) - 1(3) = 1 \qquad \textbf{A.27}$$

which completes the solution.

This algorithm can be stated formally as

Forward elimination

$$a_{pj}' = a_{pj}/a_{pp} \text{ and } b_p' = b_p/a_{pp} \quad j = p, p+1 \ldots n \qquad \textbf{A.28}$$

$$a_{ij}' = a_{ij} - a_{ip}(a_{pj}') \qquad i = p+1 \ldots n \qquad \textbf{A.29}$$

$$b_i' = b_i - a_{ip}(b_p') \qquad i = p+1 \ldots n \qquad \textbf{A.30}$$

Back substitution

$$x_n = b_n \text{ for the last row} \qquad \textbf{A.31}$$

$$x_k = b_k - \sum_{j=k+1}^{n} a_{kj}(x_j) \quad k = n - 1 \ldots 1 \qquad \textbf{A.32}$$

In equation A.32, for example, a_{kj} refers to the last determined value for this entry in the matrix, ie equations A.28–A.30 overwrite the entries in the matrix with new values and the dash superscripts are used to emphasise this.

A useful way of evaluating the determinant of a matrix follows from Gauss reduction and simply involves multiplying the pivots together. Applying Laplace's rule to the triangular matrix formed at the completion of the forward elimination procedure, readers may wish to verify this statement generally in algebraic terms. In the example of equation A.22 we obtain

$$|A| = (2)(1)(-3) = -6$$

which is the correct result.

The use of Gauss reduction, followed by pivot multiplication in this fashion, to evaluate a determinant is more computationally efficient than Laplace's rule. This procedure is used in connection with the computation of eigenvalues, by certain methods, and is known as Chio's rule.

A.9   Gauss–Jordan reduction

Gauss–Jordan reduction is a more practical and economical method of inverting a matrix than the cofactor method; it is an extension of Gauss reduction. Each column of the matrix is reduced to unit form leaving unity in all leading diagonal positions and reducing the original matrix to a unit matrix. The row subtraction operations necessary to so reduce the original matrix A to a unit matrix I are made clearer if we write the product of the augmented matrix [A   I] and a matrix B, which will eventually become the inverse, in the form

$$B[A \quad I] = [BA \quad BI]$$

Because B is constructed such that BA = I, it follows that B = A^{-1} and thus

$$B[A \quad I] = [BA \quad BI] = [I \quad A^{-1}]$$

To construct the B matrix as indicated it is necessary to perform the row elimination operations of Gauss reduction on rows above and below the pivot row of the augmented matrix.

Taking, as an example, the matrix of equation A.2, we begin with the augmented matrix

$$\left[\begin{array}{ccc|ccc} 2 & 2 & 2 & 1 & 0 & 0 \\ 2 & 3 & 4 & 0 & 1 & 0 \\ 2 & 4 & 3 & 0 & 0 & 1 \end{array}\right]$$

The first step involves subtracting multiples of the first row from all other rows to reduce the first column to unit form. Operating across the entire augmented matrix, we obtain

$$\left[\begin{array}{ccc|ccc} 1 & 1 & 1 & \frac{1}{2} & 0 & 0 \\ 0 & 1 & 2 & -1 & 1 & 0 \\ 0 & 2 & 1 & -1 & 0 & 1 \end{array}\right] \qquad \textbf{A.33}$$

We now subtract multiples of the second row from all other rows, including the first row, to reduce the second column terms of all rows, other than row 2, to zero, ie

$$\begin{bmatrix} 1 & 0 & -1 \\ 0 & 1 & 2 \\ 0 & 0 & -3 \end{bmatrix} \begin{array}{|ccc} \frac{3}{2} & -1 & 0 \\ -1 & 1 & 0 \\ 1 & -2 & 1 \end{array} \qquad \textbf{A.34}$$

Finally we reduce the third column giving

$$\begin{bmatrix} 1 & 0 & 0 \\ 0 & 1 & 0 \\ 0 & 0 & 1 \end{bmatrix} \begin{array}{|ccc} \frac{7}{6} & -\frac{1}{3} & -\frac{1}{3} \\ -\frac{1}{3} & -\frac{1}{3} & \frac{2}{3} \\ -\frac{1}{3} & \frac{2}{3} & -\frac{1}{3} \end{array} \qquad \textbf{A.35}$$

and the right hand half becomes the required inverse.

The computer code required to implement this technique is similar to that for Gaussian reduction, except that reduction extends above and below the pivot row and laterally into the newly forming columns of the inverse matrix. Two examples of such coding, which involve some modification of the basic procedure described above, are given at the close of the chapter.

This same approach, in a slightly modified form, can also be used to solve the equations $A\{x\} = \{b\}$. Following the same notation used for inversion, we write

$$B[A \quad \{b\}] = [BA \quad B\{b\}] = [I \quad A^{-1}\{b\}] = [I \quad \{x\}] \qquad \textbf{A.36}$$

but actually do not bother to record the inverse matrix. However, this approach is not as computationally efficient as reduction to triangular form by Gauss elimination followed by back-substitution as described in Section A.8.

A.10 Eigenproblems

Eigenproblems arise in finite element analysis in the general form

$$A\{x\} = \lambda B\{x\} \qquad \textbf{A.37}$$

where A and B are square symmetric. Equation A.37 states that the product of matrix A by vector $\{x\}$ is equal to λ times matrix B by vector $\{x\}$ with the vector $\{x\}$ non-null. Such solutions exist only if

$$\det|A - \lambda B| = 0 \qquad \textbf{A.38}$$

If A and B are (n $\times$ n) matrices, because the expansion of equation A.38 leads to an nth order polynomial in λ, such non-null solutions exist only for n values of λ; these values are known as the eigenvalues. Corresponding to each such eigenvalue, λ_i, all of which are real if A and B are real and symmetric, is the associated non-null solution vector $\{x\} = \{e_i\}$ known as an eigenvector. It is possible for eigenvalues to be equal while having different eigenvectors.

The computation of these eigenpairs, the eigenvalue and its eigenvector, is not a trivial exercise as considerable effort is required to compute just one eigenpair. The technique used is invariably, in the final stages at least, iterative since it involves the solution of an nth order polynomial for which no closed form solution exists for $n > 4$.

We consider only two techniques.

Jacobi diagonalisation

In Jacobi diagonalisation the matrices A and B are transformed to diagonal matrices in such a way that the eigenvalues are unaltered by the process. Each transformation can be represented symbolically in the form

$$A_{n+1} = T_n{}^t A_n T_n \qquad B_{n+1} = T_n{}^t B_n T_n \qquad \textbf{A.39}$$

where T_n is a unit matrix modified by placing entries α and β in the positions ij and ji respectively where α and β are given by

$$\alpha = -M/P \qquad \beta = N/P \qquad \textbf{A.40}$$

and

$$M = a_{ii}b_{ij} - b_{ii}a_{ij} \quad N = a_{jj}b_{ij} - b_{jj}a_{ij}$$
$$Q = a_{ii}b_{jj} - b_{ii}a_{jj} \quad P = \tfrac{1}{2}Q + \text{sgn}(Q)\sqrt{(Q^2 + MN)} \qquad \textbf{A.41}$$

This procedure has the effect of making the terms a_{ij} and b_{ij} zero although, once they have been forced to zero, they can become non-zero during later transformations. Row i and column j may be chosen on any basis but it is most effective to select the largest off-diagonal term. However, because searching to find this term is time consuming, other strategies are sometimes used. For example, proceeding by rows or columns and only transforming if the absolute value of an off-diagonal term is above a small threshold value. The threshold value is progressively lowered and iteration concludes when it reaches a small limit. The technique is known as the threshold Jacobi method and proceeding once through the A and B matrices is known as a sweep.

After the matrices have been diagonalised and the off-diagonal terms reduced below the final threshold value the eigenvalues are given by $\lambda_i = a_{ii}/b_{ii}$ etc. and the eigenvectors by

$$E = T_1T_2T_3 \ldots T_n \qquad\qquad \textbf{A.42}$$

in which column i of E contains the ith eigenvector $\{e_i\}$.

There are two major disadvantages of the Jacobi method, namely, it computes all eigenpairs even though not all may be required and advantage cannot be taken of banding. For these reasons, it is a slow method, especially for large systems.

Determinant search

An algorithm which overcomes these disadvantages is the determinant search method in which eigenpairs are computed successively from the smallest to the largest. Space does not permit a full explanation of the underlying techniques but brief details are as follows.

1 *Implicit polynomial iteration* is used to shift the origin of the eigenvalues, see Fig A.1, and solve subsequently, by inverse vector iteration, the problem $(A - \mu B)\{x\} = \lambda'B\{x\}$ where $\lambda = \lambda'_1 + \mu$. For two trial values μ_n and μ_{n-1} of an eigenvalue, we compute values D_n and D_{n-1} of D $(= \det|A - \mu B|)$ and adjust μ using

$$\mu_{n+1} = \mu_n - \alpha D_n(\mu_{n-1} - \mu_n)/(D_{n-1} - D_n) \qquad \textbf{A.43}$$

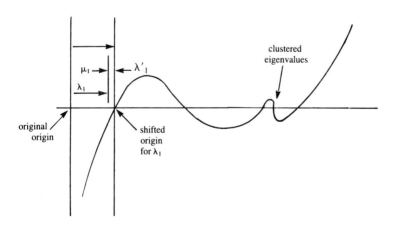

Figure A.1 Characteristic polynomial illustrating shifting

The accelerator α is set equal to 1 initially but doubled every iteration until μ_{n+1} jumps over an eigenvalue as indicated by applying the sign count technique; see 4 below. As soon as this occurs, one further iteration is undertaken and μ_{n+1} is adopted as the shift for inverse vector iteration.

2 *Inverse vector iteration* in which, describing the process in principle only, we iterate using

$$(A - \mu B)\{x\}_{n+1} = B\{x\}_n \qquad \textbf{A.44}$$

This process eventually causes $\{x\}_{n+1}$ to equal $\lambda'\{x\}_n$ where, usually, λ' is the eigenvalue of lowest absolute modulus. If two eigenvalues are nearly equal, the eigenpair to which the process converges depends on the vector $\{x\}_0$ chosen to commence iteration.

3 *Gram–Schmidt orthogonalisation* is used to precondition the starting vector so that, where two eigenvalues are close, the inverse vector iteration does not continue to converge back to the same eigenvalue. If k eigenvalues have been obtained already we start iterating with

$$\{x\}_0 = \{x\}_0 - \sum_{i=1}^{k} \{e_i\}^t B \{x\}_0 \{e_i\} \qquad \textbf{A.44}$$

4 *The Sturm sequence property* leads to a procedure known as the sign count technique, by which the number of negative pivots encountered in the Gaussian reduction of $(A - \mu B)$ equals the number of eigenvalues less than μ. This enables us to determine whether all eigenvalues in a cluster have been extracted. If they have, we return to polynomial iteration to jump to the next cluster.

A program is given in Section A.11 which carries out a determinant search. Further details of the individual techniques mentioned above may be found in Reference 4.

A.11   Coding of simple matrix operations

In FORTRAN, BASIC and other popular computer languages matrices are stored in carefully mapped arrays and each entry in an array accessed by using the same type of subscript notation as in equation A.4, for example.

Matrix multplication C = AB

For premultiplication of matrix A(N × L) and B(L × M), for example, typical coding is

```
FORTRAN                  BASIC

   DO 20 I=1,N           10 FOR I=1 TO N:FOR J=1 TO M
   DO 20 J=1,M           20 S=0:FOR K=1 TO L
   S=0                   30 S=S+A(I,K)*B(K,J)
   DO 30 K=1,L           40 NEXT K
30 S=S+A(I,K)*B(K,J)     50 C(I,J)=S
20 C(I,J)=S              60 NEXT J:NEXT I
```

where the statement S = 0 initialises the elements of the product matrix C and the assignment statement, 30, calculates a cumulative result for each entry.

Congruent transformation S = B^{t}DB

For the congruent transformations S = B^{t}DB, which occur frequently in finite element analysis, typical coding for D(M × M) and B(M × N) follows.

```
FORTRAN                      BASIC

                          10 FOR I=1 TO N:FOR J=1 TO N
   DO 30 I=1,N            20 C=0:FOR K1=1 TO M
   DO 30 J=1,N            30 FOR K2=1 TO M1
   C=0                    40 C=C+B(K2,I)*D(K2,K1)*B(K1,J)
   DO 40 K1=1,M           50 NEXT K2:NEXT K1
   DO 40 K2=1,M           60 S(I,J)=C:NEXT J:NEXT I
40 C=C+B(K2,I)*D(K2,K1)*B(K1,J)
30 S(I,J)=C
```

In the code given above it will be noted that the matrix B is not specifically transposed. The coefficients are simply accessed directly in their transposed position by nominating the appropriate subscripts.

Inverse by Gauss−Jordan reduction

The following is a simple and very compact BASIC code for Gauss–Jordan reduction. Rather than store an augmenting unit matrix, only a single additional variable is used first to store the pivot and later the row multiplier. The original matrix is overwritten by its inverse.

```
10 FOR I=1 TO N
20 X=C(I,I):C(I,I)=1
```

```
 30 FOR J=1 TO N
 40 C(I,J)=C(I,J)/X:NEXT J
 50 FOR K=1 TO N
 60 IF K=I GOTO 100
 70 X=C(K,I):C(K,I)=0
 80 FOR J=1 TO N
 90 C(K,J)=C(K,J)-X*C(I,J):NEXT J
100 NEXT K
110 NEXT I
```

Equation solution by Gauss–Jordan reduction

If, on the other hand, we wish to solve the equations $C\{x\} = \{V\}$ then the above routine can be modified to operate upon the RHS vector, $\{V\}$, and provide a direct solution. In this case we do not need to form the inverse matrix C^{-1} and can halve the amount of calculation by sweeping only to the right of the pivot in the reduction operations. The routine then becomes

```
 10 FOR I=1 TO N
 20 X=C(I,I):V(I)=V(I)/X
 30 FOR J=I+1 TO N
 40 C(I,J)=C(I,J)/X:NEXT J
 50 FOR K=1 TO N
 60 IF K=I GOTO 100
 70 X=C(K,I):V(K)=V(K)-X*V(I)
 80 FOR J=I+1 TO N
 90 C(K,J)=C(K,J)-X*C(I,J):NEXT J
100 NEXT K
110 NEXT I
```

This routine, because of its brevity, is very useful in the study of small frame and truss problems. For larger problems, account must be taken of the fact that stiffness matrices are both symmetric and banded. The programs used in such cases are based on Gauss elimination, an example occurring in Chapter 8 as part of a program for plane stress analysis.

Inverse by Gauss–Jordan reduction using row and column interchange

The following is a Gauss–Jordan reduction routine in FORTRAN. It is capable of storing a column in addition to those of the original matrix and overwrites the original matrix with its inverse. To improve the numerical accuracy of the solution, a search is made at each elimination stage, for the largest element in the remaining unreduced part of A; columns are interchanged to make this element the pivot. After the inversion is complete the address matrix M( ) has recorded the column swaps; the rows of the inverse matrix are swapped in the same way as the columns to obtain the final inverse.

```
      SUBROUTINE INVERT(N)
      DIMENSION A(6,6),M(6),COL(6)
      DO 1 I=1,N
    1 M(I)=-I
      DO 7 II=1,N
      D=0.
      DO 4 J=1,N
      IF (M(J).GT.0) GO TO 4
      DO 2 I=1,N
      IF (M(I).GT.0) GO TO 2
      IF (ABS(D).GE.ABS(A(I,J))) GO TO 2
      L=J
      K=I
      D=A(I,J)
    2 CONTINUE
    4 CONTINUE
      TEMP=-M(L)
      M(L)=M(K)
      M(K)=TEMP
      DO 3 I=1,N
      COL(I)=A(I,L)
      A(I,L)=A(I,K)
    3 A(I,K)=COL(I)
      AMIN=1.0E-20
      IF (ABS(D).LE.AMIN) WRITE(6,20)
      DO 11 J=1,N
   11 A(K,J)=-A(K,J)/D
      DO 6 I=1,N
      IF (I.EQ.K) GO TO 6
      DO 5 J=1,N
    5 A(I,J)=A(I,J)+COL(I)*A(K,J)
    6 CONTINUE
      COL(K)=1.
      DO 7 I=1,N
    7 A(I,K)=COL(I)/D
      DO 10 I=1,N
      IF (M(I).EQ.I) GO TO 10
      DO 8 L=1,N
      IF (M(L).EQ.I) GO TO 9
    8 CONTINUE
    9 M(L)=M(I)
      M(I)=I
      DO 10 J=1,N
      TEMP=A(L,J)
      A(L,J)=A(I,J)
      A(I,J)=TEMP
   10 CONTINUE
   20 FORMAT(10HA SINGULAR)
      RETURN
      END
```

Gauss reduction

We now give a simple Gauss reduction routine in BASIC for the direct solution of the equations $A\{D\} = \{Q\}$.

```
10 DIM A(10,10),D(10),Q(10),C(10)
20 READ N:FOR I=1 TO N:FOR J=1 TO N
30 READ A(I,J)
40 NEXT J:NEXT I
60 FOR I=1 TO N:READ Q(I):NEXT I
90 FOR K=1 TO N
100 P=A(K,K)
110 L=Q(K)/P
120 Q(K)=L
130 FOR J=K TO N
140 C(J)=A(J,K)
150 A(K,J)=A(K,J)/P
160 NEXT J
170 FOR I=K+1 TO N
180 Q(I)=Q(I)-L*C(I)
190 FOR J=K TO N
200 A(I,J)=A(I,J)-C(I)*A(K,J)
210 NEXT J
220 NEXT I
230 NEXT K
240 K=N
250 D(N)=Q(N)/A(N,N)
260 K=K-1
270 D(K)=Q(K)
280 FOR J=K+1 TO N
290 D(K)=D(K)-A(K,J)*D(J)
300 NEXT J
310 IF K=1 THEN GOTO 330
320 GOTO 260
330 FOR I=1 TO N:PRINT I,D(I):NEXT I
340 END
400 DATA 3
405 DATA 1,1,1
410 DATA 2,3,4
415 DATA 2,4,3
420 DATA 6,20,19
```

Jacobi eigensolver

A program which employs the Jacobi method to extract eigen-pairs of $(K \doteq \lambda M)$, follows. In its current form it does not take advantage of symmetry but has the advantage that it can be used for vibration and buckling problems, ie M may also be a geometric matrix. The input data required is

Line	Data
1	Dimension of K and M − (M1), Accuracy parameter (A5)
N lines	Elements of K (SS) in row or column order
N lines	Elements of M (SM) in row or column order

```
5000 DIM SS(10,10),SM(10,10),E(10,10),S(10),SMH(10,10)
5010 READ M1,A5
5020 FOR I=1 TO M1:E(I,I)=1:NEXT I
5030 FOR I=1 TO M1:FOR J=1 TO M1:READ SS(I,J):NEXT J:N
EXT I
5040 FOR I=1 TO M1:FOR J=1 TO M1:READ SM(I,J):SMH(I,J)
=SM(I,J)
5050 NEXT J:NEXT I
5060 REM
5070 REM INPUT SECTION COMPLETE
5080 REM
5090 FOR I9=1 TO 100
5100 REM
5110 REM SEARCH FOR MAX ABS(SS(I,J))
5120 REM
5130 M5=0
5140 FOR I5=1 TO M1:I1=I5+1:FOR I6=I1 TO M1
5150 M6=ABS(SS(I5,I6)):IF M5>M6 THEN 5170
5160 M5=M6:I=I5:J=I6
5170 NEXT I6:NEXT I5
5180 REM
5190 REM ESTABLISH TRANSFORMATION MATRIX
5200 REM
5210 M=SS(I,I)*SM(I,J)-SM(I,I)*SS(I,J)
5220 N=SS(J,J)*SM(I,J)-SM(J,J)*SS(I,J)
5230 Q=SS(I,I)*SM(J,J)-SM(I,I)*SS(J,J)
5240 Q1=SGN(Q):IF Q1=0 THEN Q1=1
5250 P=.5*Q+Q1*SQR((.5*Q)^2+M*N)
5260 C1=N/P:C2=-M/P
5270 I5=I:I6=J
5280 REM
5290 REM TRANSFORMATION
5300 REM
5310 FOR J=1 TO M1
5320 A4=SS(J,I5):B5=SM(J,I5):E5=E(J,I5)
5330 SS(J,I5)=SS(J,I5)+C2*SS(J,I6)
5340 SM(J,I5)=SM(J,I5)+C2*SM(J,I6)
5350 E(J,I5)=E(J,I5)+C2*E(J,I6)
5360 SS(J,I6)=SS(J,I6)+C1*A4
```

```
5370 SM(J,I6)=SM(J,I6)+C1*B5
5380 E(J,I6)=E(J,I6)+C1*E5
5390 NEXT J
5400 FOR J=1 TO M1
5410 A4=SS(I5,J):B5=SM(I5,J)
5420 SS(I5,J)=SS(I5,J)+C2*SS(I6,J)
5430 SM(I5,J)=SM(I5,J)+C2*SM(I6,J)
5440 SS(I6,J)=SS(I6,J)+C1*A4
5450 SM(I6,J)=SM(I6,J)+C1*B5
5460 NEXT J
5470 REM
5480 REM CHECK FOR ANOTHER ITERATION
5490 REM
5500 IF I9=5*INT(I9/5) THEN PRINT "ITERATION ";:PRINT
I9:PRINT
5510 FOR I=1 TO M1:I2=I+1:FOR J=I2 TO M1
5520 IF ABS(SS(I,J)/SS(I,I))>A5 THEN 5770
5530 NEXT J:NEXT I:FOR I=1 TO M1:I2=I2+1
5540 FOR J=I2 TO M1:IF ABS(SM(I,J)/SM(I,I))>A5 THEN 57
70
5550 NEXT J:NEXT I
5560 FOR I=1 TO M1:S(I)=0:FOR L=1 TO M1:FOR K=1 TO M1
5570 S(I)=S(I)+E(L,I)*E(K,I)*SMH(L,K):NEXT K:NEXT L:NE
XT I
5580 PRINT S(1),S(2),S(3)
5590 FOR I=1 TO M1:FOR J=1 TO M1:E(J,I)=E(J,I)/SQR(S(I
))
5600 NEXT J:NEXT I
5610 REM
5620 REM OUTPUT SECTION
5630 REM
5640 LPRINT "EIGEN-VALUES":FOR I=1 TO M1:E1=SS(I,I)/SM
(I,I)
5650 LPRINT I,E1,SQR(E1):NEXT I
5660 LPRINT:LPRINT:LPRINT "EIGENVECTORS"
5670 I5=5*INT(M1/5):I4=INT(M1/5)
5680 IF I5<>M1 THEN I4=I4+1
5690 I1=1
5700 FOR I=1 TO I4
5710 FOR J=1 TO M1
5720 LPRINT E(J,I1),E(J,I1+1),E(J,I1+2),E(J,I1+3),E(J,
I1+4)
5730 NEXT J
5740 LPRINT:LPRINT
5750 I1=I1+5:NEXT I
5760 END
5770 NEXT I9
```

Determinant search eigensolver

Finally a program is given for the determinant search technique
for the problem (K − λM). No attempt is made to take advantage of banding or symmetry and the program can only be used
for vibration problems as written. The data input required is

Line	Data
1	Dimension of K − (M1), Number of eigenpairs sought (N1), Accuracy parameter (A5)
N lines	Elements of matrix K in row or column order
N lines	Elements of matrix M in row or column order.

```
5000 DIM K(10,10),M(10,10),E(10,10),H(10,10)
5010 REM ****  E = MATRIX OF EIGENVECTORS  ****
5020 REM ****  H = K - LAMBDA*M            ****
5030 DIM B(10),X(10),Y(10),C(10),G(10)
5040 SC=0:N6=2:READ M1,N1,A5
5050 FOR I=1 TO M1:FOR J=1 TO M1:READ K(I,J)
5060 H(I,J)=K(I,J):NEXT J:NEXT I
5070 FOR I=1 TO M1:FOR J=1 TO M1:READ M(I,J):NEXT J:NE
XT I
5080 GOSUB 6500
5090 I9=0:IC=0
5100 I9=I9+1
5110 REM
5120 REM **** ESTABLISH TWO LOWER BOUNDS FOR LAMBDA1
****
5130 REM
5140 IF I9<>1 GOTO 5280
5150 GOSUB 6040
5160 Q1=D:P1=0:FOR I=1 TO M1:B(I)=1:NEXT I
5170 FOR J8=1 TO 2:GOSUB 6040
5180 GOSUB 6220
5190 NEXT J8:P2=P
5200 SHFT=P2:GOSUB 6170
5210 I4=0:GOSUB 6040
5220 Q2=D:IF N5<>0 GOTO 5240
5230 GOTO 5350
5240 P2=.99*P2:GOTO 5200
5250 REM
5260 REM **** ESTABLISH TWO LOWER BOUNDS FOR LAMBDA(I9
+1) ****
5270 REM
5280 CT1=0:J9=1:SHFT=P3+M8:GOSUB 6170
5290 GOSUB 6040
5300 P=SHFT:GOSUB 6300
5310 J9=2:CT2=0:P1=SHFT:Q1=D:SHFT=P3+M7:GOSUB 6170
5320 GOSUB 6040
5330 P=SHFT:GOSUB 6300
5340 P2=SHFT:Q2=D:F5=0
5350 REM
5360 REM **** POLYNOMIAL ITERATION ROUTINE ****
5370 REM
5380 FOR J9=2 TO 20:CT2=0:P3=P2-N6*Q2*(P2-P1)/(Q2-Q1)
5390 SHFT=P3:GOSUB 6170
5400 GOSUB 6040
5410 P=SHFT:IF I9<>1 THEN GOSUB 6300
5420 P1=P2:Q1=Q2:P2=P3:Q2=D
5430 N6=2*N6:IF F5=1 GOTO 5500
```

```
5440 IF N5<I9 GOTO 5460
5450 F5=1:N6=1
5460 NEXT J9
5470 REM
5480 REM **** PREPARE FOR VECTOR ITERATION ****
5490 REM
5500 N6=1:F5=0
5510 IC=IC+1:FOR I=1 TO M1:B(I)=1:NEXT I:IF I9=1 GOTO
5530
5520 L5=I9-1:GOSUB 6390
5530 SHFT=P3:GOSUB 6170
5540 I4=0
5550 REM
5560 REM ****  VECTOR ITERATION ROUTINE ****
5570 REM
5580 FOR I8=1 TO 100
5590 IF I8<>3 OR I9=1 GOTO 5610
5600 GOSUB 6390
5610 CT2=0:GOSUB 6040
5620 GOSUB 6220
5630 P3=P
5640 IF ABS((P2-P3)/P3)>A5 GOTO 5710
5650 P3=P3+SHFT:M8=.01*P3:G(I9)=P3:M7=.025*P3
5660 PRINT "EIGENVALUE ";:PRINT I9,P3
5670 FOR I=1 TO M1:S=0:FOR J=1 TO M1:S=S+X(J)*M(I,J):N
EXT J
5680 Y(I)=S:NEXT I
5690 S=0:FOR I=1 TO M1:S=S+X(I)*Y(I):NEXT I:S=SQR(S)
5700 FOR I=1 TO M1:E(I,I9)=X(I)/S:NEXT I:GOTO 5750
5710 P2=P3:NEXT I8
5720 REM
5730 REM **** END VECTOR ITERATION PREPARE FOR NEXT EI
GENPAIR ****
5740 REM
5750 GOSUB 6460
5760 P3=M*(1+50*A5):HOLD=SHFT:SHFT=P3:GOSUB 6170
5770 GOSUB 6040
5780 IF N5<=I9 GOTO 5800
5790 I9=I9+1:SHFT=HOLD:P3=SHFT:GOTO 5510
5800 J5=I9:IF I9>=N1 GOTO 5820
5810 I9=I9+1:GOTO 5140
5820 REM
5830 REM ****  OUTPUT SECTION  ****
5840 REM
5850 PRINT:PRINT:PRINT "EIGENVALUES":PRINT
5860 FOR I=1 TO IC:PRINT I,G(I),SQR(G(I)):NEXT I:PRINT
5870 IF SC=0 GOTO 5950
5880 S1=INT((SC+.0001)/2)
5890 FOR I=1 TO IC:IF S1=0 GOTO 5930
5900 S=0:FOR J1=1 TO S1
5910 FOR J=1 TO M1:E(J,I)=E(J,I)/1E+10:NEXT J:NEXT J1
5920 IF SC=2*S1 THEN 5940
5930 FOR J=1 TO M1:E(J,I)=E(J,I)/SQR(1E+10):NEXT J
5940 NEXT I
5950 PRINT:PRINT"EIGEN-VECTORS":PRINT
```

```
5960 I5=5*INT(N1/5):I4=INT(N1/5):IF I5<>N1 THEN I4=I4+
1
5970 I1=1:FOR I=1 TO I4:FOR J=1 TO M1
5980 PRINT E(J,I1),E(J,I1+1),E(J,I1+2),E(J,I1+3),E(J,I
1+4)
5990 NEXT J:PRINT:PRINT:I1=I1+5:NEXT I
6000 END
6010 REM
6020 REM ****  EQUATION SOLVING ROUTINE  ****
6030 REM
6040 N5=0:D=1:FOR I=1 TO M1:P=K(I,I):IF P<0 THEN N5=N5
+1
6050 D=D*P:IF I4=1 GOTO 6080
6060 P=1/P
6070 FOR J=I TO M1:K(I,J)=K(I,J)*P:NEXT J:K(I,I)=P
6080 B(I)=B(I)*P:L=I+1:FOR K1=L TO M1:IF I4=1 GOTO 610
0
6090 FOR J=L TO M1:K(K1,J)=K(K1,J)-K(K1,I)*K(I,J):NEXT
 J
6100 B(K1)=B(K1)-K(K1,I)*B(I):NEXT K1:NEXT I
6110 X(M1)=B(M1):M2=M1-1:FOR I=1 TO M2:I1=M1-I:I2=M1-I
+1:S=B(I1)
6120 FOR K1=I2 TO M1:S=S-K(I1,K1)*X(K1):NEXT K1:X(I1)=
S:NEXT I
6130 I4=1:RETURN
6140 REM
6150 REM **** SHIFT ROUTINE ****
6160 REM
6170 I4=0:FOR I=1 TO M1:FOR J=1 TO M1:K(I,J)=H(I,J)-SH
FT*M(I,J)
6180 NEXT J:NEXT I:RETURN
6190 REM
6200 REM **** INVERSE VECTOR ITERATION ****
6210 REM
6220 FOR I=1 TO M1:S=0:FOR J=1 TO M1:S=S+M(I,J)*X(J):N
EXT J
6230 Y(I)=S:NEXT I
6240 S1=0:S2=0:FOR I=1 TO M1:S1=S1+X(I)*C(I):S2=S2+X(I
)*Y(I)
6250 NEXT I:P=S1/S2:P5=SQR(S2)
6260 FOR I=1 TO M1:B(I)=Y(I)/P5:C(I)=B(I):NEXT I:RETUR
N
6270 REM
6280 REM **** POLYNOMIAL DEFLATION ****
6290 REM
6300 FOR I=1 TO J5:D=D/(P-G(I)):IF J9=1 GOTO 6340
6310 IF CT1=CT2 THEN GOTO 6350
6320 IF D>1E+20 OR D<9.999999E-21 THEN GOSUB 6620
6330 GOTO 6350
6340 IF D>1E+20 OR D<9.999999E-21 THEN GOSUB 6600
6350 NEXT I:RETURN
6360 REM
6370 REM ****  GRAM-SCHMIDT ORTHOGONALISATION  ****
6380 REM
6390 FOR J1=1 TO L5:FOR I=1 TO M1:S=0:FOR J=1 TO M1
```

```
6400 S=S+M(I,J):NEXT J:X(I)=S:NEXT I
6410 S=0:FOR I=1 TO M1:S=S+E(I,J1)*X(I):NEXT I
6420 FOR I=1 TO M1:B(I)=B(I)-S*E(I,J1):C(I)=B(I)
6430 NEXT I:NEXT J1:RETURN
6440 REM
6450 REM **** SELECT MAXIMUM EIGENVALUE ****
6460 REM
6470 M=0:FOR I=1 TO I9:IF G(I)>M THEN M=G(I)
6480 NEXT I:RETURN
6490 REM
6500 REM **** SCALING OF MATRICES ****
6510 REM
6520 FOR I=1 TO M1:D=1:FOR J=1 TO M1:D=D*K(J,J)
6530 IF D>1E+20 GOTO 6550
6540 NEXT J:RETURN
6550 SC=SC+1:FOR J1=1 TO M1:FOR J2=1 TO M1
6560 H(J1,J2)=H(J1,J2)*1E-10
6570 K(J1,J2)=K(J1,J2)*1E-10:M(J1,J2)=M(J1,J2)*1E-10
6580 NEXT J2:NEXT J1
6590 NEXT I:RETURN
6600 CT1=CT1+1:F1=1E+10:IF D>1E+20 THEN F1=1E-10
6610 D=D*F1:RETURN
6620 CT2=CT2+1:F1=1E+10:IF D>1E+20 THEN F1=9.999999E-2
1
6630 D=D*F1:RETURN
```

References

1 Y K Cheung and I P King, 'Computer Programs and Computer Methods', in O C Zienkiewicz (ed), *The Finite Element Method in Engineering Science*, McGraw–Hill, London, 1971.

2 L A Pipes and S A Hovanessan, *Matrix Computer Methods in Engineering*, Wiley, New York, 1969.

3 J S Przemieniecki, *Theory of Matrix Structural Analysis*, McGraw–Hill, New York, 1968.

4 K J Bathe and E L Wilson, *Numerical Methods in Finite Element Analysis*, Prentice–Hall, Englewood Cliffs, NJ, 1976.

Glossary of symbols

a,b	local co-ordinates in quadrilateral element
a,b,c	natural co-ordinates (ie parallel to the sides) in triangular element
A	element area
B	strain interpolation matrix
c,s	direction cosines for line element
c_{ax},c_{ay}	direction cosines of side 12 of triangular element
c_x,c_y	direction cosines of normal to element boundary
{c}	coefficients of interpolation polynomial
C	capacitance (Chapter 3 only), element interpolation matrix, damping matrix (Chapter 6 and Appendix A)
D	modulus matrix
{d}	nodal displacements for an element
{D}	system nodal displacements
E	Young's modulus
{e}	eigenvector
f_x,f_{xx}	$\partial\{f\}/\partial x, \partial^2\{f\}/\partial x^2$
F_c,F_t	permissible compressive and tensile stresses
F_{ul},F_{u2}	Cartesian forces at nodes
{f}	element interpolation functions
G	conductance (Chapter 3 only), shear modulus
h	characteristic length of element
I	electrical current (Chapter 3 only), moment of inertia, unit matrix
j	$\sqrt{-1}$
J	Jacobian matrix, St Venant's torsion constant (Chapter 7 only)
k	element stiffness matrix
k_x,k_y	coefficients of thermal conductivity in x, y directions

L	length of line element
L_a, L_b	side lengths of rectangular element
L_a, L_b, L_c	side lengths of triangular element
L_1, L_2, L_3	area co-ordinates in triangular element
m	nodal mass
M	mass matrix (Chapter 6 and Appendix A), moment force
M_b	bending couple
$\{M\}$	interpolation function modes for an element
p	pressure head (Chapter 3 only), distributed load intensity
P	axial force in line element
q_x, q_y	heat fluxes parallel to Cartesian axes
$\{q\}$	nodal loads on element
$\{Q\}$	total nodal loads on system
R	resistance (Chapter 3 only), residual error
s	dimensional co-ordinate in line element
S	strain interpolation matrix in terms of Cartesian or local co-ordinates
t	element thickness, time co-ordinate (Chapter 6 and Appendix A)
T	temperature (Chapter 3 only), transformation matrix
u,v	Cartesian velocity components (Chapter 7 only)
u,v,w	Cartesian displacement components
V	voltage (Chapter 3 only), element volume
x,y,z	Cartesian co-ordinates
Y	complex admittance
Z	complex impedance
α	slope of line element
γ	damping ratio
δ	extension of line element
$\triangle$	area of triangular element
$\varepsilon_x, \varepsilon_y, \varepsilon_{xy}$	direct strains and shear strain in Cartesian system
θ	slope freedom, torsional angle of twist per unit length (Chapter 7 only)
λ	eigenvalue
μ	trial eigenvalue in iterative solution

π	total potential energy
ρ	mass density
$\sigma_x, \sigma_y, \sigma_{xy}$	direct stresses and shear stress in Cartesian system
ν	Poisson's ratio
ϕ	phase angle (Chapter 6 only), potential function, Prandtl stress function (Chapter 6 only)
ϕ_x, ϕ_y	Cartesian slope freedoms in thin plate
$\Phi_x, \Phi_y, \Phi_{xy}$	direct curvatures and twist curvature in Cartesian system
ψ	stream function
ω	angular frequency of vibration, vorticity (Chapter 7 only)
ω_i	integration point weight
Ω	diagonal matrix of eigenvalues
$( )_a, ( )_b, ( )_c$	natural quantities referred to sides of triangular elements
$( )_e$	element quantity
$( )_i$	nodal quantity
$( )^*$	quantity referred to local axes of initial basis
$o( )$	order of truncation error
$\mathrm{sgn}( )$	sign of $( )$
$\delta( )$	increment in $( )$
Σ	summation
Π	chain product
$\int dx$	integration with respect to x
$d( )/dx$	derivative with respect to x
$\partial( )/\partial x$	partial derivative with respect to x
$\nabla^2( )$	Laplacian operator $= \partial^2( )/\partial x^2 + \partial^2( )/\partial y^2$

Note concerning matrix notation:
Matrices are denoted by capital letters to simplify notation and this should be clear in context, scalar quantities within matrix expressions frequently being enclosed in brackets ( ) to identify them (eg equation 4.21).

Where the entries of a matrix are to be indicated square brackets are used.

{ }	denotes a vector
< >	denotes a row matrix
| |	denotes determinant of a matrix

Superscript t denotes transposition of a matrix, eg $\{\ \}^t = <\quad>$

Index